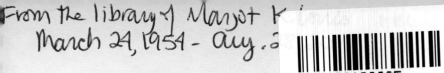

Amazons and Mili
Women Who Dressed as Men in the Pursuit
of Life, Liberty and Happiness

Julie Wheelwright was born in Farnborough, Kent and emigrated to Canada as a young child. While studying at the University of British Columbia she wrote for the *Vancouver Sun* and later worked for Canadian University Press in Ottawa. In 1986 she graduated with an M.A. in history from the University of Sussex and has since worked as a freelance writer. Her articles have appeared in magazines and newspapers throughout Canada, the United States and Britain. She is currently developing a drama documentary about the life of Flora Sandes. She lives in London.

For my mother, Patricia Doreen Wheelwright

Photographs, captions and credits:

Front Cover – Vesta Tilley, Britain's best-known music hall male impersonator, dressed for her 1917 performance of 'Six Days Home on Leave' at London's Coliseum theatre.
(*Raymond Mander and Joe Mitchenson Theatre Collection.*)

Back Cover – American naval recruitment poster by Howard Chandler Christy from the First World War acknowledged that women might covet not only the sailor's uniform but the freedom and adventure it was supposed to symbolize. (*Trustees of the Imperial War Museum.*)

Amazons and Military Maids

Women Who Dressed as Men in the Pursuit of Life, Liberty and Happiness

Julie Wheelwright

PANDORA

London   Boston   Sydney   Wellington

First published in Great Britain by Pandora Press,
an imprint of the Trade Division of Unwin Hyman Limited, in 1989.
First published in paperback in 1990.

PANDORA PRESS
Unwin Hyman Limited
15–17 Broadwick Street
London W1V 1FP

Allen & Unwin Australia Pty Ltd.
POBox 764, 8 Napier Street, North Sydney, NSW 2060

Allen & Unwin NZ Ltd. (in association with the Port Nicholson Press)
Compusales Building, 75 Ghuznee Street, Wellington, New Zealand

Unwin Hyman Inc.
8 Winchester Place, Winchester, Mass. 01890, USA

BRITISH LIBRARY CATALOGUING IN PUBLICATION DATA

Wheelwright, Julie
    Amazons and military maids: women who dressed as men in the pursuit of life,
    liberty and happiness.
    1. Female transvestism — 1700-1918
    1. Title
    306.7'7
ISBN 0–04–440494–8

Printed in Great Britain by Cox & Wyman Ltd, Reading

A Vagrant Heart

O to be a woman to be left to pique and pine,
When the winds are out and calling to this vagrant heart of mine,
Whisht! it whistles at the windows, and how can I be still?
There! The last leaves of the beech-tree go dancing down the hill.

All the boats at anchor, they are plunging to be free —
O to be a sailor and away across the sea!
When the sky is black with thunder and the sea is white with foam,
The grey gulls whirl up shrieking and seek their rocky home.

Low his boat is lying leeward, how she runs up in the gale,
As she rises with the billows, and shakes her dripping sail;
There is danger in the waters — there is a joy where dangers be —
Alas to be a woman and the nomad's heart in me.

Ochine! to be a woman and only sighing on the shore —
With a soul that finds a passion for each long breakers' roar,
With a heart that beats as restless as all the winds that blow —
Thrust a cloth between her fingers and tell her she must sew;
Must join in empty chatter and calculate with straw —
For the weighing of our neighbour — for the sake of social law.

Oh chatter, chatter, chatter when to speak is misery,
When silence lies around your heart and might is in the sea.
So tired of little fashions that are root of all our strife,
Of all the petty passions that upset the calm of life.

The law of God upon the land shines steady for all time;
The laws confused that man has made, have reason not nor rhyme.
O bird that fights the heavens, and is blown beyond the shore,
Would you leave your flight and danger for a cage to fight no more?

No more the cold of winter, nor the hunger of the snow,
Nor the winds that blow you backward from the path you wish to go,
Would you leave your world of passion for a home that knows no riot?
Would I change my vagrant longings for a heart more full of quiet?
No! — for all its dangers, there is joy in danger too;
On, bird, and fight your tempests, and this nomad's heart with you.

The seas that shake and thunder will close our mouths one day,
The storms that shriek and whistle will blow our breaths away,
The dust that flies and whitens will mark not where we trod,
What matters then our judging? we are face to face with God!

Dora Sigerson Shorter, 1907.

Contents

List of Illustrations

1. Valerie Arkell-Smith, dressed as her alias Colonel Barker, 1926.
2. Female music hall impersonator Vesta Tilley in uniform during the First World War.
3. Etching of 'Nancy', an eighteenth-century British female soldier.
4. Hannah Snell, disguised as James Gray, British soldier and sailor, 1750.
5. The frontispiece of Murray's 1915 novel, *Fanny Campbell or the Female Pirate Captain*.
6. Mary Anne Talbot, eighteenth-century English soldier and sailor.
7. Sarah Emma Edmonds, the Civil War soldier, nurse and spy, as Franklin Thompson.
8. Christian Davies, an Irish publican turned soldier, the most popular of eighteenth-century heroines.
9. Maria Bochkareva, leader of the Russian Women's Battalion of Death.
10. Russian soldier Marina Yurlova *en route* to Japan from Vladivostock, 1919.
11. Flora Sandes circa 1881.
12. Flora Sandes in fencing gear, Thornton Heath, Surrey, circa 1894.
13. Flora Sandes with her 'motor car', Thornton Heath, Surrey, 1907.
14. Flora Sandes with her sisters, Fanny, Sophia and Mary.
15. *The Vagrant Heart*, by Irish poet Dora Sigerson Shorter, copied from Flora Sandes' diary, circa 1910.
16. Mary Anne Talbot, British sailor and soldier, disguised as John Taylor.
17. Mary Read and Ann Bonny, eighteenth-century pirates.
18. Princess Kati Dadeshkeliani in the uniform of Prince Djamal.
19. Sergeant Flora Sandes with her Serbian comrades at the Serbian Camp in Nador, near Bizerta, Tunis, February 1917.
20. Portrait of Sergeant Flora Sandes wearing the Kara George Star for non-commissioned officers, Bizerta, Tunis, 1917.

Acknowledgements

Amazons and Military Maids began as an M.A. History thesis at the University of Sussex and, with the helpful nurturing of many colleagues, friends and a thoughtful editor, has grown into a fully-fledged book. But my first interest in historical cases of these extraordinary women and the enduring fantasy they spawned began in the summer of 1985. Professor Sylvia Van Kirk first sparked my interest in the subject when she mentioned the story of the Orcadian Isabelle Gunn — the only known female cross-dresser in the Hudson's Bay fur trading Company — during a lecture to her University of Toronto class on the History of Women in Canada. I found only a few scattered references to Isabelle Gunn in the Kirkwall parish records in Orkney, but it was enough to open up a stream of questions about why, how, when and where women masqueraded as men.

The ideas in this book evolved with the assistance and encouragement of a great number of people. My first debt is to Candida Lacey at Pandora Press for her skilled and thoughtful editing, for consistently raising important issues, contributing invaluable insight and dispelling doubts at the crucial moment. I would equally like to thank Dea Birkett not only for her comments on my original draft but for taking the journey across the psychological terrain of these intrepid women with me and for all her support. I am also indebted to Rob Turrell for his intellectual encouragement, accomplished skills as a copy editor and for his typesetting on the Apple Macintosh. Arthur and Nan Baker of Sudbourne, Suffolk played a very important role in this project and I am extremely grateful to them for their kindness, encouragement and for providing me with access to Flora Sandes' personal papers and photographs. A special thanks to Julian Putkowski for all his help on the First World War material; to Dianne Dugaw for her generosity in sharing her extensive knowledge of eighteenth-century warrior heroines and to Cynthia Enloe, Rudolf Dekker, Jane Schultz and Lydia Sklevicky for their insightful comments and invaluable references. Dorothy Sheridan pointed me in the direction of the 'Colonel Barker' material in the Tom Harrison Mass Observation archive at the University of Sussex and Mandy Wheelwright made my news hunting at Colindale Newspaper Library an unquestionably more pleasant task. I would like to thank my brother, Geoff Wheelwright, who first introduced me to the world of computers, and encouraged me to have my book set on an Apple Macintosh.

I am also grateful to Eva and Zika Antonijevic and Louise Askew for translating documents from Serbo-Croatian. Mira Harding, another translator to whom I am indebted, also shared with me her childhood memories of Flora Sandes and encouraged my interest in the English in Serbia.

For translations from Dutch I am grateful to Henk van Kerkwijk. For their always stimulating views and thought-provoking questions, I would like to thank Lyndal Roper, Dagmar Engels, Diane Hamer, Anna Clark, Clare Midgley, Susan Thorne, Carol Barash and Rachel Weil and all the women who attended the London Feminist History Group and Women's History seminar at the Institute of Historical Research.

I am also obliged to the following libraries and archives for their assistance; the Hudson's Bay Company Archive in Winnipeg, Manitoba; the Imperial War Museum; Central Michigan University; the Masters and Fellows of Trinity College, Cambridge for the A. J. Munby collection; the Bentley Historical Library, the University of Michigan; the Southern Historical Collection, the University of North Carolina at Chapell Hill; the William R. Perkins Library, Duke University; the Robarts Library at the University of Toronto; the Royal Anthropological Institute; Orkney Parish Records and Archives, Kirkwall; Senate House, the University of London; the Institute of Historical Research and the Tom Harrison Mass Observation Archive at the University of Sussex.

1

The Persistence of a Phenomenon

❦

The influence of the costume penetrates to the very soul of the wearer.
Oscar Wilde[1]

Whoso doth the breeches wear lives a life as free as air.
French proverb[2]

VALERIE ARKELL-SMITH, while living as Colonel Victor Barker, married Elfrida Haward at St. Peter's parish church in Brighton in 1923. The ceremony was witnessed by the wife's parents and the proceedings were conducted by Reverend Laurence Hard, who like the witnesses was innocent of the groom's real identity. Afterwards the portly 'Colonel' with the demure, dark-haired Elfrida, swathed in her white veil, departed for a modest wedding breakfast and honeymoon at Brighton's Grand Hotel.

Six years later, having changed her rank and expanded her name to Captain Leslie Ivor Victor Gauntlett Bligh Barker, the 'Colonel' was arrested in connection with a bankruptcy charge and put down for trial at London's Old Bailey court.[3] While she was on remand at Brixton Prison her true sex was uncovered by a doctor and, in addition, she was charged with perjury in connection with her marriage to Elfrida Haward. During the trial the prosecution and defence grappled with the complexities of a woman who had successfully masqueraded as a man for six years, convincing even public officials that 'he' had served as a messing officer in the British Expeditionary Force in France and had received the Distinguished Service Order. When the 'Colonel' was found guilty before an astonished court in

1929, the judge called hers a case 'of an unprecedented and very peculiar nature.' He then sentenced her to nine months in Holloway prison for women.

The trial, like the 'obscenity' trials involving the works of Radclyffe Hall and D.H.Lawrence, was sensationalized in the press. Tabloids featured the 'Colonel' on the front page with headlines that screamed, 'Woman's Strange Life as Man' and 'Duped Wife of Bogus DSO.' The court rooms were packed each day. Even before the morning sessions began the doors of the court were locked to prevent overcrowding; every available seat was occupied and 'many fashionably dressed women stood in the gangways and between the seats.'[4] As Sir Earnest Wild, the prosecutor, probed deeper into the 'Colonel's' life the revelations became increasingly shocking. Not only had Valerie Arkell-Smith married Miss Haward as a bogus officer, but two years earlier she had been tried — as a man — in a London court on a charge of possessing a forged firearm certificate. The 'Colonel,' eyes swathed in bandages, had been guided into the court room on the arm of a friend, who explained in soft tones that Victor suffered from 'hysterical blindness' as the result of war injuries and when exposed to undue stress the 'Colonel's' eyesight temporarily failed. On 14 July 1927 Judge Atherely-Jones found Victor Barker, 'a retired army officer,' not guilty of possessing the falsified document.[5]

Mr Freke Palmer, the 'Colonel's' defending counsel in 1929, explained what he saw as the public interest in the case to the court.[6] 'There has been a great deal of publicity in this matter,' he said:

> because a woman has been bold enough and has succeeded in earning her living as a man when she found that she could not do it as a woman. It seems to shock some people but there is no law against it.[7]

As the 'Colonel', she pursued an acting career, managed a boxing club, bought an antique and second-hand furniture business, managed a dog kennel, a dairy farm, an orchard, purchased a café and worked as a desk clerk in London's Regent Palace Hotel. Posing as a retired officer she relied on her employers' willingness to assist a returned war hero in need of steady and honest work. 'Although there was something mysterious about the new reception clerk,' an official at the Regent Palace Hotel said, 'we accepted him as what he pretended to be, an ex-army officer down on his luck.'[8] Such pursuits were not beyond the reach of women in the 1920s, but the court needed little persuasion that it was all so much easier for Valerie Arkell-Smith as an officer and a gentleman.

Perhaps surprisingly, no connection was made during the trial between the 'Colonel's' relationship with Elfrida Haward and the explicit lesbian love depicted in Radclyffe Hall's novel, *The Well of Loneliness*, which had been the centre of publicity only a few months earlier. On 9 November 1928 the novel was deemed obscene and banned only six weeks after the book — the first in Britain to explicitly describe a lesbian relationship — went on sale. Radclyffe Hall herself was dismayed by the 'Colonel' and thought the trial gave the cause of free sexual expression the very worst publicity. 'I would like to see [Colonel Barker] drawn and quartered,' she wrote to her agent, Audrey Heath. 'A mad pervert of the most undesirable type . . . and then after having married the woman if she doesn't go and desert her.'[9] Both the novelist and the bogus 'Colonel' were interested in claiming male social privileges, including the right to sexual relationships with women, but they remained diametrically opposed in their methods: Valerie Arkell-Smith continued her masculine disguise and lesbian relationships even after her release from prison, while Radclyffe Hall never pretended to be anything but 'a woman with a masculine psyche.'[10]

The word lesbian was never used during the 'Colonel's' case and there was no attempt to charge her and Elfrida Haward under the amendments to the 1920 Sexual Offences Act. Despite the sensational nature of the newspaper coverage of the trials, some press reports portrayed the 'Colonel' with surprising sympathy. She was seen, unlike Radclyffe Hall, as an eccentric merely imitating male behaviour rather than appropriating it in the name of sexual freedom and enlightenment. 'Colonel' Barker's relationships were presented as oblique and confusing because Elfrida Haward claimed she did not know her husband was 'anything but a man' until the trial. In an interview Haward said she met the 'Colonel' first in her father's chemist shop in Littlehampton and had no reason to believe the tall, good-looking and entirely charming officer was a woman. However, later testimony revealed that Elfrida knew the 'Colonel' first as Mrs Pearce-Crouch, mother of two, who came into the shop dressed as a Land Army girl in trousers and an open-shirt. This prior female friendship, however, was irrelevant to the romance. 'Because she courted me as a man,' Elfrida told the court, 'I believed she was a man.'[11] Moreover, Barker told her 'there could be no normal relations,' because of an abdominal injury the 'Colonel' had suffered during the war. The 'Colonel' even managed to convince Elfrida's father that she was really a baronet named Sir Victor Barker. For most of her life she had lived, she told him, as a woman because her mother had always wanted a daughter, and so when Sir Victor Barker, her father, had died she, his son, was dressed as a girl by her mother. On the strength of this story the 'Colonel' proposed and was accepted by Elfrida and her father.

The following day's testimony of the sensational trial, however, revealed yet another twist. Elfrida admitted that the couple had only married after her father had discovered them living together in Brighton's Grand Hotel in 1923. At this point in the trial Sir Earnest Wild's questioning contained more than a note of disbelief. He asked Elfrida if she and the 'Colonel' had lived together at the Grand 'apparently as husband and wife?'

"Yes," replied Elfrida.
"Did you sleep in the same room and bed?" he queried.
"Yes," replied Elfrida who began to show signs of fainting as Wild pressed on.
"When did you discover she was a woman?"
"Not until I read about it in the newspapers."[12]

More upsetting than the possible motives for two women wanting to marry, Wild believed, was the couple's deception of the church. In his summing up he thundered:

If ['Colonel' Barker] had wanted to marry another woman she could have gone through a ceremony in a register office. There is no justification for her abusing the church.[13]

Valerie Arkell-Smith's greatest crime was, in the eyes of the prosecution, her refusal to carry out her deception with discretion and anonymity. Instead she flaunted the confidence she gained as the 'Colonel' in British society, choosing ever grander sights for her masquerade and taking ever greater risks. 'As the weeks slipped by,' she wrote of her transformation from Mrs Arkell-Smith to Sir Victor Barker, 'I began to experience a sense of exhilaration at the knowledge I was getting away with it.'[14]

There was more. *The Sketch* reported that she had successfully used her officer's guise to deceive a man who had witnessed her first wedding to an Australian officer, Harold Arkell-Smith, in 1918. Barker's knowledge of military manoeuvres so convinced Colonel R. Neave that he helped 'him' organize a dinner for survivors of the Battle of the Mons at the Adelphi restaurant in London. 'It is perhaps the biggest and most complex hoax the West End has ever known,' Neave said of her exploits, 'and I was completely deceived by "Colonel" Barker.' The *Daily Express* portrayed Barker as a romantic figure who 'received a man's welcome among men, smoked, drank, worked and played as a man with men.' For her astonishing ability to mimic male behaviour and blend into these quintessential masculine environments, reporters could only praise her. When her confidence faltered and she cried piteously as Elfrida Haward entered the court room, their pronouncement was that she 'broke down and showed that she was, indeed, a woman.'[15] She became a pathetic figure, who bordered on collapse during the trial and when asked to stand murmured, 'Oh God, I cannot.' After she was charged, 'with tears streaming down her face and leaning heavily on two policemen, she was almost carried through a side door to another room.'[16]

But even though the 'Colonel' billed herself as an exception, divorcing herself from any connection with Radclyffe Hall's cause of sexual tolerance, she acknowledged that financial inequality had partly prompted her disguise. Making a living as a man was simply easier and more satisfying, and the Recorder of London accepted this. However, he also believed the 'Colonel's' short-cut to economic security was unique, but even as the trial was in progress another case came to light. On 24 April, two days before sentencing, The *Daily Herald* reported that a 16-year-old servant, Elsie Carter, had appeared in North Holland Police Station charged with stealing a man's suit and bicycle. No motive was given for Elsie Carter's masquerade except that in her employer's clothes she could venture into Boston and Skegness by night. Her actions spoke for themselves since a man's suit clearly afforded a domestic servant access to another world and escape from the drudgery of her labour. Unfortunately the court had little sympathy with Elsie Carter's restless spirit and remanded her to Nottingham jail, 'with a view to Borstal treatment.'

Despite his belief that the 'Colonel's' case was unique, Wild worried that it might set other precedents. 'You are an unprincipled, mendacious and

unscrupulous adventuress,' Wild solemnly addressed the 'Colonel' before
her sentencing:

> You have profaned the House of God, you have outraged the decencies of
> Nature and you have broken the Laws of man. . . . You have set an evil exam-
> ple, which, were you to go unpunished, others might follow.[17]

Underlying his vociferous condemnation of her actions was a fear that it
might give encouragement to other forms of female resistance to subordi-
nate social conventions. With Radclyffe Hall's trial and public debates about
whether women had been made more belligerent by their work in 'masculine' jobs during the Great War fresh in public minds, the woman in male
clothes had become a potent symbol of female rebellion. Typical was a
Daily Sketch cartoon that depicted a pinch-faced woman wearing a suit and
tie questioning a blimpish campaign candidate. 'Do you believe in sex
equality?' she asks. He replies: 'Certainly, but leave us the neckties.'[18] In
1929 male power still resided in ties, trousers, short hair-cuts and, of
course, officer's uniforms.

Wild was wrong in thinking of the 'Colonel's' adoption of her military
guise as an anomaly. Her decision to live as a man — to escape an unhappy
home, to find release from the bonds of womanhood and to acquire the
social power of men — was grounded in a long tradition. The warrior heroines of popular literature echoed the 'Colonel's' decision to leave her husband by adopting a new identity. 'Behind the change from woman to man,'
she wrote in 1956, 'I would be able to screen myself against all the tortures,
miseries and difficulties of the past and work out my own salvation.'[19] Her
marriage to Elfrida Haward which gave financial security and social legitimacy to their relationship had its parallels in the lives of many earlier
female-husbands. Contrary to Wild's belief, women had been breaking the
laws of men and outraging the decencies of nature for a very long time.

It is impossible to know how many women actually chose to live as men
by adopting male clothing and assuming a 'masculine' occupation throughout British history. Only those women whose identity was discovered or
who, for various reasons, publicly surrendered their masquerade have come
to light. Aside from newspaper reports that recorded an occasional discovery,
there is rich material evidence of these womens' existence in ballads, songs,

dramas, and court cases from earlier centuries. Court records also reveal cases of women charged with stealing male clothes, and prosecutions for fraud or miscellaneous crimes that their deception involved. Since some female soldiers were awarded medals, pensions and retired to army hospitals there are scattered references to them in military publications.

Some idea of the common occurrence of female cross-dressing can be gleaned from the diary of the writer, A. J. Munby, who was keenly interested in Victorian working women. In February 1866 Munby met Helen alias Richard Bruce in Stroud where she had been discovered to be a woman in disguise. Helen had worn male clothes for seven years and told Munby she knew of a girl from Downham Market who was working as a sailor, and a week before Bruce's arrest the Ipswich police had found 'a lass tramping West her way in sailor's clothes.' Bruce began her adventure with another woman who dressed as a boy and ran errands from St. Paul's churchyard in London. During her seven years living as a man Bruce had met a Scots girl from Aberdeen serving as an ordinary seaman but after discovery continued her male disguise and worked at the Gateshead Iron Works. The two met in a pub, found out each other's sex and became fast friends.[20]

The theme of female cross-dressing is not confined to Britain but has been common throughout European and North American folk literature. Beginning with the legendary Amazons, a tribe of Syrian women who vowed to defend themselves and to forsake marriage when their husbands were killed and they were driven from their homeland, female soldiers' stories have persisted for centuries.[21] However, anthropologists and historians have argued that these stories of gender reversal also perform an important function within their given social context. Sexual inversion as a widespread form of cultural play in literature, in art, and in festivity has served to disrupt and ultimately to clarify often fluid or evolving concepts of sexual difference.[22]

Female soldiers in seventeenth-century English drama also reflected a growing concern about appropriate male and female roles. According to one estimation of the more than 300 plays first performed in London between 1660 and 1700, 89 contained roles in which actresses donned male clothes.[23] The 'roaring girls' of the stage disrupted the ordered scheme that depended on each sex maintaining its proper function; dress and appearance operated as political shorthand. During this period of enormous economic, social and political transition in Britain, the women warriors were symbols of threatening female aggression — another sign of the world gone topsy-turvy.[24] But although they appeared to rebel against women's position in society, these characters were ultimately resigned to it. The inverted women of these dramas accepted marriage as a preferable alternative to prostitution which was considered the only option for sexually independent women. Female soldiers in this context advocated change, not revolution and served to clarify the importance of sexual difference. By satirizing or mocking deviants, the drama defined norms and by the eighteenth century the female warrior had become a popular, even conventional, heroine.

Although there is mounting evidence of women donning men's clothes to enter a wide-range of occupations, the best-documented cases are those of women soldiers and sailors.[25] The long years of war in the eighteenth century when naval press gangs roamed Britain produced more than 100 female warriors who surface in more than 1,000 variations of Anglo-American ballads.[26] However, the dream of escape from the increasingly oppressive confines of femininity was a phenomenon that developed beyond North America and Britain. While living on an estate near Stockholm in 1813 Fredrika Bremer, who later became a well-known travel writer, was caught up in an adolescent desire to join Sweden's Prince in the battle against Napoleon. 'She wept bitterly for not having been born a man,' wrote her sister Charlotte, 'so that she could have joined her countrymen against the general disturber of peace.' A decade earlier Russian Nadezhda Durova, disguised as a man, was granted a commission in Alexander I of Russia's hussar's campaign against the French in 1807 and served nearly ten years in the light cavalry during the Napoleonic wars.[27] Some French, Prussian, German and Austrian women also took up their country's cause disguised as volunteers in a similar bid to quell a 'restless, passionate' soul.[28] In Holland, working-class women living in seaports were even advised by relatives to take up a career, in male guise, as a sailor and many enlisted in the Dutch East India Company during the early modern period.[29]

In England Henry Addington, first Viscount of Sidmouth, received a petition from the women of Neath in 1803 responding to rumours about a French invasion. The townswomen requested permission:

> to defend ourselves as well as the weaker women and children amongst us. There are in this town about 200 women who have been used to hard labour all the days of their lives such as working in coal-pits, on the high roads, tilling

the ground, etc. If you would grant us arms, that is light pikes . . . we do assure you that we could in a short time learn our exercise.[30]

Even though the women pleaded with Addington that, 'we are not trifling with you but serious in our proposal,' their request was denied. In Devon and Cornwall women helped defend the ports from the French and Spanish by disguising themselves in soldiers' dress. They wrapped themselves in red cloaks and stood at the headlands in military formation to frighten the enemy.[31]

Throughout the nineteenth century, collections of stories about some of these famous Amazons appeared on booksellers lists and peppered the pages of antiquarian magazines. Collected editions of their life-histories, sanitized to conform to the prevailing notions of Victorian morality, were still produced at the end of the century. The warrior heroine continued to draw audiences into Britain's music-halls where the lass in breeches swaggered in a caricature of masculinity. Pleasure Gardens provided another outlet for this powerful fantasy. At these venues in working-class neighbourhoods of London, women could rent male costumes at the door or came dressed as seamen or soldiers, rough-housed with their male companions, while they smoked and drank at the bar.

The female soldier was given a new prestige during the Great War when photos and reports of women fighting as soldiers, disguised as men or serving in an all-female battalion in Russia, began to filter back to Britain and North America. Debates raged on both sides of the Atlantic about whether women were fit to become combatants and what devastating consequences this might have on relations between the sexes. As Dr. Dudley Sergeant, physical expert at Harvard University said in 1917: 'The average, normal woman . . . is biologically more of a barbarian.'[32] Unleashed, it was feared, a monstrous regiment of women might dominate the earth. As women were increasingly catapulted into traditionally male spheres of work during the war, the female soldier came to symbolize the ultimate liberation. It was falsely assumed that entry into the military, the most masculine of occupations, would herald a new dawn of equality. If women could now defend their country, went a popular argument, they must be guaranteed political power.

It is tempting to claim these women as our feminist forebears and to read into their acts an intentional and self-conscious desire to defy the prevailing notions of sexual difference. But their lives demand a more complex analysis. Their life-histories and popular representations present a myriad of contradictions that raise questions about understandings of gender and heroism that are not easily resolved. Their individual stories must also be understood within their historical circumstances — their rebellion was qualitatively different over time and place. Attempts to recast these women merely as unconventional heroines, simplifying their actions and motives, would be equally intellectually stifling. The richness of these stories lies in the problems they present.

During the course of their entry into the masculine world many became so immersed in their male identity that women became 'the other' in their eyes. Women, such as the music hall male impersonators of the late nineteenth century, were forced to admit that they were different but would prove their 'womanliness' whenever it was required.[33] In the military, women experienced an individual liberation that dissolved any sense of sisterly solidarity as they became 'one of the boys.' Often the only way for women to cope with the contradiction of being both female and a soldier was to actively deny their connection with the feminine world. Disguised as men they engaged in acts of imitation love-making, flirted, teased, abused and insulted other women to secure their own position. To expect these female warriors to challenge an institution in which they held such a precarious position is unrealistic. Even their fictional representations, who subverted concepts of sexual difference, could claim no nascent feminist understanding, and instances where authors used the female soldiers' exploits to illustrate the unrealized, potential power of women are rare. It is, rather, their very presence in such male spheres that often speaks louder than their words.

'Colonel' Barker presents the complexities of this phenomenon very starkly. While we may applaud her courage in fleeing from a drunken and brutal husband in the safety of a male guise, and admire her ability to flaunt her newly-found confidence, her political involvement with the National Fascisiti, a breakaway branch of Britain's fascist movement in which she became a 'leading light,' is much more difficult to understand. In 1927 she joined, according to a friend, 'not so much from patriotic motives as from the spice of adventure it introduced into life.'[34] The 'spice' it lent to Barker's life included running the boxing programme — designed to whip members into top physical condition to combat 'the reds and the pinks' — and participating in the Sunday afternoon disruptions of the Communist Party meetings in Hyde Park.[35]

The National Fascisiti were a more militant element of the British Fascists who broke away from the party in the autumn of 1924 to pursue 'positive fascism.' Small in number and largely confined to London, they adopted the black shirt as a uniform and other prevalent fascist symbols and myths. They boasted a larger membership than the British Fascists because of their active and violent pursuit of the Communists. Their programme was ill-defined but clearly anti-Semitic, anti-communist, and supported the mainte-nance of the monarch, the preservation of Empire and the development of a 'truly national spirit.'[36] The party proposed a government of experts with a governing executive of men (of British birth and breeding) with the will and power to rule. Overall their influence on the public order, policy and opin-ion was negligible and 'Colonel' Barker became its best-known member.

The 'Colonel's' story is not unusual in the contradictions she embodied. As a woman taking on a masculine identity she made a mockery of the mili-tary officials and judges she deceived. As a woman escaping from a brutal common-law husband to live with her female lover the disguise afforded her the individual liberation she was seeking. But, as her involvement in the National Fascisti so clearly demonstrates, her own rebellion against the con-straints of her gender did not translate into a broader social analysis of oppression. Rather she allied herself with the most hierarchical and authori-tative ideology of the day, embracing an extreme of masculinity.

Cross-dressing for women often remained a process of imitation rather than a self-conscious claiming of the social privileges given exclusively to men for all women. Their exploits challenged existing categories of sexual difference but the terms of the debate usually remained the same. Was women's real oppression challenged by these heroines who felt only capable of grasping an individual liberation? The female sailors who were discov-ered working on British naval and merchant ships were described as prov-ing themselves 'as good a man as any other' or even performing their duties so skillfully they 'caused a degree of envy in the other lads.'[37] They were known to run up the mast with expertise, could hold their grog like any other tar and never shirked the most arduous of duties. They proved that women were equally capable of excelling in the masculine sphere but since the female soldiers and sailors remained such staunch individualists, they presented little threat to the established order.

Women who entered male occupations, passing as men or known to their workmates, often coped with the contradictions of their position by developing a strong male-identification. They refused to accept the traditional, socially-assigned fate of their sex and managed a 'basic feminine protest.' But these women appear largely unconcerned about changing the society that produced the inequity which they felt most keenly in their own lives.[38] Moreover, their rejection of the female role was often accompanied by a high degree of self-denial because this process did not allow them selectively to disregard sex-assigned characteristics. They traded roles rather than forged new ones so their rebellion was never without a heavy price.

Ironically, the crux of the disjuncture between masculine and feminine identities surfaced most poignantly for these women in their sexual relations. The real Amazons took from prevailing concepts of masculinity what they needed to survive in extremely difficult circumstances. But, as the case of long-standing heroine St. Joan illustrates, women have yet to attain a third order or a state of 'genderlessness.'[39] The female warrior's acceptance was often based on denial of her sexuality and great emphasis was placed on her virginity or sexlessness in popular representations. Her passport into the world of male experience was usually issued on a temporary basis, to be revoked during peacetime or if she overstepped the boundaries of the behaviour allowed her. This was an individual rebellion rather than a tactic for social revolution that took place on the highly-contested, constantly shifting ground of gender-identity.

The Amazons' actual sexual experience is often masked behind literary convention and the fantasy of male authors. Eighteenth-century biographers describe the female soldiers visiting brothels, wooing female suitors and indulging in overt, sexual teasing. However, neither they nor their readers' understanding of these actions conforms to contemporary notions about lesbian identity. This is not to deny the experience of women who loved each other but to pose the difficulty in evaluating how the women themselves understood their sexual relations. Since the scenario of an innocent female falling for a woman in soldier's disguise is so clichéd, the sources themselves cannot be trusted to give a realistic portrayal. These passages were possibly intended solely to titillate male audiences although this too remains speculative. The letters, diaries and newspaper interviews with 'real-life' soldiers and the purely fictional representations of women in battle provide few clues about this aspect of life. It is, however, clear that women expressed a desire not for the physical acquisition of a male body but for a male social identity.

The context of the female warrior's masquerade points to another important contradiction. For many women their only liberation from the confines of domestic responsibilities was experienced during wartime. They exercised skills, travelled with security, socialized freely, found comradeship and acceptance; the male world became accessible in an exciting way. The military gave them an identity and, under the guise of patriotism or wifely devotion, an understandable motive for rejecting hearth and home. Many never readjusted after this experience but found their awareness of female oppression doubled when their superior status was snatched away from them after war ended.

The excitement these stories still generate, and the reasons for their persistence, lies at the heart of their relevance. Theresa Russell's portrait of an officer in the 1987 film, *Aria*, the cross-dressing American forces pilot of Marge Piercy's novel about the Second World War, *Gone to Soldiers*, the Confederate female soldier in Rita Mae Brown's *High Hearts* and Fa Mau Lan, the heroine of Maxine Hong Kingston's novel, *Warrior Women*, provide a few contemporary examples.[40] Political scientist Jean Bethke Elshtain has recently written about her childhood fantasy of 'becoming a leader of men' after watching Ingrid Bergman in the film, *St. Joan*. 'I dreamed of action,' she wrote, 'of Joan, of myself in male battle attire, fighting for morally worthy ends. Oh yes.'[41]

The interest in female soldiers endures partly because we lack so few powerful, mocking heroines and because they live out an adventure that transgresses sexual boundaries. Deborah Sampson, a soldier in the American War of Independence who published her memoirs as *The Female Review* and conducted a public speaking tour in 1802, was commemorated a century later by leading suffragettes such as Mary Livermore. When Flora Sandes, an English woman who became a Serbian officer in 1915 went to Australia on a public speaking tour in 1920, women packed the halls in Kempsey, Darrigo, Coff's Harbour and Sydney. In 1750 Hannah Snell's biographer acknowledged in his introduction that the 'fair sex,' for whom his treatise was chiefly intended, would benefit most from its telling.[42]

The female swashbucklers of popular literature provided an alternative image of women and inspired others to challenge the rigid definitions of sexual difference. Emma Edmonds, a 19-year-old soldier in the American Civil War, was inspired to 'step into the glorious independence' of masculinity after reading Lieutenant Murray's novel, *Fanny Campbell or The Female Pirate Captain*.[43] Although Fanny went to sea to find a lost lover, Emma Edmonds used her disguise as Franklin Thompson to avoid marriage to a New Brunswick farmer by running away from home. Christian Davies, Britain's most famous eighteenth-century soldier, even received poems from adoring women who knew of her exploits and declared, 'the Amazonian race begins again.'[44]

If Emma Edmonds was disappointed in her heroine Fanny Campbell, who disguised herself merely to follow a man, there were other heroines who were more explicit in their desire for adventure. Hannah Snell first went in search of her husband, who had deserted her, out of financial necessity rather than sentiment and when Christian Davies found her long-lost love, she demanded that they live as brothers until the end of the campaign because she was enjoying her life as a man. Female sailors in nineteenth-century London often cited economic need as their primary motive for signing aboard while others, their masquerade stripped away, supported themselves earning only a meagre subsistence.

There was little need to convince audiences before this century that a woman could withstand the hardships of the ship or army camp. A report in 1813 from a London newspaper, *The Weekly Dispatch*, illustrates both the violence of that age and women's involvement in what we might consider male arenas. On a quiet Sunday morning in early October a crowd gathered to witness 'a kind of pitched battle' between boxers Mary Flaharty and Peggy Carey for the prize of £17 10s at a small field in South London. Although Peg Carey won after the final round, 'both ladies were much punished and Mary was taken away senseless in a tilbury [cart].'[45] The women in this age who rode, hunted, played cricket, boxed and participated in other tough, dangerous sports made the female soldier and sailor infinitely more believable than she appears today.

Inadvertently the women warriors generated debate and discussion, even if it was only within the confines of whether women should or could be combatants. When Flora Sandes toured Australia in 1920 the press speculated whether her appearance at the Melbourne race track, in her uniform, unabashedly smoking a cigarette, would not inspire other women to flaunt social conventions. Her 1916 autobiography of life in the Serbian army was met with cries of 'she's the new woman' and 'a modern girl' from British reviewers.[46] The Russian female soldiers of the Great War prompted American experts to comment on what impact this new phenomenon would have 'on our ideals, our chivalry and of all that has grown out of them.'[47] In 1950 military officials still used the image of Polly Oliver, a female sailor from an eighteenth-century ballad, to discuss the 'comical fancy' of women's earlier historical and future participation in warfare.[48]

As these few examples demonstrate, the meaning of the Amazons' stories has inevitably been highly contentious. Just as the issues involved in the debate about sexual difference change over time so does the larger framework of our understanding. The stories reflect the shift in the eighteenth-century concept of this difference as an outwardly defined, fluid entity to the Victorian's reliance on the theory that biology dictated destiny. By the mid-nineteenth century a woman's nature was believed to anchor her to the home where her reproductive role could best be fulfilled. The shifts and fluctuations across this terrain affirm the notion of sexual difference as a quality dictated more by society than biology.[49] However, it is in the military — arguably the most male of institutions — that what was historically involved in a woman 'becoming a man' is most clearly discernible. Since the Amazon's shedding of her 'femininity' is never static the retelling of her story over time is also a useful indicator of society's changing understanding of male and female roles. Above all it is striking that this phenomenon of women literally claiming trousers for their own has persisted for centuries, across cultures, occupations and classes. Moreover, an examination of their stories reveal that their motives and experiences were remarkably similar.

It would appear that women have simply borrowed male dress as an avenue to gain power denied them elsewhere in their lives. However, the differences in women's circumstances must also be considered in articulating the significance of male imitation in different historical periods. I hope to highlight the voice of the women themselves, to illuminate what prompted them to leave behind their homes, families, friends, indeed their very identity for the danger and discomfort that inevitably accompanied a military or naval life. Where that voice is muted and distorted we can at least discern what an audience was willing to believe about these female adventurers and the significant role they played in the popular imagination.

Another contradiction the warrior heroine presents is simply in her role as a soldier that often filled her with a heady blood-lust. The Amazons' experience defined within a period of warfare raises questions about the importance of sexual difference to military ideology. At a time when many nations, including Canada, the United States and Britain, are considering increased recruitment of women into the armed forces to shore-up labour shortages this issue takes on an increasing relevance.[50] During the 1980s opposition to nuclear weapons and the arms race have also become an important focus for the feminist movement in western capitalist countries. But the argument, produced by some feminist theorists to explain the connection between sexual difference and military ideology, is ambivalent about the identification of a basic biological or at least some essential psychological difference between the sexes.[51] The experience of the female combatants in this book contradict the notion that women are inherently more pacifist than men. It is simply naive and untrue. Moreover such an approach does not help us understand the military's continual dependence on women: on their labour and practical skills as soldiers, nurses, munitions workers and their support as wives and mothers of uniformed men.

By linking women's role as housekeepers and mothers to pacifism, existing social relations are reinforced rather than challenged; the real experience of women during times of war is denied and so is the military's appeal to them. This argument that often relies on biology to explain gender differences only masks the real complexities and inconsistencies that women in such 'masculine' environments face. It is equally misleading to condemn the actions of these military women as a form of 'false consciousness.' Women like Christian Davies, Hannah Snell, Maria Botchkareva and Flora Sandes inherited rather than chose the circumstances in which they made their own history. Given the limitations of their options it is perhaps surprising there were not more women who chose this rebellion against the strictures of their time.

These stories are not about women's involvement in auxiliary or support units but are largely confined to the experience of women who served, openly or disguised, in all-male fighting units. The contemporary debate about the danger for feminists of pushing for women's increased access to the armed services has exposed the importance of rigid definitions of sexual difference to military ideologies. Policy makers, historically and currently, use women to achieve their goals and the key to their control is to define women's function as marginal to the military's identity, no matter how crucial their role actually is.[52] Excluded from participation as combatants, women have been relegated to the sidelines and fighting remains the ultimate test of masculinity, a chance for men to assert their control, their capacity for domination, conquest and even immortality.

But what of those women who have been allowed into battle and given guns? What happens to their need to prove their 'manhood' and why has this historically been regarded as unthreatening to the nature of masculinity? What circumstances permitted women access to that exclusively male preserve, the front? These questions will be raised by focussing on the process that gave women an ability to cope with the duality of being a female soldier. The social value of militarism, changing concepts of sex roles, women's material circumstances, the importance of nationalism and patriotic sentiments are all crucial variables in these stories. The nature of warfare, military organization and its relations to the general society have undergone significant changes over the period of this study. These factors also play a part in the story. War allows men to assume their role as patriarchs; to become the defenders of the nation, the protectors of 'their' metaphorical and actual women and children. It confers a homogeneity upon their aims, pursuits, identities and rewards them with a short-lived glory. During times of war sexual difference becomes heightened even as the sexual divisions of labour become blurred. But it is only relatively recently that gender has assumed such a prominent role during times of war.

Women have always played an important part in the British military as the stories of the warrior heroines illustrate. They served aboard ships, although unofficially recognized, worked in cannon crews, nursed and even gave birth while at sea. Women also formed an integral part of camp life in early modern armies, performing a wide variety of tasks including foraging for food, selling meats and wines, laundering, nursing or looting as well as working as prostitutes.[53] At Britain's largest military battles in the eighteenth and nineteenth centuries women's presence is also well-documented. Sergeant-Major Edward Cotton in his account of the battle of Waterloo in 1815 mentions the women who died on the field including a female officer of the French hussars who had been shot dead:

> Many women were found amongst the slain although not of the same class as the heroine alluded to. As is common in the camp, the camp followers wore

male attire, with nearly as martial a bearing as the soldiers and some were even mounted and rode astride.[54]

Women also sailed with the 'first rates' during the Napoleonic wars and performed a variety of jobs during the large-scale operations. But their function within the military was rarely officially recognized and only organized in the mid-nineteenth century. By the early part of the century three-quarters of Britain's infantry was stationed overseas and the decline of soldier's use in civilian service alongside the construction of large-scale buildings further removed them from public view. The new barracks excluded soldiers' relatives, sutlers and hangers-on, including women. Sexual and marital relations were brought under the military's direct control for the first time in this period. As the army became increasingly professional and bureaucratic, regiments assumed control over all aspects of a soldier's life and became more exclusively male.[55]

At the same time other military heroines began to emerge. Descriptions of Florence Nightingale's work in the Crimea were accompanied by stories of brave wives and heroic mothers who found themselves in battle but never strayed from their supportive role.[56] With the concurrent change in ideals of sexual difference were real changes in women's role within the British military which was being reorganized to conform more fully with Victorian concepts of marriage and family responsibility. Soldiers' overcrowded and communal housing, their high mobility and reputation for promiscuous sexuality were all regarded as outward manifestations of their potential or real failure to adhere to the prevailing moral code.[57]

A dramatic rewriting of history subsequently took place. In addition to women's long and diverse performance as auxiliaries within the military, the female soldiers and sailors were erased from the record or reduced to the occasional footnote. The female soldiers who were hailed as heroines, albeit exceptions a century earlier, became portrayed as amusing freaks of nature and their stories examples of 'coarseness and triviality.'[58]

This suspicion of women who aspired to the ranks was reinforced by contemporary studies on morality. In 1897 Havelock Ellis, an early sexologist, wrote in his *Studies in the Psychology of Sex* about the British soldier's willingness to engage himself as a prostitute. The private soldier would usually prefer women for pleasure, but Ellis noted that, 'on summer evenings Hyde Park and the neighbourhood of Albert Gate is full of Guardsmen and others plying a lively trade, with little disguise — in uniform or out . . . it means a covetable addition to Tommy Atkin's pocket.'[59] Such revelations reinforced the perception that soldiers and military families lived on the very margin of social respectability. In 1913 the author, A. R. Hope Moncrieff, summed up the Victorian middle-class attitude toward the female desire for a military life: 'In our day a certain ridicule attaches itself to the character of a woman in arms, made admirable only by such religious enthusiasms as inspired Joan of Arc.'[60] It was only when nationalist military glory gained a new lease of life during the Great War that such 'characters' could claim more admirable motives and find a new place of honour.

The circumstances in which women signed on as soldiers, sailors or found themselves in battle as combatants through other means is another important variable in the Amazons' stories. Some of the women in this book were asked to sign on as women; others lived their entire lives as men and their sex was only revealed upon their deaths. Some were 'ladies' and joined as the wives or daughters of officers where their privilege spared them the dangers and extreme discomfort in which the enlisted men and their families lived. Yet others were working-class women who found the shift from physically-demanding farm or domestic labour to the rigours of army life quite unproblematic. The army became the only home some ever knew, while for others the adventure lasted only a few days.

The thread that pulls these stories together is women's desire for male privilege and a longing for escape from domestic confines and powerlessness. Many vividly describe a lifelong yearning for liberation from the constraints they chafed against as women. They were unconventional women who spent their lives rebelling against their assigned role before they pursued a male career. Most could only conceive of themselves as active and powerful in male disguise. Some were lesbians who bravely risked ostracism and punishment by symbolically claiming the right to women's erotic love through their assumption of male clothing. Many, when the initial purpose for their masquerade had been served, continued to pass as men or deeply longed for a return to their male role. Happy endings are all too rare in these stories.

Today dress has lost its potency as an indicator of gender and social status but the rewards of 'male' imitation remain. The business woman's suit which mimics its masculine counterpart is one contemporary example.

What we share with the warrior heroine is a recognition that the social construction of our sexual difference is still an enormously important determining factor in our lives. The barriers to equality between the sexes have yet to be eliminated and our struggle for what is still deemed male power is far from over. The Amazons, while uneasy heroines, can lay claim to be our feminist predecessors, by virtue of their battle against those powerful ideas that still maintain territories marked outside women's reach. They also dramatically illustrate how, with courage and imagination, women have always found ways of overcoming even the most seemingly impossible restrictions.

2

And Then Annie
Got Her Gun

❦

*You have expressed a desire to know what led me to assume male attire. I will
try to tell you. I think I was born into this world with some dormant antagonism toward man. I hope I have outgrown it measurably but my infant soul
was impressed with a sense of my mother's wrongs before I ever saw the light
and I probably drew from her breast with my daily food my love of
independence and my hatred of male tyranny.*
Sarah Emma Edmonds[1]

THE AMERICAN CIVIL War's most famous female soldier, Emma
Edmonds, claimed after her retirement from the army that her inspiration to take up arms came from a nascent understanding of her oppression as a woman. But along with her 'hatred of male tyranny' she
remembered being struck forcefully by the imaginative power of a character
in a favourite childhood book. Dreaming of escape from drudgery and her
father's volatile temper, Emma turned to her heroine, a female pirate,
for hope.

Fanny Campbell, female pirate captain, blue stocking and bold saviour of
deserving men, graces the frontispiece of Lieutenant Murray's 1815 novel.
The intrepid heroine stands defiantly on the wood-planked deck of her ship
gazing out into some foreign sea. She grasps a black flag embossed with a
skull and cross bones in her left hand and in her right she sports a menacing
sabre that reaches to the floor in a graceful arch. The captain's hips are hid-
den beneath a short but modest skirt, a hint of short curls adorns her pea-
cock-feather hat and frames the delicate features of her face. Her lips are
touched with the faintest hint of a smile.

Murray succeeded in creating an appealing figure. So thought teenaged Emma Edmonds, who surreptitiously read the novel on a spring day when she should have been planting potatoes with her sister on the family farm in Prince William parish, New Brunswick in 1854. Emma's copy of *Fanny Campbell or the Female Pirate Captain* was a gift from her mother. It was the first novel Emma had ever read and she felt honoured that of her four sisters, she the youngest, had been the recipient of this kind gesture. Unlike Emma, her heroine Fanny's parents spared no expense in educating their daughter — hers was a life of writing poetry rather than planting potatoes. But Fanny was no effete intellectual. She was equally adept at rowing a boat, shooting a panther or riding the wildest horse in the state. She wrote thoughtful prose and her friends respected her talents as a scholar. 'Fanny Campbell was none of your modern belles, delicate and ready to faint at the first sight of a reptile,' wrote Murray, 'No Fanny could . . . do almost any brave and useful act.'[2]

Thirteen-year-old Emma was delighted with the novel and intoxicated by the simple ingenuity of Fanny's disguise; with just a blue sailor's jacket, breeches, a haircut shorn of her long, brown curls she stepped 'into the freedom and glorious independence of masculinity.'[3] While Emma scorned Fanny's low ambition to masquerade merely to rescue her lover William Lowell, the heroine's ability to transcend her femininity seemed, to her, touched with genius. As the realization that Fanny's adventure lay open to her as well, Emma tossed her straw hat in the air and let a lusty cry of sheer delight ring out into the surrounding fields — salvation was hers. 'All the latent energy of my nature was aroused and each exploit of the heroine thrilled me to my fingertips . . . I was emancipated! and could never again be a *slave.*' As she crossed the fields home that evening she plotted that, one day, she would emulate Fanny's brilliant scheme. Like many of her fellow female warriors, a longing to escape was the central theme of her early life.

While still in her teens, Emma became a partner of Miss Henrietta Perrige in a Moncton millinery store, giving her some degree of independence from her tyrannical father. But her moment for escape came when he announced her impending engagement to a local farmer. She consented to the engagement but only 'in obedience to orders' and covertly planned her escape. *Fanny Campbell* was a novel of her youth but at the age of 19 Emma self-consciously followed her heroine's plot and 'unceremoniously left for parts unknown' in male clothing.[4]

She began a new life as Frank Thompson selling family bibles door-to-door for a publishing house in Hartford, Connecticut. During her transition from Emma to Frank she ventured out canvassing the good book only by night and sleeping in the woods by day until she became accustomed to her new identity. Frank began selling bibles 'in earnest' only when New Brunswick was a safe distance behind her. She settled in Flint, Michigan for a year where she lived in the home of Reverend Mr. Joslin, a Methodist pastor. She sold her books in the surrounding area with great success and spent her free time taking her lady-friends on country rides in her stylish, horse-drawn buggy. Her friend Damon Stuart, who knew her first as Frank Thompson, described 'him' as, 'glib of tongue, thoroughly business-like, and had an open persuasive manner that was particularly attractive.'[5]

She returned to visit her mother in New Brunswick after a year. She recounted in 1883 that her family had failed to recognize her when she ate supper with them, although when she stepped into the barn, the farm animals greeted her. 'My mother,' she said, 'looking up through a mist of tears asked my sister, "Fanny, don't you think this young man looks like your poor sister?"'[6] Emma then burst into tears and was forced to prove her identity before her mother would accept her miraculous transformation. But her visit was brief because she feared encountering her father and she left that afternoon.

Frank Thompson, 'after a strange catastrophe,' lost all her worldly possessions except a bible which she sold for $5 to see her through to Hartford, Connecticut. Frank then found work with a publishing company selling books in Nova Scotia. Her sales throughout the province were highly successful, clearing $900 in 10 months. While on the road she stayed in good houses, ate well and 'came near marrying a pretty little girl who was bound I should not leave Nova Scotia without her.' During this period Frank Thompson was buoyed with confidence and recalled later: 'Oh how manly I felt; and what pride I took in proving (to my employers) that their confidence in me was not misplaced.'[7] But Frank left 'his' sweetheart in Halifax for the lures of the West and returned to Michigan at the beginning of the American Civil War.

On 12 April 1861 Confederate forces fired upon Fort Sumter and President Abraham Lincoln swiftly called for 75,000 military recruits. Five days later Frank Thompson enlisted in a local militia unit that was accepting men for the second Michigan volunteers. While living in Flint, Frank had befriended William Morse, captain of the Flint Union Greys and enlisted in time to attend a mass meeting and to help choose its officers — Morse among them.[8] The Greys' departure was marked by a parade of the 'boys' and an address from Morse. Each soldier was ceremoniously presented with a bible courtesy of the Methodist Episcopal church, the Flint ladies pinned a rosette inscribed, 'The Union and The Constitution' on each volunteer and Reverend Joslin pronounced the benediction.[9]

The reasons for Emma Edmonds' decision to enlist remain obscured by her own writing on the subject. In her autobiography, *Nurse and Spy in the Union Army*, she recounted ironically that she was working for a foreign missionary society when war broke out. As a Canadian she could easily have returned home but instead turned to 'the Throne of Grace' for advice.[10] Her prayers directed her to sign up as a field nurse for the Union army. In her autobiography, however, she carefully veils the fact that she was actually disguised as a man when she joined the Greys and she never acknowledges Frank's previous existence. Although religious moral conviction as the sole motive for enlisting wears slightly thin, her story is typical of many female soldiers.

Emma is vague about her childhood yearning for freedom that lead to her initial metamorphosis into Frank. Quite possibly she thought her readers would be less sympathetic toward a woman whose decision to join up was stimulated more by a need to perpetuate her deception than to fight for the Unionist cause. The first edition of *Nurse and Spy*, published in 1865 while the war was still raging, has the quality of a polemic. Emma's adventures are seen through the lens of patriotic sacrifice rather than feminine liberation. Though the warrior heroine was well-known in balladry and in popular literature in Britain and the US during this period, none of these heroines openly declared Edmonds' 'dormant antagonism' towards male tyranny.[11] Even Emma Edmonds' earlier incarnation as Frank and her proto-feminist statements came to light years after her Civil War experience when she spoke from the perspective of wife and mother. But the published testimony of her enlistment, her motives and their later popular representations and misrepresentations shed much light on the warriors' experience.

What Emma Edmonds shares with her fellow female combatants is her sense that, like Fanny Campbell, she too could grasp 'the freedom and glorious independence of masculinity.' Like those women who went before and after, she sensed that donning trousers, a transformation as simple as changing a suit of clothes, would transport her to another, more privileged, world. Shorn of their long, flowing locks and no longer encumbered by stays, bodices, skirts and petticoats these women discovered new freedom of movement. They shed any concern for their appearance along with their feminine modesty. In shirts and breeches they strode forward, capable of expressing themselves in ways they had only dreamed about. As late as 1929 clothing still carried such significant value that this miraculous shift was convincingly made. No audience had difficulty believing that clothing, literally, made the man.

In eighteenth-century ballads, the warrior heroine's transformation is often described with striking understatement.[12] The life-history of Christian Davies, Britain's best-known Amazon of that period, spent little time describing her transformation from Mrs. Welsh to Christopher Welsh because it was unimportant to the audience. The plausibility of the masquerade was taken for granted as Christian Davies says simply:

> I cut off my hair and dressed me in suit of my husband's having had the precaution to quilt the waistcoat to preserve my breasts from hurt which were not large enough to betray my sex and putting on the wig and hat I had prepared I went out and brought me a silver hilted sword and some Holland shirts.[13]

Equally acceptable was the claim by Christian Davies' biographer that a dildo had completed her masculine outfit. Readers puzzled about 'how a woman could so long perform a certain natural operation without being discovered,' were assured that she used 'a silver tube painted over, and fastened about her with leather straps.' It was further claimed that Christian had inherited the 'urinary instrument' from a Captain Bodeaux, a friend of her father's, who stayed one night in their family home and accidentally left it behind in the bed. The Captain and Christian's father left suddenly that night to rejoin their troops headed for the battle of the Boyne. After Bodeaux's death on the field, it was discovered that she was a woman.[14]

In a period when sexual difference and social status were so highly encoded in clothing, audiences easily accepted the desire for such changes of identity. An example of the eighteenth century's rigid adherence to the class significance of clothing is reflected in the sailor, Mary Anne Talbot's, arrest for wearing powder in her hair without a licence. She confessed to her crime but stated: 'It is true that I have worn a little powder in my hair whenever I have had occasion to call at the house of noble persons . . . but I have much more frequently made use of it in defence of my King and country.'[15] Divisions between the sexes and social strata were considered so great that a change of costume could affect a remarkable transformation. Female warrior ballads and stories abound with parents, lovers, sisters, brothers and friends who are completely deceived by her disguise. Safely ensconced in her new role the heroine often explored her 'masculine freedom' with a vengeance.

Madeline Moore, heroine of an 1862 book on the 'thrilling adventures' of a lady lieutenant in the Kentucky Home Guards during the Civil War, used a 'small pair of whiskers and moustache' to complete her outfit. Suitably attired she fooled not only her miserly aunt ('a hypocritical blue stocking') but the lover she set out to find.[16] Madeline admired herself in a full-length mirror for the first time in her new clothes and mused: 'I looked in the glass and must say I fell in love with myself — that is, I should have been apt to take a fancy to just such a youth as I appeared to be.' At one level the heroine convinces herself she has literally become a person who is so different that 'he' can be narcissistically, sexually objectified. Rather than merely exchanging one identity for the other, the heroine creates a 'masculine' self, a fully-fleshed twin. Her femininity is only temporarily obliterated in many stories; it is put on ice until her aim — to win a battle, find her lover, wreak revenge, or complete a journey — has been accomplished.

Declaring herself 'perfectly wild about war,' Loreta Janeta Velasquez disguised herself as Harry T. Buford and joined the Independent Scouts of the Confederate Southern Army in the spring of 1860. In a coat heavily padded with cotton in her back and under her arms to her hips, she set off to follow her husband in the war. After she had made initial adjustments to her new clothes, Loreta Velasquez wrote, 'I lost all fear of being found out and learned to act, talk and almost to think like a man.'[17] Buoyed with this confidence, Velasquez experienced more difficulty in resisting condescending comments about her height rather than anxiety about accidental discovery.

Although Madeline Moore and Loreta Velasquez's stories were fictionalized, first-hand accounts of women who appeared in battle during the Civil War lent legitimacy to their stories.[18] Philip Sheridan, an officer with the Army of the Potomac, once received a report from Colonel Conrad of the Fifteenth Missouri about the shocking behaviour of two women who belonged to his detachment. Conrad said that these two female soldiers 'had given much annoyance by getting drunk and to some extent demoralizing his men.' The women had 'in some mysterious manner' attached themselves as soldiers but were found out when they got drunk on a foraging expedition, had fallen into a river and, half-drowned, were taken to the army surgeon for an examination. Although Sheridan found Conrad's story astonishing, the women were only dismissed because they had become 'disturbers of Conrad's peace of mind.'[19] In 1864 A. Jackson Crossley wrote to his friend Samuel Bradbury from the Army of the Potomac headquarters that among the prisoners brought in was a woman dressed in male clothes. 'She was mounted just like a man and belonged to cavalry though she was taken as a spy; she wore her hair long and did not like to have our men looking at her.'[20] Mary Livermore, a nurse with the Union army, estimated the number of female soldiers who fought in the Civil War at 400. But she adds in her 1888 autobiography of her experiences:

> I am convinced that a larger number of women disguised themselves and enlisted in the service, for one cause or other, than was dreamed of . . . Some startling histories of these military women were current in the gossip of army life; and extravagant and unreal as were many of the narrations, one always felt that they had a foundation in fact.[21]

Though Livermore provides no information about the actual process of enlisting, she states that some women joined simply by appearing in uniform and no further questions were asked.

It is significant that later versions of Emma Edmonds' story question the ease of her recruitment. In response to an article in the Detroit *Post and Tribune*, Edmonds corrected a statement by her friend, Damon Stuart, that the Greys initially rejected her because of her height. According to Stuart, she was only accepted on her second attempt to enlist when many volunteers had dropped out after their initial three month service.[22] A later newspaper article by Delia Davis, written during the Great War, adds another permutation to the episode:

> Although volunteers in those days were not subject to the strict examination of our recent recruits, Frank felt rather nervous and apprehensive over this part of the programme, particularly when he noted how the man ahead of

him in the line was treated. However, the examiner merely looked into the frank honest face, took hold of the firm, strong, but fair hand and asked, "Well, what sort of a living has this hand earned?"

With the dash native to her Frank replied, "Well up to the present that hand has been chiefly engaged in getting an education." And the examiner passed on.[23]

By 1937 Edmonds was described as a 'smart, handsome lad' who convinced recruiting officers that 'he' was 20 although 'he' looked no more than 17. In an article, written in the 1960s, Emma got through the cursory physical examination 'by looking "his" examiner square in the eye and gripping his hand in a firm handshake.'[24]

More contemporary writers struggled to make sense of the evidence that women were able to deceive officers and recruiters in gaining admission in the ranks. But this confusion that begins to appear in the late nineteenth century, rests upon a set of assumptions about constructions of sexual difference. For the woman who so easily disguises herself makes transparent those fixed and immutable barriers between the sexes. She blurs distinctions and raises questions about how they are maintained. Writers of our century emphasize the female soldier's supposed physical weakness (her height, her youthful face) and her *unique* powers of deception because her exploits seem too fantastic. In reality, Emma Edmonds, Flint's well-known lad about town, friend of the Grey's captain, probably had little trouble signing up. She may have looked youthful but her power and social status in the community would have rendered her reputation impeccable. Emma, according to her own testimony, grew up on a farm, spent her childhood working in the fields and was an expert with a horse and rifle. Frank Thompson probably appeared as a sterling candidate for the Greys. Frank's refusal or indifference to joining up would probably have created greater suspicion or even hostility.

Many female soldiers are painted as patriots in glorious colours in contemporary ballads. The reality of their motives for going to war are often very different but, like Edmonds, most were sensitive to the reception their explanations would receive. Others never had an opportunity to tell their stories which were refashioned according to prevailing heroic ideals of love lost, and love found. In these songs love is the province of women while glory is the terrain of men. The female warrior of the ballads, however, embodies both through her devotion to her lover and her inclinations to a valorous soldiering masquerade.[25]

The duality of female love and male glory is frequently reflected in the given and ascribed motives for the female warrior's inspiration to enlist. Maria Bochkareva, leader of Alexander Kerensky's ill-fated Women's Battalion of Death, combined both elements in her biography of her first military experiences. Before forming the Battalion in 1917 Bochkareva fought on the western front in the Tsar's army. She was never disguised but was an oddity in her all-male regiment.[26]

She had married Afansi Bochkarev at the age of 15 in Tomsk, Siberia to escape from her parent's home but soon found her husband matched her father in his brutality. Together Maria and Afansi worked as day labourers on a construction site in Siberia. Maria, however, soon rose to become assistant foreman which bolstered her confidence and financial position but annoyed her husband. She left him to join her sister in Barnaul where Maria found employment on a steamship. But Afansi followed her there and, against her will, they returned to Siberia. In Tomsk she found work considered more appropriate for a woman — baking bread — which earned her enough money to escape again.[27] Maria returned to her sister and her work as construction foreman on a site where her boss was extremely pleased with the efficiency of her operation. Twenty-five men worked under her and although she was regarded as a 'queer novelty' she appealed to their 'sense of fairness' for their co-operation. The height of her employer's praise was to acknowledge her right to that ubiquitous symbol of masculine power — trousers. As Maria Bochkareva remembered, he said, 'Look at this *baba*! She will have us men learning from her pretty soon. She should wear trousers.'[28]

But again Afansi found her and they returned to Tomsk. It was only when Afansi was safely ensconced in the Tsar's army that Maria was free to leave and to find another lover. But her second husband, with whom she was legally married by civil agreement, became as abusive as her first.[29] While he was delirious with fever in hospital Maria cut her hair, dressed in men's clothes and ran away. Once shed of the feminine identity that seemed to have brought her so little happiness, she described her desire to fight with the fervour of a religious convert:

My heart yearned to be there [at the front], in the boiling cauldron of war, to

be baptized by its fire and scorched in its lava. The spirit of sacrifice took pos-
session of me. My country called me. And an irresistible force from within
pulled me . . . [30]

The language of her description — her 'baptism of fire,' her 'spirit of sacrifice' and even her mysterious 'irresistible force from within' — all allude to
ideals of heroic glory. The religious symbolism of the fire would cleanse
Maria of her painful past and purify her soul. Like a novice nun, she felt
'called' by her country to serve. It was Bochkareva's careful nurturing of this
exemplary image that prompted a newspaper correspondent to write of her
in July 1917: 'The woman that saved France was Joan of Arc — a peasant
girl, Maria Bochkareva, is her modern parallel.'[31]

According to Isaac Don Levine, to whom she told her story, there were
many false rumours about her military career and her history in the Tsar's
army. The most persistent, however, was the belief that she joined to avenge
Afansi's death.[32] Bochkareva never contradicted this story, says Levine,
because she knew what the journalists wanted to hear and were willing to
believe.

A version of Bochkareva's ideal love resurfaces in an Australian newspaper in 1920. Lt-Col R. F. Fitzgerald, in an article on women's work during the
Great War, cites Bochkareva as an example of admirable female bravery:

Madame Bochkareva had originally fought alongside her husband, who was
a private, in the trenches, where he was killed. They belonged to the peasant
class and she had little education but a wonderful capacity for organization
and great pluck.[33]

The image of the husband and wife team linked Bochkareva with more
appropriate concepts of feminine sacrifice and made sense of her desire for
the masculine deeds of war. Even American journalist Bessie Beatty, who
covered the Russian civil war and revolution for *The San Francisco Bulletin*
and lived in the Battalion's barracks for 10 days, perpetuated the myth
about Bochkareva's husband. Beatty wrote that Bochkareva was working at
a Tomsk butcher shop when she learned that her husband had been killed in
action and she immediately asked to join the army.[34]

In reality, Bochkareva, like Emma Edmonds saw the assumption of a
male role as an escape from a feminine identity that ensnared and even

enslaved her. Bochkareva petitioned the Tsar to join his army and when permission was granted she said: 'I was so happy, so joyous, so *transported* . . . It
was the most blissful moment of my life' (my italics).[35] Just as Edmonds
explained the discovery of cross-dressing as a path into 'the freedom and
glorious independence of masculinity,' Bochkareva felt literally transported
into another world. At first Maria was 'confused and somewhat bewildered,
hardly being able to recognize myself,' but the men soon regarded her as 'a
comrade and not a woman.'[36] In this other world she was freed of emotional
and sexual vulnerability.

When Beatty interviewed the women of the Battalion during her stint in
the barracks, many echoed Bochkareva's ideals of glory. The former stenog-
raphers, dressmakers, servants, factory hands, university students, peasants
and even bourgeois ladies who surrounded her said they joined 'because
they believed that the honour and even the existence of Russia were at stake
and nothing but a great human sacrifice could save her.'[37] But Beatty added
that others came because 'anything was better than the dreary drudgery and
the drearier waiting of life as they lived it.'[38] A Japanese woman said her
reasons for joining were so varied she would rather not tell them and a 15-
year-old Cossack girl from the Ural mountains signed up after her father,
two brothers and her mother [a nurse] had all died in battle. '"What else is
left for me?" she asked with a pathetic droop to her young, strong shoulders,' wrote Beatty. But the Battalion publicly wore the face of feminine love,
sacrifice and duty.

Beatty noted that Bochkareva appealed to her potential recruits as mothers and natural-born nurses. In June 1917 Bochkareva addressed Russian
women on the steps of St. Isaac's Cathedral in Petrograd. She spread her
arms and in a deep, booming voice cried into the crush before her: 'Come
with us in the name of your fallen heroes. Come with us to dry the tears and
heal the wounds of Russia. Protect her with your lives.' Bochkareva then
turned to her 250 young soldiers and said: 'We women are turning into
tigresses to protect our children from a shameful yoke — to protect the freedom of our country.'[39] There was none of the transcendent joy of
Bochkareva's own experience in her appeals because feminine heroics were
only tolerated publicly if wedded to prevailing concepts of motherhood and
female sacrifice. Maternal love subsumed patriotic glory.

Ironically, the motives expressed by the Russian women soldiers bear more similarities than differences to those who disguised themselves and slipped into all-male ranks. They were escaping the same boredom of domestic life or felt compelled by the same sense of urgency to join in the struggle. But however they articulated their reasons for donning their uniform, once enlisted, the experience of shedding their female selves and adopting a male persona was almost universal.

The Russian women were also following a long tradition of fighting alongside and following male soldiers in camp. The Tsar's government had no consistent policy on female combatants but women's names continued to appear in Russian journals that recorded new recruits throughout the war. Many women found joining their brothers was a matter of being in the right place at the right time.[40] Marina Yurlova quite literally began her military career when she was shoved accidentally onto a train packed with Cossack women from her village following their men to war in 1915. But Marina wrote that she felt more excitement than fear, as she assumed her father was also on board. Fourteen years old, separated from her family and bound for an unknown destination, Marina felt secure in her position as camp follower. She wrote of her experience:

> I am not exaggerating when I say that I felt no remorse and no fear. I was a Cossack. As with my companions, so with me it was a blind instinct to follow men to war. And beside that, to me — caught up in all this violence and carried helplessly along — here was an adventure, the sort of adventure I had dreamed about . . . [41]

Yurlova's military induction followed haphazard lines. When the train reached its destination and the contingent of men from her village encamped, her father was not among them. Like any other adolescent, Marina let out a howl of misery at her plight and attracted the attention of a 'big Cossack'. Once befriended by Sgt Kosloff, Marina was outfitted in army regulation trousers, khaki shirt, boots and a lamb's wool hat. As she put on her new uniform, Kosloff promised her: 'All right synok (sonny),' he laughed, 'before I die, I'll make a Cossack out of you.' In the camp Marina found her new clothes 'made all the difference in the world.'[42]

But because of her age Marina made few distinctions between the men in the camp and herself. To her they were just older people who lived in a different world, gave her work to do and tolerated her presence.[43] For two months, before her adopted company moved to the bare plateau of Armenia, her work consisted of grooming the horses. But thereafter, equipped with a sabre, the elimination of Marina's pigtails was her final initiation as a Cossack soldier. Then her company awaited their orders.

Marina Yurlova's autobiography is the story of her gradual evolution as a soldier who depended on the army's lax attitude toward women in the ranks. In part this indifference stemmed from a recognition among the soldiers, who were mostly peasants, that women were as physically capable of enduring the privations of war as they were of other hardships.[44] Russian peasant men and women worked side-by-side in the fields and, as Maria Bochkareva's example illustrates, at other manual labour. Yurlova had been harvesting sunflowers and potatoes with other girls and boys from her village the morning the Cossack troops left for the front.

By 1915 the British and American press began carrying reports about the Russian women who had disguised themselves as men to enter the war. New York's *Literary Digest* quoted the *London Graphic*'s report that there were about 400 women bearing arms in Russia, most in Siberian regiments. But rather than pointing out the relative disarray that enabled women to penetrate military ranks more easily, reports stressed the Russian women's patriotism:

> The sex of 50 [women] has been revealed by death or wounds. This number is quite remarkable when one considers the obstacles to be surmounted in eluding or circumventing the recruiting officials. For even in Russia women are not supposed to be soldiers. One can but feel that the passion of the Russian woman to fight side by side with their men is not only patriotic but symptomatic of a fine sense of comradeship.[45]

Such accounts neatly tied together the ideals of female devotion to husband and country. The women's more complex, less sanguine reasons — the desire for escape, the longing for independence and excitement that a masculine identity appeared to offer — were overlooked. Simplified, the female warrior embodied more familiar visions of perfection. Undoubtedly women have been and are just as susceptible to the rhetoric of patriotism as men. Many of these women simply believed they were compelled to go. As a former Russian Red Army soldier told the English journalist, Rosita Forbes: 'I had to go to the front. The whole of my village went. I didn't think about [whether I liked fighting]. I had to do it.'[46] Undeniably the Russian women were also moved to fight by a genuine desire to protect their homes, their children's future and all that their nation meant to them. But reading between the lines of these and other women's stories about their experience of soldiering, consistent patterns and themes of rebellion against female restrictions appear that belie other motives.

Though wholly imbued with her belief in fighting for the British Empire and for Serbian nationalism, the autobiography of Captain Flora Sandes also reveals explicitly her frustration with the suffocating life of a middle-class woman in Edwardian Britain. She begins her 1927 recollection of her transition from nurse to soldier in the Serbian army with a lament:

> When a very small child I used to pray every night that I might wake up in the morning and find myself a boy . . . Many years afterwards, when I had long realized that if you have the misfortune to be born a woman it is better to make the best of a bad job and not try to be a bad imitation of a man, I was suddenly pitchforked into the Serbian army and for seven years lived practically a man's life.[47]

Only 50 years before Flora Sandes wrote this description of life as the only woman in an all-male regiment, Loreta Velasquez penned remarkably similar thoughts. 'I wish I had been created a man instead of a woman,' she wrote in 1876. 'This is what is the matter with nearly all the women who go about complaining of the wrongs of their sex. But being a woman, I was bent on making the best of it.'[48] Although Flora Sandes was never disguised, as Loreta Velasquez was, they shared the same individualism and desire to succeed in a masculine world despite the disadvantages of their sex.

Sandes, the youngest daughter of a rector's large family, was born in 1876 at Poppleton in Yorkshire. Her life before the war was marked by her attempts to escape from the confines of her gender. Flora spent her week days working as a secretary but at weekends drove along the narrow, green lanes near her home at Thornton Heath, Sussex in a second-hand French motor car. In her adolescence Flora would don a pair of pantaloons for short camping trips equipped with a bicycle and tent, and sometimes accompanied by the family dog. Flora posed with her canine companion as an intrepid traveller for a newspaper photograph in 1905. The caption read: 'This tent which weighs under three pounds has sheltered its owner Miss

*Valerie Arkell-Smith, dressed as her alias Colonel Barker, 1926. (*Munsell Collection.*)

*Music hall impersonator Vesta Tilley whose repertoire included 'The Bold Militiaman' and 'Six Days Home on Leave' during the First World War, in uniform. (*Raymond Mander and Joe Mitchenson Theatre Collection.*)

*Etching of an eighteenth-century British female soldier 'Nancy', who was also heroine of a popular ballad in London, entitled, *Wounded Nancy's Return*, 1780. (*Mansell Collection.*)

*Hannah Snell, disguised as James Gray, British soldier and sailor, 1750. (*The British Library.*)

Above left The frontispiece of M.M. Ballou's 1915 novel, *Fanny Campbell or the female pirate captain*, that inspired Sarah Emma Edmonds to masquerade as Franklin Thompson. (*Library of Congress.*)

Above right Mary Anne Talbot, eighteenth-century English soldier and sailor after her discovery. (*The British Library.*)

Left Civil War soldier, nurse and spy Sarah Emma Edmonds as Franklin Thompson, taken at Fort Scott, Kansas. (*Clarke Historical Library.*)

*Christian Davies, the Irish publican turned soldier, the most popular of the eighteenth-century warrior heroines. (*The British Library*.)

Below Maria Bochkareva, leader of the Russian Women's Battalion of Death in 1917, stands in the background as her members practice shooting, at their Petrograd headquarters. (*Trustees of the Imperial War Museum*.)

Above left Russian soldier
Marina Yurlova *en route* to
Japan from Vladivostock, 1919.

Above right Flora Sandes,
second from right, bottom,
dreaming that she might wake
up and find herself a boy, at
Monewden, Suffolk, circa 1881.
(*Flora Sandes Collection,
Sudbourne, Suffolk.*)

Right Flora Sandes in fencing
gear, Thornton Heath, Surrey,
circa 1894. (*Flora Sandes
Collection, Sudbourne, Suffolk.*)

*Flora Sandes with her 'motor car', Thornton Heath, Surrey, 1907 (*Flora Sandes Collection, Sudbourne, Suffolk.*)

*Flora Sandes, top right with her sisters (counter-clockwise), Fanny, Sophia and Mary, Thornton Heath, Surrey. (*Flora Sandes Collection, Sudbourne, Suffolk.*)

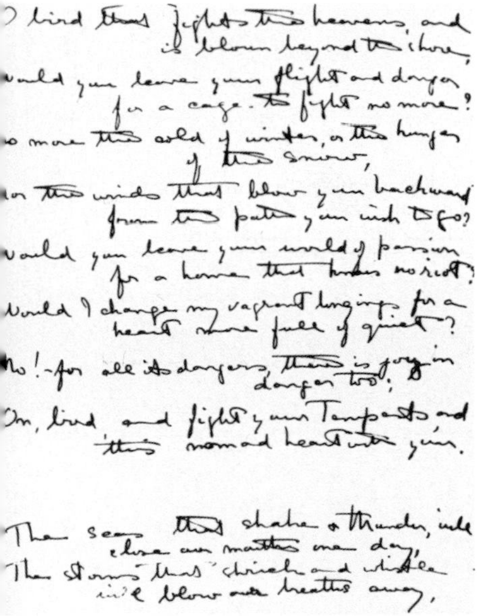
O bird that fights the heavens and
is blown beyond the shore,
Would you leave your flight and danger
for a cage — to fight no more?
No more the cold of winter, or the hunger
of the snow,
Nor the winds that blow you backward
from the path you wish to go?
Would you leave your world of passion
for a home that knows no riot?
Would I change my vagrant longings for a
heart more full of quiet?
No! — for all its dangers, there is joy in
danger too;
On, bird, and fight your tempests and
the nomad heart with you.

The seas that shake and thunder will
close our mouths one day,
The storms that shriek and whistle
will blow our breaths away.

he Vagrant Heart, by Irish
›et Dora Sigerson Shorter,
›pied from Flora Sandes'
ary, circa 1910. (*Flora Sandes
›llection, Sudbourne,
ıffolk.*)

*Mary Anne Talbot, British sailor and soldier who was pressed into service by an unscrupulous guardian, disguised as John Taylor. (*British Library*.)

'irates Mary Read and Ann Bonny who roamed the Caribbean with the infamous
aptain Rackham in the eighteenth century.
tching by B. Cole, the Mansell Collection.)

*Princess Kati Dadeshkeliani in the uniform of Prince Djamal who served in Russia as a field ambulance nurse, 1915 and 1916.

*_Below_ Sergeant Flora Sandes with her Serbian comrades at the Serbian Camp in Nador, near Bizerta, Tunis, February 1917. (_Flora Sandes Collection, Sudbourne, Suffolk._)

Sandes in many parts of the world from Surrey to the Rocky Mountains.'[49] Despite her journeys abroad, a *wanderlust* persisted and in her diary Flora copied out a poem by Dora Sigerson Shorter that seemed to capture her unfulfilled desire:

> O to be a woman to be left to pique and pine
> When the winds are out and calling to this vagrant's heart of mine
> There is a danger in the waters — there is a joy where dangers be —
> Alas to be a woman and the nomad's heart in me
> Ochine! To be a woman only sighing on the shore
> With a soul that finds a passion for each long breaker's roar.[50]

The First World War eventually transported Flora Sandes from the confining shores of Edwardian womanhood to the dark, dangerous waters of masculine experience.

As Flora Sandes told an Australian audience on a speaking tour in 1920, when she signed on as a St. John's Ambulance nurse bound for Serbia in August 1914, it was 'with no more idea of going as a soldier than any other lady now in the hall.'[51] Despite her experience in the Ladies' Nursing Yeomanry and first aid training, the War Office rejected Sandes as a nurse for the Volunteer Aid Detachment. The seven woman unit that American Madame Mabel Grouitch, wife of Serbia's Secretary of State for Foreign Affairs, hastily assembled was definitely Flora's second choice. She left London on a three-month contract on the morning of 12 August aboard the first boat to follow the British Expeditionary Force across the English channel. She was 38 years old.

The journey was fraught with difficulties; France was still mobilizing troops, trains were disrupted, platforms chaotically crowded with soldiers on their way to the front and boats difficult to find. Among other less serious mishaps Flora noted in her diary that during a train trip along the Adriatic coast, a 'Miss Saunders lost her purse' and her friend Emily Simmonds, a surgical nurse known affectionately as Americano, 'lost her reputation — neither ever found again.' In Athens a war correspondent identified only as 'Mr. X' in Flora's diary for security purposes, sent the women a bouquet 'which nearly caused a battle.'[52] In the sultry evening air Americano and Flora drove through the streets till about midnight accompanied by 'Mr X' and 'sundry others.' But the nurses arrived safely in Serbia after a memorable 36-hour voyage on the deck of a Greek cattle ship in a raging thunderstorm from Piraeus to Salonika. From there they travelled by slow train through the rugged Vardar valley to Kragujevatz.[53] When she arrived, there was a telegram waiting, stating that her father, the Reverend Samuel Sandes with whom she had lived until her departure, had died on 23 August. Flora made no notes in her diary until the middle of November.

The conditions in the First Reserve Hospital where Flora spent her first few months in Serbia were extremely basic. The seven English women were the only nurses working with Serbian doctors and orderlies to tend more than 1,000 sick and wounded soldiers. They were casualties of the Serbs' efforts to repel the Austrian invasion across the Danube. Many patients travelled more than three days in a bullock cart over rough terrain with only their first bloodstained field dressings on their wounds. Those who survived the journey arrived in terrible condition.[54] After exhausting hours on duty, the nurses took turns sleeping on straw mattresses, sharing one army blanket and eating all in one small room. The hospital was desperately short of medicine and other supplies so that only the worst cases were treated with anaesthetic.

At the end of her contract Sandes returned home to London and 'Americano' to New York to raise money for medical supplies. In only six weeks Sandes' campaign raised more than £2,000 and she returned to Serbia in early 1915 literally sitting on the packing cases that contained 120 tons of desperately needed materials. The supplies were gratefully received as she and Emily Simmonds arrived back in the midst of a typhus epidemic. When the packing crates were safely delivered to Nish, the President of the Serbian Red Cross asked the women if they could accompany them to a town in northern Serbia that was particularly hard hit by the epidemic and now entirely cut-off. Sandes had read only vague rumours of the illness in the English press and agreed to the journey.[55] *En route* to Valjevo — known as the death trap of Serbia — they met an American doctor who had come to help fight the epidemic. He predicted the women would be dead within a month if they did not turn back. 'Americano and I chewed it over together,' wrote Sandes, 'and finally left for Valjevo on the 8 p.m. train.'[56] Flora and Emily Simmonds' bravery was mixed with their deeply-felt patriotism as they boarded the carriage.

A visit to the English consul had influenced their decision. The consul handed them a letter from the British Foreign Minister, Sir Edward Grey, addressed to all nurses working in Serbia. Whatever assistance they gave Serbia, he said, 'was helping Britain and the Allies and was of inestimable benefit to the common cause.' It was a shrewd move by Grey because on 24 September he pledged England's assistance to Serbia 'without qualifications and without reserves.' Grey, however, quickly reversed his position and clarified his earlier statement by saying it was intended 'in a political and not in a military sense.' This left the Serbs without the support and supplies they had anticipated and badly needed. The British nurses were at least a highly visible sign of some allied concern and assistance.[57]

When Flora and Emily arrived in Valjevo two days later they found only one doctor well enough to work in a town where soldiers and civilians were dying at a rate of 200 a day. The mortality rate among those who contracted typhus was 70 per cent and there were 5,000 suffering from the disease. Sandes and Americano heard at the train station that two American doctors were lying sick in a nearby hotel:

> We went at once and found that one doctor had died the day before and been taken away and at the same time as they carried him out they brought in the coffin for his pal and laid it down beside his bed ready for him. He was lying there with his coffin beside him having completely given up all hope.[58]

The doctor eventually recovered but the losses of medical staff were enormous. Twenty-one doctors died in Valjevo in three weeks. Both Sandes and Emily Simmonds were stricken but survived. Each evening meal became a celebration as the staff at the Serbian hospital where the women worked fought against the enveloping doom. There were 14 at the long wooden table when Sandes first arrived and over each place hung a large, black-edged funeral notice of the person who had formerly sat there. All were typhus victims. '[The staff] won't let us go to bed early,' Sandes wrote in her diary, 'they say you never know which will be your last night and why waste it in bed.' At the end of a month only the Serbian doctor, one other man and the two women remained.[59]

During her time in Valjevo Flora's Serbo-Croatian improved, her commitment to the Serbian cause grew stronger and she took increased responsibility in the hospital. One day just after finishing an operation the Chief Military Surgeon of Serbia walked in on an inspection visit. He looked round the room and asked her, 'Who's the surgeon here?' When Flora replied meekly that she was, 'he just crossed himself three times and said, "Carry on, do the best you can, there's no one else to do it."'[60] Flora became adept at managing with few resources. She noted in her diary on 1 March 1915: 'Cut off a man's toes with a pair of scissors this afternoon.' Two days later she caught her first louse — the insects that carry typhus — and between 16 and 21 March she wrote 'sick with typhus, kept no diary.' It was not until 2 April that she rose from her bed for the first time.

By the spring of 1915 the typhus epidemic had abated, both Emily and Flora had recovered and became anxious to find a hospital where their skills were more urgently needed. That summer the two women visited the local military headquarters and inquired about joining a regimental ambulance unit. As Flora explained, it was a position barred to women under ordinary circumstances because, as the only first-aid dressing station, it was frequently shelled and it required the nurses to live with the regiment. Flora's first attempts to get an ambulance position were thwarted and so in August 1915 she returned to England.

Her stay, however, was brief and on 18 October Flora left London to return to Serbia via Marseilles, Sardinia and Athens aboard the *Mossoul*. Dr. Isabel Emslie Hutton, also destined for relief work in a Serbian hospital, became friends with Sandes on a journey marked by submarine chases and a seasick crew. She described her companion as, 'a tall handsome woman with short grey hair and skirt.'[61] Sandes and the other English medics arrived at Salonica — 'a scatty mess of soldiers and officers of all nationalities' — in early November.[62] After much wrangling Flora was attached to the Ambulance of the Second Infantry Regiment in Southern Macedonia as a dresser, undoubtedly a reward for her services in Valjevo and a sign of trust from the Serbs. A commandant arrived with papers assigning her to the regiment while she was working at a military hospital in Prilep, and against the advice and wishes of Mr. Grieg the British Consul, she accepted.

When Dr. Hutton wrote about her time spent in Serbia she remembered vividly a conversation with Flora Sandes aboard the *Mossoul*. Despite Flora's public protestations that she had no intention of 'going for a soldier' when she left London in 1914, Dr. Hutton was only mildly surprised at her friend's transformation from nurse to combatant. On that ship, so crowded with French soldiers that the English women stole cushions from the smoking room and slept underneath the stars, Flora whispered her real ambition to Isabel. When Dr. Hutton saw Flora again in 1916, she wrote in her diary:

> She has got what she wanted without much difficulty for I remember that on the Mossoul she told me that she had always wished to be a soldier and fight . . . she got caught in the retreat, however, shouldered a gun and was made a soldier . . . she looks well and in good spirits.[63]

Later Flora commented on the seemingly incongruous shift from her role as nurse to soldier: 'Looking back I seem to have just naturally drifted, by successive stages, from a nurse into a soldier.'[64] The change was gradual but from the Serbian's perspective completely reasonable. There were other women in their army; enlistment was often haphazard and Flora possessed extremely valuable skills — she could shoot and she could ride — and she was English.

In her diary, only six days after her introduction to the regiment, she commented: '[the men] seem bent on turning me into a soldier and I expect I'll find myself in the trenches next battle.'[65] To her eldest sister Sophie, she wrote in a letter the following day:

> I threw my lot in with the second regiment and they seem to think I've done something wonderful whereas . . . I've done absolutely nothing except share their grub, ride their horses and they've adopted me as a kind of mascot.

She added that the regiment considered her ability to shoot, to ride and to go anywhere with them more valuable 'than the fact that I'm supposed to be a nurse.' To her comrades, however, her most distinguishing feature was her nationality.

Her position as a nurse came to an abrupt end when the Second Regiment was ordered to withdraw from the area. The enemy was pushing from the north, most of Serbia had fallen and the regiment was expected to move into a retreat position any day. The last battle for Serbia before the Bulgarian invasion was fought at Babuna Pass but overwhelming numbers slowly drove back the Serbian army; the Germans and Austrians were pressing from the north, the Bulgarians from the east; and the south was blocked by neutral Greece. Refusing a separate offer of peace the Serbs' only route out lay through retreat into Albania.[66]

When the regiment pulled back to within a few miles of Monastir, Flora was transferred to the regimental field unit attached to army headquarters. Dr. Nikolitch, a Serb, warned her darkly that the journey through Albania would be terrible and the army's difficulties experienced so far would be nothing compared with what lay ahead. Undaunted Flora told him she would stay with the regiment unless she was asked to leave. Her regimental commander Colonel Milic said it would be better for Serbia if she stayed, but it would be better for Flora Sandes if she left. Nikolitch said she would encourage the soldiers as 'I represented England!'[67] Flora ceremoniously stripped the Red Cross badge from her arm while Milic laughingly took the small brass figure '2' from his own epaulettes and fastened them on her shoulder straps.[68] Equipped with her violin, three cases of cigarettes, jam and warm helmets (gifts for the soldiers), Flora Sandes, now the living promise of Allied rescue, motored back to her regiment's camp. Along the way she breathed a sigh of relief: 'for me it [was] too good to be true, having fully expected to be ignominiously packed back to Salonique as a female encumbrance.'[69] A hurried line to her family at home and in half an hour she had disappeared into a howling blizzard, *en route* for Albania.

Flora's awareness of her political importance and her unique position provide another explanation for her motives and for the Serbian military officials' acceptance of her. Grey's promise of military aid had been sadly lacking and each night when the second regiment sat around the camp fire Flora was asked, 'when are the British coming to help us?'[70] Considerations of sexual difference were overridden by larger questions of social position and the politics of war. Flora's comments about a Serbian woman soldier in another battalion, Milunka, underlined the importance of being English. The 17-year-old Milunka had a reputation for extraordinary bravery and for having shot a man in her village who insulted her sister. But according to Flora, Milunka was always in trouble and 'being a peasant like themselves the men did not treat her at all in the same way they treated me.'[71] Flora was neither Serbian nor a peasant, but an English *lady* and an invaluable asset.

Like Edith Durham, an English woman traveller who became an unofficial but extremely important representative of Albania before and during the Great War, Flora Sandes served an important function in the Balkans.[72] By 1915 Flora had already shown her flare at fundraising for the Serbian cause. When she returned home on leave a year later, fresh from the front line, where she had lived with and fought alongside the Serbian soldiers as a comrade, she spoke with the irrefutable voice of authority. In the English press she was catapulted from Red Cross nurse to the 'Serbian Joan of Arc,' stopped in the street by cab drivers, dined by British generals and lunched with Royals. Her 1927 autobiography was hailed as 'important to students of Balkan affairs and to those diplomats whose duty is to preserve the peace of the Near East.'[73] Her ventures were phenomenally successful in raising funds and in publicizing the plight of the Serbs.

Flora was not alone in serving a dual political function as combatant and diplomat. Forty years before she joined the Second Regiment another foreigner, Jenny Merkus, had enlisted in the Serbian ranks after participating in the revolt against Turkish rule in Herzegovina and Bosnia. At the age of 36, Jenny Merkus, a wealthy Dutch heiress, befriended the Herzegovinian chief, Liubibratic, and purchased Krupp cannons for the rebels. French, German and Slavic journalists wrote about the unusual sight of Merkus riding through Belgrade wearing a Montenegran cap on her unruly blond hair and a man's cape slung across her shoulders. But she was quick to refute their claims that she had joined the cause to lend aid in any domestic capacity. 'I did not wish to nurse wounded soldiers, but to help liberate Christian people, and also Christ's land from the sovereignty of the Turks,' wrote Jenny who had once pushed a 'large, beautiful bible in Arabic' into the hands of Jerusalem's Turkish governor. The revolt was successful but when the Austrians invaded Jenny Merkus was recruited as a volunteer in the Serbian army.[74] Hers was solely a religious and political mission.

The motives and ability of women to embark on a military career and to successfully disguise themselves within an all-male regiment were inevitably influenced by their class and social position. Flora Sandes' equestrian skills, familiarity with a gun and her knowledge of French and German were products of her middle-class background which did not dictate but certainly influenced her acceptance as a foreign woman in the Serbian army. Although patriotic ideals, a tremendous courage, a yearning to travel and to loosen the bonds of female restriction are universally expressed by or attributed to the female warriors, there are discernible class-based differences in their experience. Women who enlisted as soldiers and sailors were most often from the labouring classes where they were used to hard, physical work. They came from communities where the women were confident of their strength as they worked side by side with men in the fields. Watching their brothers 'going for a soldier,' being pressed into naval service or taking to sea further persuaded these women that they too could withstand its hardships.

The navy and the army offered them different risks and very different rewards. In 1759 Mary Lacey disguised herself in men's clothes and entered the Royal Navy where she served until the end of 1766. Aboard the *Royal William* she was apprenticed to the ship's carpenter for seven years and then gained a permanent position as shipwright in the Portsmouth yard.[75] Elizabeth Taylor —known as Happy Ned — served as a sailor during the American Civil War and became immortalized in a well-known ballad. At the end of her service, she continued to live as Ned, working for many years on the Liverpool docks, then as a navvy and a farm labourer. Her sex was only discovered upon her death in 1887.[76]

Mary Anne Arnold, whose mother was widowed in 1835, began supporting herself by working as a farm labourer and running errands at the age of ten. She found a permanent job in a rope-making factory in Sheerness, Kent where she earned a pittance. Her brothers were both sailors in the Royal Navy and she realized that boys of her age who went to sea were better fed, more highly valued and 'in every way in a superior condition to her.' Mary Anne then persuaded a friend to lend her his old jacket, trousers and a shirt 'for a lark' after she promised to return them. To her great joy and her friend's dismay she was employed as a cabin-boy aboard the *Williams* — a Sutherland coal ship docked in Sheerness harbour.[77] When Isabelle Gunn signed on with the Hudson's Bay Company as John Fubister, a labourer, at Kirkwall, Orkney in 1806 she was guaranteed wages higher than anything she would have earned at home as a woman.[78] In early modern Holland, army and naval recruiters, parents in sea ports, garrison towns or on farms encouraged their daughters to take up a military career for its financial benefits.[79]

The female soldier's story often illustrated the extent of women and children's involvement in eighteenth- and nineteenth-century warfare. An 1825 account of Phoebe Hessel claimed her father, a drummer in the King of England's service, took his young daughter with him to Flanders when her mother died. He disguised Phoebe as a boy, taught her to play the fife and enlisted her in the 5th Regiment of Foot. She fought in the ranks as a private soldier, unsuspected, until she was wounded in the battle of Fontenoy in

1745.[80] In a variation on this theme Confederate officer Loreta Velasquez claimed that, disguised as Harry T. Buford, she enlisted her son Bob in the ranks at Columbus, Tennessee where they dug entrenchments side by side.[81]

Although the majority of women who cross-dressed to enter a male occupation were young and single, there were also exceptions to this rule. Almira Paul went to sea to support her two young children after her sailor-husband William was killed aboard the British privateer *Swallow* on 20 February 1812. She decided to leave her children in Halifax with her mother, dressed in one of her husband's suits and shipped herself as a cook's mate aboard a cutter, the *Dolphin*. She claimed that when the ship set sail in June 1812, she took the precaution of wearing a close-fitting vest and kept a suit of women's clothes close at hand.[82] Another widow, Elsa Jane Guerin, began her career at sea when she was left penniless with two children to support after her husband's death. After thinking through her options, Elsa Jane decided 'to dress myself in male attire and seek for a living in this disguise among the avenues which are so religiously closed to my sex.'[83]

It was not only working-class women, however, who passed as men to enter an exclusively-male profession. Dorothy Lawrence, an eighteen- year-old English woman, attempted to further her journalistic aspirations by joining the Royal Engineers as a sapper in 1915. Dorothy Lawrence was living in Paris when war was declared and offered to get front line coverage to several London newspapers but all flatly refused her. Snarling down telephone lines the editors barked with one voice: 'Do you suppose we're going to send a woman out there when even our own war-correspondents can't get out for love or money?' Only one hinted vaguely that he might run something if she did make it to the front line.[84] But Dorothy remained undeterred. As she wrote in her autobiography:

> I'll see what an ordinary English girl, without credentials or money can accomplish. If war correspondents cannot get out there, I'll see whether I cannot go one better than those big men with their cars, credentials and money. I'll see what I can manage as a war-correspondent.[85]

In a Parisian café she befriended two English soldiers who agreed to provide her with a uniform. It was smuggled into her flat in small, discretely wrapped brown paper parcels and Dorothy reciprocated by taking the

Tommies on guided tours of the city. Once all the necessary parts were assembled Dorothy took Christian Davies' route and bound her chest with bandages to hide a 'robust figure.' She padded her back with cotton wool and sacking. Despite her uncanny resemblance to the Michelin Man, who even then was a household figure in France, her friends taught her to drill and march.[86] She persuaded two Scots policemen to cut her hair and she used a weakened Condy's fluid (a dark stain for furniture) to produce 'the requisite, manly bronzed complexion.'[87] As Private Denis Smith of the First Leicestershire Regiment, with a forged pass and a real identification disc, she headed for the front.

Dorothy Lawrence, when she was exposed, completely confounded the British military authorities. Her frank admission that a by-line and a potential furthering of her career — considered to be less than noble motives — lay behind her masquerade may also partly explain why her story received so little attention in Britain when published in 1919. While some women began using a male disguise to enter a profession through the army, navy or a quasi-military organization like the Hudson's Bay Company, other cross-dressing women joined up to prevent detection. Emma Edmonds probably joined the Union Greys as Franklin Thompson for this reason.

Unlike Dorothy Lawrence another woman, Albert F., was discovered attempting to enlist in North London in 1916 to protect her career in a male occupation. Albert F. was working as a skilled printer in a North London shop, 'earning very high wages even for a man' when war broke out in 1914. Five other printers had already joined the forces before Albert was called up for national service. But because 'his' work was so highly valued, 'his' employer lodged an appeal arguing that Albert was indispensable. Albert, described as 'a slightly-built, fair-haired, and smooth faced conscript dressed in a neat, navy-blue suit, brown cap and patent-leather boots' appeared before the Mill Hill Medical Examining Board in August 1916. The sergeant was surprised when Albert asked permission for a private medical examination because of a cardiac condition and produced a National Health Insurance form to substantiate this. 'His' request was denied and the surgeon immediately discovered that Albert F. was a woman. The sergeant, who had refused Albert a private consultation, said later that he had no reason to question the conscript's sex. 'The voice was soft and rather gentle,' he said, 'but no notice was taken of that. Plenty of young fellows — and she looked like a young man of 24 — have effeminate voices, and when a great many men are being dealt with. . . individual characteristics are passed without comment.'[88]

London newspapers reported that Albert was previously married to a man in a northern seaport where the couple lived for several years. The marriage crumbled after two children died in infancy. She moved into a nearby lodging house and met a woman who later became her 'wife.' But Albert still feared her husband might find her so she assumed a male identity, began a new life in North London and found a job. Albert's employer launched an appeal claiming: 'He was one of the best "workmen" at this particular job I have ever had — punctual, quick and with just the touch of imagination needed to make a success out of that particular line. . . "he" was my right hand "man."'[89]

The notion that a woman would and could masquerade as a man to enlist or to earn a better living was picked up by the columnist, Berta Ruck, in the *Illustrated Sunday Herald* — the newspaper that first ran Albert F's story. Berta Ruck invented a conversation between two women —'of opposing types (but) full of character and independent ways'— discussing an unspecified news article about a cross-dressing woman:

> THE BRUNETTE: Another of them? Only lately I heard about that girl who ran away from home dressed as a boy to earn her living as a plumber's mate. Then there was that doctor 'man' in America. There was the woman who served in the ranks and became a Chelsea pensioner. Quite often these cases seem to crop up.
> THE BLONDE: I suppose it's because as men, the women get better jobs and earn better money than they would do as members of their own sex.[90]

The discussion gives a hint of the popular equation between women taking over previously exclusive male spheres of work and the achievement of equality between the sexes. Since the military was considered the ultimate citadel of masculine experience, women's involvement as actual combatants, it was argued, symbolized true liberation. The American navy also played on the popular notion that the new, emancipated woman was eager to enter the ranks. A United States Navy recruitment poster showed a woman, with ringlets peaking out from underneath a sailor's cap and pulling at a pair of invisible suspenders, who exclaimed: 'Gee! I wish I were *a man*. I'd join the

Navy.' If the image of the coquette appropriating the sailor's duty was not enough to induce potential recruits to flock to the nearest station, the poster further urged: 'Be a Man and Do It.'[91]

Albert F., although a highly skilled worker, and valued by her employer, found that once her sex was revealed, she was barred from a profession in which she had excelled. However, financial security and a skilled trade were only partial reasons for Albert's disguise. Throughout her four years in London she was dogged by a fear that one day, somehow, her husband would find her. In an interview Albert said that when the call-up notice came she considered it 'a godsend.' She explained: '[I] felt that here was a chance, at any rate, of getting where my husband would never find me.'[92] But once her story was publicized Albert left London to live with relatives in the North of England and went into hiding.

It would be wrong to suggest that every woman who found herself enlisted as a soldier was there because she wished to be. But even when women did not choose a military life the theme of escape often figured largely in their motives for signing up. There are accounts of women forced into their role because of unscrupulous husbands and guardians. In the eighteenth and nineteenth centuries stories emerged of young women disguised as cabin or foot-boys who played a pseudo-sexual role. A popular nineteenth-century ballad, *The Handsome Cabin Boy*, satirized this mythical character and her sexual availability. The practice of keeping a young mistress disguised as a male servant was by no means widespread because many naval captains kept their lovers or wives aboard ship quite openly and subterfuge was hardly necessary.[93] There were, however, many more women who worked at rougher, more physically demanding and higher status jobs at sea.

One of Britain's most celebrated female sailors, Mary Anne Talbot, began her naval career when pressed into service as footboy to an unscrupulous officer. She was born on 2 February 1778, one of 16 illegitimate children of Lord William Talbot, Baron of Hensol and stewart of the royal household. Her mother died giving birth to her and she was left with a wet-nurse in Shrewsbury. At the age of five she went to Mrs. Tapperly's boarding school where she lived for the next nine years, 'unacquainted with the views of the world and knew no happiness.'[94] In 1791 her elder sister who had acted as a surrogate mother to Mary Anne died leaving her a fortune.

But since she was not of age, Mary Anne was placed in the care of a Mr. Sucker in Newport.

Mary Anne was then introduced to Captain Essex Bowen of the 82nd Regiment of Foot and he became her new guardian. She was taken to London on a pretext of improving her education but on the journey Bowen became increasingly malevolent. Eventually Mary Anne felt she had no choice but to submit to his attempts at seduction. 'Intimidated by his manner and knowing that I had no friends near me, I became everything he could desire,' she recalled years later. '[I] so far aided his purposes as to become a willing instrument to my future misfortunes.'[95] Enlisted 'in the menial capacity of footboy' and using the name John Taylor, Mary Anne set sail with Bowen from Falmouth on the *Crown* destined for Santo Domingo.

Fifteen years later Marianne Rebecca Johnson was brought before the Lord Mayor of London at Mansion House with a similar story. A master bricklayer in Bishop's Gate had found her sitting in the pouring rain, shivering with cold, weeping bitterly and generally 'in a forlorn and distressed condition.' The daughter of a seaman killed in action during the Napoleonic wars she was raised by an abusive stepfather who bound her as an apprentice aboard a coal-ship. He had threatened her with murder if she revealed her identity to anyone. It was no idle threat, she said, and showed the bricklayer a scar just below her left ear that was the result of a blow her stepfather gave her with a poker. Marianne worked aboard a Sutherland collier, the *Mayflower*, for four years without detection but eventually she fled. One morning she lay in her bunk after the morning call because she was ill and was flogged for her laziness.

Moreover, three years before she went to sea her mother had been forced by her stepfather aboard a man-o-war. She served seven years on different ships before she was mortally wounded in the British capture of Copenhagen in 1807. But in a letter to her daughter written just before her death, she said she 'preferred the hardships of her situation to returning to her friends at the risk of meeting her unnatural husband.'[96]

The themes of escape and reward are tightly bound together in these narratives. As the differences in Marianne and her mother's story suggest, however, freedom could quickly turn into another form of captivity. Life at sea or in camp was, for many women, only the lesser of evils. But however difficult life was in male guise there appears, in these stories, a recognition that it was better than being a woman. They inevitably accepted that experience is always mediated by sexual difference. Even Marianne, the runaway apprentice, shrank from travelling without an escort on a collier once she resumed female clothes. Lost was that small protection her trousers afforded her and in its place was a renewed awareness of her vulnerability.

Financial security, steady employment, patriotism, rejection of femininity, freedom from domestic responsibilities, independence, fame and infamy form a complex web of motives. There are no clear and simple answers to that ringing question — why did she do it? The warriors are the stuff of legends and even those who laid claim to simple motives did not remain untouched by history. Few women wrote their own stories and those who did not, found that task left to historians, journalists, ballad writers and to popular imagination. Each generation and place refashioned these heroines to fit the prevailing ideals of female love and male glory that arose during periods of war.

The life-histories of these women, as will be discussed in later chapters, pose their own problems of interpretation. Whose voice is really telling the story and for what purpose? The heroines who starred in the immensely popular eighteenth-century ballads about female warriors stemmed from 'real-life' stories but where did the fiction begin and reality end? Even Emma Edmonds, who later in life became more forthcoming about her earlier existence as Frank used romantic conventions to make her story more plausible. Flora Sandes wrote her first autobiography as a polemic for the Serbian cause and the second, in part, to supplement a military pension. Every female warrior was viewed within a tradition that stretches back to the Amazons and no matter how vibrantly she described her own life, it was inevitably recast and distorted.

But if the 'facts' of these stories are elusive, the myths are not. It is because of their enduring quality that the female warrior, in life and in fiction, has survived for so long. Fiction drew from myth which drew from fact in a rhythmic cycle. If Fanny Campbell, the inspiration for Emma Edmond's cross-dressing, was fictional, the sixteenth-century Irish pirate captain, Grace O'Malley, was not.[97] Neither were Mary Read and Anne Bonny — pirates who roamed the seas in the eighteenth century with the infamous Captain Rackham — mere figments of a colourful imagination.[98] Their persistence kept alive an alternative image of female heroism and convinced women that an entrance into the masculine world was possible.

However recast and refashioned, the female warrior still conveyed inspiration, hope and optimism that women could find release from boredom, from the monotonous waiting for a lover's return and from their own female vulnerability. In every period they too reveal a different plot for women and suggest another ending to an all-too mundane and predictable story of acquiescence. The freedom they gained was often paid at a very high price.

3

Becoming
One of the Boys

❧

Trousers make a wonderful difference in the outlook on life. I know that dressed as a man I did not, as I do now I am wearing skirts again, feel hopeless and helpless . . . Today when the whole world knows my secret I feel more a man than a woman. I want to up and do those things that men do to earn a living rather than to spend my days as a friendless woman.
Colonel Barker, *The Sunday Dispatch*, 31 March 1929.

A N ENTIRE GENERATION of British women shared a belief with Valerie Arkell-Smith, alias Colonel Barker, that an active independent life could only be imagined in male terms. Battling against the dominant image of the weak, passive feminine ideal they plotted alternative lives in male costume. During the Great War many nurses dreamed of becoming soldiers while music hall singers Bessie Bonehill, Hetty King, Dorothy Raynor, Vesta Tilley and others in snugly fitting trousers strutted the London stage in varieties of male uniforms.[1] Suffragette leader Christabel Pankhurst self-consciously inserted military metaphors into her militant speeches encouraging women to action. The idealized woman was often portrayed as a knight leading civilization into a better future — the only alternative to passivity lay in emulating those with real political power in the public sphere.[2] Caught up in the rhetoric of empire and Britain's need to defend her interests, some women envisioned participating in war as nurses but also as soldiers, carrying out a vital task that would be rewarded with equality.[3] In the guise of Colonel Barker, Valerie Arkell-Smith never saw battle but her statements reflect a prevailing female fantasy that, as a man, the unattainable was always within reach.

The stories of female soldiers from this and earlier periods encouraged the idea that freedom was only one costume change away. The fantasy had a strong basis in reality, recognizing the complex limitations of all women's experience and the difficulties in overcoming them. The rigid exclusion of women from male spheres made that world ever more exotic and enticing. Male approval among her comrades became the ultimate sign of the cross-dressed woman's rejection of her suffocating femininity and security of her acquired, privileged position. The constant need for male acceptance is a feature of autobiographies written by both disguised women warriors and those fighting as the lone female in an all-male regiment. Because their lives were dependent on their comrades' approval, it was never something they could take for granted. Rather, the women endured endless self-imposed tests of their masculinity, proving over and over again that they measured up. Their feminine weakness that they feared might well up like so many unwanted tears spilling out in some wretched public display, was kept tightly controlled. They struggled with the contradictions, harbouring both male and female identities within themselves.

A female warrior would most keenly feel the contradiction of a woman living as a man in undramatic moments. It struck Marina Yurlova, a soldier with the Russian Army in 1915, with force as she lay in her bunk one night in crowded quarters and watched the men strip off their clothes, searching for lice. The fourteen-year-old Marina had never seen a naked man before and watched the hunched figures with a horrified fascination. 'I lay curled up in my bunk,' she wrote years later, 'with an entirely new feeling: modesty.' She suddenly realized the impossibility of joining the men as she flushed hot with shame and with a new-found self-consciousness about her female body. Smells of the soldier's damp foot wrappings hanging to dry, the stale tobacco smoke, the singeing shirts, unwashed bodies and feet pressed menacingly upon her. Mingled with these pungent smells was her feeling of instantly recognized sexual vulnerability.[4]

It was only when embarrassment about her body, her revulsion of close quarters and fear of naked men disappeared that Marina believed she was becoming a true soldier. The men, although they knew she was a woman, respected her work. They accepted her as a soldier and thus Marina began to trust that her innocence would not be exploited. She learned to accept the intimacy of the dug-out and when she was given sentry duty she realized, 'that meant that [the men] really considered me as one of them, or they wouldn't have trusted me with so much responsibility.'[5]

For Flora Sandes the transition from nurse to soldier was also fraught with small but significant transitions. On her first night spent with the Second Regiment of the Serbian army as an ambulance nurse, she moved her tent off by itself for modesty's sake. Flora, who was soon accustomed to sleeping in the middle of a regiment, whenever and wherever she could, laughed at her earlier concern. She so often slept fully clothed that she soon forgot that it was usual to undress before going to bed.[6] With her 'raggys' — her two close mates Sgt Miladin and Sgt-Major Mallesha — she shared her tobacco, her food, and even her overcoat at night.[7] On long marches blankets were considered a useless, extra weight. So during the winter soldiers were obliged to huddle up together. When Flora accidentally fell asleep by herself one night, a machine gun captain abruptly woke her with a gentle kick. 'Heavens Sandes, what are you thinking of, going to sleep like this by yourself, have you gone mad?' he asked. 'You'll be frozen to death by the morning.'[8] Flora quickly moved over to a group of sleeping bodies and fell back into a deep, untroubled slumber.

Living in such intimate and close quarters was characteristic of military life and the female soldiers usually adapted quickly and discretely. A soldier with the Continental Army, Deborah Sampson fought for two years in the War of American Independence disguised as Robert Shurtleff. While working as an aide-de-camp to General Paterson in 1783, she often slept with other men, usually officers, without concern. 'They as little suspected my sex,' she wrote in her memoirs in 1797, 'as I suspected them of a disposition to violate its chastity, had I been willing to expose myself to them, and to act the wanton.'[9]

'Establishing proper relations' with her fellow soldiers was much less genial for Maria Bochkareva. She reported for duty with the Fourth Company, the Fifth Regiment of the Tsar's army in 1914 filled with excitement and trepidation. When introduced to her male comrades they burst into laughter at a woman with clipped hair wearing heavy boots, foot-rags, regulation trousers and blouse, a thick leather belt, epaulets, a cap and a rifle. According to Maria, 'the news of a woman recruit had preceded me at the barracks and my arrival there precipitated a riot of fun.'[10] The men pinched, jostled and brushed up against Maria, howling stinging insults until the company Commander intervened.

Her first night in the barracks the Commander ordered the men to leave Maria alone. But since the men assumed she was 'a loose-moraled woman who had made her way into the ranks for the sake of carrying on her illicit trade' the harassment continued unabated. 'As soon as I made an effort to shut my eyes I would discover the arm of my neighbour on the left around my neck, and would restore it to its owner with a crash,' she wrote of that exhausting night. 'Watchful of his movements I offered an opportunity for my neighbour on the right to get too near me, and I would savagely kick him in the side. All night long my nerves were taut and my fists busy.'[11] To add to her humiliation the next morning Maria was so anxious to be punctual at roll-call she put on her trousers inside out, provoking another storm of hilarity.

Winning the men's respect was a gradual and difficult process but eventually Maria 'was tested by many additional trials and found to be a comrade and *not a woman* by the men.'[12] This often involved, for the undisguised soldier, a willingness to forego any exceptions made on the basis of her sex. When the regimental train left Tomsk, Maria Bochkareva insisted on sleeping with the men rather than in the officer's car which 'immensely pleased' her comrades because it was a sign that she considered herself one of them. In return, the men became so blind to her sex that Maria claimed she was able to join her comrades in the large communal bath without any fear of sexual harassment.[13]

The soldier's identity was so closely bound to a concept of masculinity that she risked ostracism by displaying any behaviour that might be construed as 'feminine.' The world was neatly divided by sexual difference and since the military belonged to the male sphere, a woman by definition, could only be a soldier if she was accepted as an honorary man. Conformity to what were considered masculine values — bravery, suppression of all fear, physical strength and endurance — were essential to the female soldier's survival. It was imperative that a woman 'became' a man in every sense if these attributes were to be recognized.

In almost every female warrior's story a romantic entanglement reveals the crux of this identity dilemma. Women fall for the disguised female soldier with astounding ease, manipulating her into promises of marriage, swearing undying love and vowing to follow her anywhere. These love interests aside the ultimate sign of male acceptance is usually an invitation to the female soldier from her fellow comrades to accompany them to a brothel. Maria's mates exhorted her to 'be a soldier' and accept their offer to accompany them to the Tomsk red light district. She did but only to 'learn the soldier's life so that I will understand his soul better.'[14] Smoking, drinking, playing cards, rough-housing and dancing in the red light district was not the stuff of a quiet domestic world but part of 'the soldier's life' that bound men together. It was also, as Maria indicates, part of the world entirely closed off to all but those women willing to exchange their sexual exclusivity for economic support. By refusing to be considered a sexual object Maria was allowed access to these male pleasures and intimate knowledge of the soldier's 'soul.'

The prostitutes in these stories never suspect the female soldier's real identity but do their utmost to entice the prospective customer. Bochkareva is saved from the predicament of what to do once alone with her 'youthful love-maker' when an officer steps into the room. She is ordered back to camp in humiliation and punished for breaking the 8 p.m. curfew.[15] Princess Kati Dadeshkeliani who disguised herself as Prince Djamal in a Tartar regiment in 1915 caught a nurse's attention and trouble ensued. When the nurse turned up in the Prince's bed one night 'in a state of undress' she was disappointed to receive only a lecture on professional moral conduct.[16] A soldier with the notorious Russian White Army, Lul Gardo, once woke up in a hayloft sleeping in the arms of a woman she had never seen before. 'I had not the heart to tell her that I was a woman and to witness her subsequent confusion,' wrote Gardo. 'I preferred to let her think I didn't want her caresses.'[17]

Thin and sunburnt, Flora Sandes easily passed as a man in her uniform, and found herself in a similar situation while recovering from a leg wound in Bizerta, Tunisia. In the summer of 1917 it was packed with Serbian convalescents and Sandes often visited the Serbian camp just on the outskirts of town. The Serbs were big, good-looking fellows who were considered generous with their money by the Tunisians and spent many hours drinking in local cafés to while away their boredom before returning to active service. One sultry evening Sandes' Serbian comrades took her to a 'sort-of café.' A young woman quickly planted herself on Flora's knee, put an arm round her neck and caressingly remarked: 'He doesn't look so stupid, but he's very shy.' Flora 'kept it up for awhile' but gave herself away by turning her cheek when the woman attempted to kiss her. The incident also provided insight into a female world about which Flora knew little. Sergeant-Major Sandes was impressed the next day when she and a group of her friends passed the woman in the street and 'not by the flicker of an eyelid' did she acknowledge Flora's acquaintance.[18]

This incident, described in Flora Sandes' 1927 autobiography, was probably intended as a humorous anecdote, playing on the ambiguity of her position. However, it also reinforced Flora's identification with her comrades rather than the women she happened to meet. In her uniform, working for an important cause, hailed as a convalescing hero, Flora Sandes felt she had no more in common with the woman sitting on her lap than any of the other men in the café. If she, or any other female combatant in a similar position, allowed herself to empathize with women who served the military in other capacities, her credibility was threatened.

The female soldiers' flirtations with other women, their bold caricatures of male behaviour were both mocking and affirming of male power. But they showed that the world of men was not beyond their reach. The heroines moved across the murky channels that separated male and female spheres, using their knowledge and experience of both to their own ends. When they courted women it was often to bolster their disguise and vent their resentment against the hegemony of male authority. In the eighteenth century the female soldier who took on a masculine identity generally elicited charmed admiration for her assumption of manly virtues. Her sexual play was a theatrical flaunting of her attempt at total immersion in a forbidden world.

The belle of the eighteenth-century, popular, warrior heroines was Christian Davies. According to an anonymous and widely-read account of her exploits, she both pursued and was chased by other women. Stationed at Gertruydenberg for the winter with the job of repairing dykes, Christian Davies disguised as Christopher Welsh, courted a wealthy burgher's daughter, employing all the language and actions that men had used when flirting with her. Although she was later contrite about her 'frolics' when the young woman fell in love with her, during the course of the romance Christian demonstrated that she knew exactly what her lover wanted to hear:

As I had formerly had many fine things said to myself I was at no loss in the amorous dialect; I ran over all the tender nonsense (which I look upon as the

lover's heavy cannon, as it does the greatest harm with raw girls), employed
on such attacks: I squeezed her hand whenever I could get an opportunity,
sighed often in her company; looked foolishly and practiced upon her all the
ridiculous airs which I had often laughed at, when they were used as snares
against myself.[19]

The romance with the burgher's daughter and other occasions when she visited 'houses of civil conversation' helped legitimate her disguise. But the
narrator was quick to state that Christian's infatuation was merely platonic
and Christian was delighted when she attempted to seduce her young lover
and was rebuffed. 'I own that this rejection gained my heart and taking her
in my arms I told her that she had heightened the power of her charms by
her virtue,' Christian told her narrator. 'I was now fond of the girl though
mine, you know, could not go beyond a platonic love.'[20]

   Christian Davies later added to her reputation for philandering when a
Dutch prostitute claimed 'he' had fathered her child. Christian made no
protest and happily added fatherhood to her list of masculine accomplish-
ments. When her identity was revealed a few years later, the puzzled soldier
who had shared her bed for several months protested upon interrogation
that 'he never knew I was a woman or even suspected it; it was well known
that [I] had a child lain to [me] and took care of it.'[21] Susanna Cope, an eighteenth-century soldier, 'played amongst several lasses who supposed her to
be a man, and fell in love with her, by which means she got store of putting
the bilk upon the maids, widows and wives.'[22] Even *female* soldiers were
portrayed indulging their newly-found male power by taking advantage of
love-sick women who were blamed for their impropriety.

   The Amazons often made an important distinction between the misguided but virtuous women who fell in love with them and the evil seductress.
Sailor Hannah Snell disguised as James Gray, *en route* to the West Indies
aboard the *Swallow*, went ashore in Lisbon with her mate Edward Jefferies.
To quell probing questions about how she gratified the 'lustful appetite' she
accompanied him to a local cafe frequented by prostitutes. James attracted
the notice of the pretty Portugeuse woman Edward had been eyeing and the
sailors tossed a coin for the lady's attentions. James lost and, reputation
restored, 'he' discreetly left. But on returning to Portsmouth a Miss
Catherine fell in love with James who returned her affection. Back aboard

the *Swallow* Hannah boasted of her now love to her mates who approved the choice and accepted James' excuses for avoiding the brothels.[23]

Genuine love and affection sometimes threatened the female warrior's disguise, however. Mary Anne Talbot was thrown into an awkward situation when her employer's niece developed a crush on 'him'. While on leave from their ship the *Ariel* in 1796, Captain John Field invited Mary Anne Talbot disguised as John Taylor to stay with his family in Rhode Island. During the visit, Field's niece paid great attention to John Taylor and eventually offered her hand in marriage. 'I made several excuses but could not divert her attention from what she proposed,' Mary Anne wrote of the embarrassing incident. Even Mrs. Field's arguments with her niece that the English sailor was far too young and inexperienced did little to dissuade her. John Taylor and Captain Field eventually returned to London and left behind the broken-hearted niece.[24] Later in life, however, Mary Anne Talbot became involved with a female companion who lived with her for several years. Mary Anne, who never married and continued to dress in male clothes even after her retirement from sea, wrote of her companion's support while she was languishing in a debtor's prison:

> My time in Newgate [prison] was rendered more comfortable than I had any reason to expect from the constant attention of a female who lived with me for some time previous to my arrest, for when no longer in my power to support her in a way I had been accustomed, instead of quitting me, remained in the prison and by needle work she obtained, contributed greatly to my support. She has continued with me ever since and remains a constant friend in every change I have since experienced.[25]

In this relationship, Mary Anne clearly took what she considered the masculine role of financially supporting her companion who displayed all the virtues of a faithful wife.

Deborah Sampson also developed an affectionate relationship with a female companion but only wrote about her less than platonic feelings from the perspective of a respectable wife and mother of two children. While disguised as Robert Shurtleff, she became 'mutually and tenderly attached' to a 17-year-old woman from a wealthy Baltimore family in the summer of 1783. Deborah had fought in the revolution for two years and met Miss P. while recovering from a long illness. 'Emaciated and pallid,' Deborah Sampson

was still convincing as the 'gallant young soldier' Robert Shurtleff, and former aide-de-camp to General Paterson. Her affection for Miss P. threw
Deborah into great confusion and she left Baltimore abruptly for a tour of
duty in southern Virginia. On her journey she resolved to reveal her real
identity to her friend. 'If you receive these lines remember they come from
one who sincerely loves you,' she wrote to Miss P. while languishing in a
relapse of fever. 'But my amiable friend, forgive my imperfections and forget
you ever had affection for one so unworthy of the name of *your own sex*'.[26]

When, still disguised as Robert Shurtleff, Deborah Sampson returned to
Baltimore, 'an irresistible attraction drew me again to . . . Miss P.' However,
in a melodramatic twist of fate, the confessional letter posted from Virginia
had gone astray and Robert now attempted to put off Miss P. by saying: 'I
[am] but a stripling soldier; I [have] few talents, less wealth to commend me
to so much excellence or even repay [your] kind regard and favours.'[27] Miss
P. refuted all Robert's claims and finally Deborah Sampson was forced to
reveal the truth to her startled friend. Like many other female soldiers in
similar situations, Deborah Sampson attempted to avoid revealing the truth
because an admission of her deception would end her friendship with Miss
P. These incidents illustrated the loneliness and isolation disguised women
had to confront as part of their dealings with other women. The need to
prove their masculinity forced these women to mimic male power relations,
flirting with, mocking or flattering their admirers, but reinforced their
inability to completely transform their gender. There appeared to be no
room for any real sexual intimacy.

Another sadly deceived but virtuous woman appears in Princess Kati
Dadeshkeliani's autobiography of her experiences in the Russian army, disguised as Prince Djamal. In 1916 Kati briefly took leave from the front to
visit her sister in Petrograd. One evening they attended a perfomance at the
theatre where, dressed as Prince Djamal 'my uniform and my very youthful
appearance brought me many flattering attentions.' Among her admirers
was a celebrated singer who quickly became a good friend and the two
women began to see each other every night. But the singer was soon 'entertaining too lively an affection for me . . . . The knowledge was very painful
to me as I both loved and respected her.'[28] Like Deborah Sampson, Kati
resisted telling her friend the truth but eventually felt she had no alternative.
The infatuated singer confessed to Kati's sister that she was deeply in love

with the Prince 'because he is so reserved and so respectful,' emphasizing the relationship's platonic nature. When Djamal broke down and told her, 'Mademoiselle . . . my dear friend . . . you must forgive me . . . I am a woman,' the astonished singer fainted in a heap.[29] But even as Kati became increasingly cut-off from female companions because of the danger they posed, such stories served not only to highlight an erotic tension in her story but to lend further credence to her disguise. If she was convincing enough to have a famous singer swooning at her feet, she would have no fear of detection within the ranks either.

But homo-erotic tension could also work to highlight sexuality within male relationships. When Madeline Moore, the fictional lady Lieutenant of the Grand Army of the Republic who fought in the American Civil War, met up with her lover Frank, they instantly formed an intense friendship. Although Frank was unaware that his new companion Albert was really his fiancée in disguise, he soon declared, 'I already love you as a brother.' Albert saved Frank's life but was wounded in the process and was comforted by his companion who clasped him in his arms and cried: 'Oh more than ever, Albert, do you resemble my dear, dear Madeline! Oh! would to heaven I were with her!'[30] The eroticism in this scene where Frank tenderly cradles Albert is diffused and rendered appropriately heterosexual when Madeline reveals her identity. The affection men might develop for their comrades in the ranks could be played out in this fantasy where the attractive young mate or ship's cabin boy turned out to be a woman, after all.

Discussion of the female soldier's sexuality, however, could take on another important role. The female soldiers were never portrayed actually engaged in sexual relationships with other women and their inability to do so was often mocked. The use of physical props in their masquerade — whether it was Loreta Velasquez's wire meshed shirts, Madeline Moore's glue-on whiskers and beard or Christian Davies' 'urinary instrument' — suggest that their masculinity was only artificial. The silver dildo that Christian Davies reportedly strapped onto her groin as part of her disguise is a rich metaphor for this experience. Since sexuality was understood only in phallic terms this claim implied that Christian could only adopt her masculine identity like some clumsy, mechanical device. She acquired the symbolic gun and trousers —transformative accoutrements — but since only a phallus could bring another woman the 'real' sexual pleasure of penetration the female soldier's flirtations were rendered harmless and pleasingly erotic in the popular imagination.

Moreover, those soldiers who expressed confusion and deep affection for their misguided love objects did so often in retrospect, writing from the vantage point of safe, happy, heterosexual marriage. Deborah Sampson, like Emma Edwards and Christian Davies, wrote about her female relationships from the perspective of motherhood and old age. Since there was no parallel with a gay male subculture to give weight to possible fictive transgressions by the female soldiers, their sexuality was considered devoid of any real threat .

Whether the female warriors were involved in lesbian relationships is often an extremely difficult question to answer. The societies that produced these women denied, manipulated or silenced the public expression of active female sexuality. But that some of the female combatants were lesbian is clear, as Mary Anne Talbot's appreciation of her female companion suggests. There are numerous examples of cross-dressing women who assumed the role of husband with a female lover — like Albert F. — until the middle of this century.[31] The evidence of fictionalized heroines suggests that passionate romance between women was not considered a serious threat but was used to highlight the imitative nature of the soldier's identity. Like every other aspect of the female soldier's portrait, however, her sexuality was never static but took on the prevailing ideals in each historic period.

Sexual relationships between women were considered out-of-bounds, and increasingly so into the nineteenth century, as were heterosexual relations outside the confines of marriage. It was important that the female combatants remained chaste to their fellow soldiers, as Maria Bochkareva's struggle demonstrates. Autobiographies emphasize either the soldier's extreme youth, innocence or the brotherly platonic affection she developed with her comrades. This was partly pragmatic because it was a form of protection but heterosexual romance was also incongruous with and threatening to the soldier's identity. Flora Sandes once donned an evening dress to attend an officer's party in Bizerta as a joke but it left her comrades feeling extremely uncomfortable. '[My fellow soldiers] declared they did not know how to talk to me when dressed like that,' she wrote, 'and implored me to get back into uniform at once, and be one of them again.'[32] Flora Sandes could not be both sexual object and comrade at the same time and she readily sacrificed the former.

The question remains: when was it necessary and appropriate to resort to 'female' behaviour? Flora Sandes grappled with this problem while convalescing in Bizerta and wrote: 'My own chief difficulty was that I could never be quite sure when I was supposed to behave as a "lady" and a guest and when as a plain sergeant for sometimes I was treated as one and sometimes the other.'[33] At the New Year's Eve officer's ball in Belgrade in 1919 Flora was struck once again by the ambiguity of her position. The Serbian King Alexander asked why she refused to dance and Flora explained that she would rather not dance with the women, nor they with her and in uniform, she could only do the kola [the Serbian national dance] with the men. "If you won't find a partner for yourself I am going to find one for you," laughed the King. A few minutes later he approached Sandes' friend, Dr. Katherine MacPhail, a Scottish woman doctor who had worked on the Salonique Front, and ran her own Children's Hospital in Belgrade. "I've got a partner for you for the next waltz, Dr. MacPhail," said the King. "It's Lieutenant Sandes. I was just going to leave but I shall wait to see you two dance it."[34]

Whether the King's attempt to embarrass Flora Sandes and Dr. MacPhail was intentional or not, he certainly succeeded and highlighted their awkward social position. The women were made to dance together in front of the King's dias causing Flora Sandes great embarrassment. The ill-fated ball illustrates clearly her discomfort; although she was completely accepted as a comrade amongst the men in her ranks, when larger social pressures intruded, Flora could still be called upon to fulfill a feminine sexual role. As Flora Sandes later wrote: 'it's a hard world where half the people say you should not dress as a man and the other half want to punish you for dressing as a woman.'[35] Caught between the two she constantly improvised, switching costumes and identities to suit the occasion.

Flora Sandes' ability to straddle these worlds provides insight into how women who masqueraded in the ranks were able to maintain their disguise. The female soldiers who were known to their comrades were accepted once they had 'proved' themselves and in the heat of battle, sexual difference was superseded by the larger, all-consuming struggle for survival. But Sandes' story also suggests that male soldiers might agree to protect their female counterparts for a variety of reasons. These male friends rarely appear in published accounts of the female warrior's exploits probably for fear that the relationship would be misconstrued but they undoubtedly existed.

One of the most fascinating records of friendship is revealed in the correspondence of American Civil War soldiers Emma Edmonds and Jerome Robbins. Throughout the war Jerome Robbins of the Second Michigan Infantry Regiment kept a detailed diary of his army experiences. On 30 October 1861 Jerome, then assistant surgeon, refers to his friend Frank Thompson (Emma Edmonds) who also worked at the regimental hospital. The friendship blossomed over the following weeks as Jerome found Frank an entertaining conversationalist, 'a good noble-hearted fellow' and a keen intellectual companion.[36] Together they attended prayer meetings, took long walks and on 7 November Jerome noted that he 'arose greatly refreshed after a sound sleep in a couch with my friend Frank.' Soon after Jerome's intimacy with Frank prompted him to write: 'The society of a friend so pleasant as Frank I hail with joy though foolish as it may seem a great mystery appears to be connected with him which it is impossible for me to fathom.'[37] Despite his unease, which Jerome brushed off as 'false surmises,' the friendship grew. The soldiers shared a deep religious conviction and their work kept them in close contact, occasionally filling in for each other or staying up to talk on night duty in the hospital.

Only two weeks later, after a 'long and interesting conversation' with Frank, Jerome returned to his quarters and wrote in his crabbed hand, 'my friend Frank is a female.'[38] Jerome was distraught, not from any moral conviction that women had no place in the army, but from his sense of personal betrayal. A more than platonic love for 'his' stalwart companion may have prompted Frank to reveal 'his' true identity. When Jerome spoke about his intended bride, Anna Corey, Frank volunteered an explanation for 'his' decision to leave New Brunswick in male disguise and to join the army. Frank Thompson had enlisted in the Union Greys on 17 April 1861 and Jerome was probably the first person, after eight long months of subterfuge, to learn 'his' friend's secret.

Contrary to all Emma Edmonds' published accounts about her life as Frank, Jerome Robbins states in his diary that she left her home town, Mandan, New Brunswick because of an ill-fated love affair with Thomas, a local merchant. 'My friend describes him as pleasing in manner and so won her heart as to cause the object of love to be nearly worshipped,' wrote

Robbins. 'But a change came; her lover seemed cold, reserved and exacting, which was too much for the nature of my friend.' The lovers separated, Emma became seriously ill with scarlet fever and after several weeks languishing in bed, she recovered and abruptly left Canada.[39] Emma possibly invented this story because she doubted that Jerome Robbins would believe anything else but it is equally plausible that her lover did exist. She would wisely have left the mysterious Thomas out of her published and self-censored autobiographies that fashioned her into a more conventionally acceptable war heroine. According to her own account Emma left home when her brutal father forced her into an engagement with an odious farmer and, inspired by the lively heroine of Lieutenant Murray's novel, *Fanny Campbell or the Female Pirate Captain,* she took on a new identity as Frank.

The story so far adds another dimension to Emma's own words that her alias allowed her to escape from an unhappy home life. There is no reason to doubt Jerome Robbins' record of this conversation since he carefully protected Emma's confession from accidental discovery. Jerome gummed together the pages for this entry and wrote across the top, 'please allow these leaves to be closed until author's permission is given for their opening.' Jerome kept his friend's secret throughout the remainder of his diary, never mentioned the conversation but always referred to Frank in the masculine pronoun. Though Jerome burned with resentment about Frank's deception he still regarded the friendship 'as one of the greatest events of my life.'[40]

Despite this assurance, however, Jerome Robbins found a replacement for an increasingly surly Frank. On 6 December his moody companion watched as Jerome had 'another long conversation with Russell in which he expressed to me the deepest friendship that even a brother could not.'[41] Two weeks later Jerome wrote of Frank: 'I am a little fearful our natures are not as congenial as at first supposed by me yet I feel he is the same friend.' For the next few weeks the friendship appeared to deteriorate, Jerome noting that Frank, 'acts strangely,' and was 'very much out of humour.' He suggested that Frank might be jealous of Jerome's fiancé and wrote, 'Perhaps a knowledge on her part that there is one Michigan home that I do regard with especial affection creates her disagreeable manner.'[42]

At the end of December 1861 Frank left Camp Scott to nurse at an army camp in Alexandria. According to Jerome, Frank left because of constant teasing about 'his' feminine appearance from a cook and other men in the camp.[43] But when they met again a year later in Alexandria, they resumed a warm friendship. They continued their evening walks, often discussing religion, nursed each other when sick, swapped magazines, stories and on 14 February Frank, Jerome and another soldier shared a 'pretty, warm berth' on a cabin floor. When Frank failed to pay a visit for a few days, Robbins wrote, 'I feel quite lonely without him.'[44] One evening Frank came to visit when Jerome was out but left a note between two pages of Robbin's journal saying that 'he' had read it 'for spite.'[45] Such was their intimacy that Jerome was amused rather than angry about his friend's disregard for privacy.

But on 16 April 1863 Frank deserted the army at Lebanon, Kentucky and soon after Lieutenant James Reid of the 79th New York Volunteers, followed. Throughout that spring Jerome made note of Frank's 'particular friend,' Reid, who was 'a fine fellow and seems very fond of Frank.'[46] Although Jerome knew his friend planned to leave, he felt cheated and deceived when it happened. 'He did not prepare me for his ingratitude,' wrote Robbins '. . . to repay kindness, interest and the warmest sympathy with deception [is] the petty attribute of a selfish heart.'[47] Reading between the lines of Robbins' journal it is clear that he was smitten with jealousy and wrote on 4 April while nursing Frank through an illness: 'It is a sad reality to which we awaken when we learn that others are receiving the devotion of one from whom we only claim friendship's attention.'[48]

This was not, however, the end of Jerome's friendship with Frank. During the last two years of the war they corresponded and in Emma's letters she reveals her affection for Robbins. A month after leaving the army she wrote from Washington, D. C.: 'Oh Jerome, *I do miss you so much*. There is no person living whose presence would be so agreeable to me this afternoon as yours.'[49] Two years later Emma still addressed her friend wistfully. 'I daily realize that had I met you some years ago I might have been much happier now,' she wrote from a camp in Falmouth, Virginia. 'But providence ordered it otherwise and I must be content.'[50] Reid told Emma that he and Jerome had discussed her which prompted her to ask Robbins: 'I want you to write me the import of [that conversation]. Will you please do so? [Reid] says he wants me to come and visit his wife who is very anxious to see me.'[51]

There is very little evidence of Emma's relationship with Reid but if she was in love with him, it must have been an excruciating situation. Her relationship with Reid jeopardized her position in the regiment and her friendship with Jerome. Her affair with a married man appears quite contradictory to her Christian principles and was probably the source of vicious rumours that she later took pains to quell in her published life-history. In *Nurse and Spy* and other autobiographical accounts Emma left the army because she was seriously ill with malaria and only then because a request for a leave of absence was denied. But in reality her relationship with Reid may have become uncomfortably public and since Robbins says that Frank prepared him for 'his' eventual departure it was probably not spontaneous.[52]

Apparently Reid and Robbins were not the only men who knew Emma's secret. William Boston, also of the Second Michigan Regiment, wrote in his diary on 22 April 1863: 'Our brigade postmaster turns out to be a girl and has deserted when his lover Inspector Read [sic] and [General O.M.] Poe resigned.' Several years later Poe was willing to testify that 'her sex was not suspected by me or anyone else in the regiment,' although he alludes to her fear of detection as the reason for her desertion.[53] Her comrades' extraordinary loyalty in keeping her secret (in Poe's case to help her get a pension) suggests her fellow-soldiers' acceptance of a woman in the ranks. Emma was an exception but one who had 'proven' herself in battle and in the camp, working tirelessly in the hospital. When Robbins discovered Emma's secret there was no mention of turning her in or divulging her secret to a commanding authority. Even Poe and Reid — both officers — accepted her presence. It is only later, public accounts of her story that wrestle with questions about a woman's appropriate role on the battle field.

Jerome Robbins' documentation of his relationship with Emma Edmonds reveals the complex inner workings of a double identity. Jerome struggles to make sense of his conflicting feelings for Emma as a woman *and* as a comrade in arms. He implies that Emma too yearns for more than a platonic relationship and the opportunity for physical intimacy — the nights they shared a warm berth — presented itself. Their mutual interest in religion may have provided a space where their corporeal conflict was felt less keenly. It remains surprising to a contemporary audience that Robbins' reaction to Emma's confession is confusion about his friendship with her and anger at her deception while he is unconcerned with the gender issues that figure so large in public discussion of women in war.

However, there are echoes of Robbins' confusion and anger at being deceived elsewhere. A century earlier when Deborah Sampson fought in the

Continental Army, she most feared detection because of 'the *shame* that would overwhelm me.' Wounded in the leg and shoulder during a battle near East Chester in June 1782, Deborah equated an unmasking of her disguise with death and found death preferable. 'I considered this as a death-wound, or as being equivalent to it as it must, I thought, lead to discovery,' she wrote in *The Female Review*. Would the intimate friendships she had formed with the men in her regiment withstand the shock of her discovery? She did not know and felt fortunate that her comrades were never tested.[54] Loreta Janeta Velasquez took a similar course of action in 1862 when she decided to desert the Confederate Southern Army rather than have a foot wound attended to by a surgeon who might discover her secret.[55]

There are numerous examples of women helped by a male friend, relative or lover in maintaining their disguise. When Christian Davies found her husband Richard after her 12 year search, she demanded that they live 'as brothers' until the Duke of Marlborough's campaign had ended, much to Richard's dismay. Loreta Velasquez claimed that she had a confidant while in the Confederate Army who kept, 'the secret of my transformation as faithfully as if it were his own.'[56] Princess Kati Dadeshkeliani was persuaded by a family friend Colonel Khagandokov to enlist during the First World War as her cousin.[57] Twelve Muscovite high school girls, who fought in the Russian army in 1914, were aided by soldiers who 'treated the little patriots quite paternally and properly having concealed them in [railway] cars took them off to the war.'[58]

British Tommies aided Dorothy Lawrence at every step of her foray to the Western Front in 1915. The conspirator who found her a place in a mine-laying company within 400 yards of the front line was a Lancashire coal miner, Tom Dunn. After establishing that Dorothy was 'English right enough,' and not wandering among the soldiers to solicit business, this 'small soldier' delivered the following lecture to his charge:

> Now I see thoroughly the sort of girl yer are, I'll help yer. Yer no bad 'un. You're a lady. I followed yer to see what sort of gal yer was. I ain't no better than the rest. All the same I ain't agin to harm any gal. You're straight, that's what yer are. I can see that. So I'll help yer.[59]

Tom then found an dilapidated but abandoned cottage for Dorothy to hide in. During the day she worked in the trenches laying mines and at dusk took the precaution of hurrying back to her hide-out. To avoid detection she stayed away from the other men, eating only what Tom managed to bring her and sleeping in her clothes on a pile of straw. She worked with Tom laying mines but, 'I declined, after thought, the duty of setting light to the fuse, preferring that *murder* should not rest on my conscience.'[60] In her mind this disqualified her from being a *bona fide* soldier although the refusal aroused no suspicion among her comrades.

At this stage during the Great War the trenches were disorganized enough that Lawrence could slip easily into a newly-formed tunnelling company made up of miscellaneous soldiers from other regiments. She wrote in her autobiography that officers did not expect to be paid any particular notice nor was discipline rigidly enforced so there was no worry of breaching the rules. Since engineers regularly moved from company to company no one noticed a stranger in their midst. Nor was Dorothy Lawrence the only women to visit the front unofficially. Australian author Louise Mack produced a 300 page book of her journey to see the 'Boche' in 1915; Lady Isabelle St John went to Bethune, France the same year looking for a son missing in action and found him; and an English nurse, Mary Wilkinson, got her pilot's certificate from the United Aero Club and volunteered for the Russian Army Air service in 1916.[61] These stories parallel those of the Russian women soldiers who appeared in the midst of battle and stayed. They are all testimonies to the chaos of the war and the inefficiency of military security in keeping determined women at bay.

Just as there were numerous women who found their way into the military or behind lines with the help of a comrade, there is an equally long list of women who managed a disguise without detection for many years. Authors of anecdotal life-histories, however, often suffer from a compulsion to write about a successfully maintained disguise because it disallowed accusations that the woman soldier was working as a military prostitute. It also made for a much more exciting story which could be shot through with *double-entendres* and near-misses. The case of Emma Edmonds sheds light on the actual complexity of these situations. But there were those who, by all accounts, convinced even their closest mates of their assumed identity.

For those women who were known to their fellow soldiers or sailors immersion in a male persona was imperative. Rather than forcing their comrades to accept a woman doing a man's job they became 'one of the boys' — a much less threatening position.[62] In the process, all female combatants sloughed off their feminine selves for the duration of their military careers. According to the biographer of an American woman who joined the U.S. Merchant Marines in the 1970s as 'Mike,' she was convincing as a male sailor because she managed to create a sense of the reality of her masculinity for those with whom she interacted. In practical terms some women managed by making themselves indispensable, developing an expertise or a flamboyant, eccentric personality.

W. H. Davies, while waiting on a Baltimore dock for work aboard a freight steamer in the 1890s, met a sailor whose 'vitality of spirits seemed overflowing every minute of the day.'[63] The sailor was almost a caricature of the rolling, jolly tar, who entertained the men by singing with 'surprising sweetness,' deftly rolling cigarettes, spitting tobacco and swaggering about the dock. Back in Baltimore, a few weeks later, Davies met his friend Blackey who had worked a cattle steamer back to England with the strange sailor. Though Blackey worked side by side with the 'cattleman' for 11 days it was only when his companion had an accident on board and was taken off the ship that he discovered his friend was a woman. 'By his singing, laughing and talking, he made a play of labour,' Blackey told Davies. 'Down in the forecastle at night he sang songs and in spite of our limited space, and the rolling of the ship he gave many a dance and ended by falling into his low bunk exhausted and laughing still.' Though Blackey always thought his friend 'a queer man' and Davies had the impression she was 'playing a part, all this cigarette smoking, chewing tobacco and swaggering,' neither man had the slightest suspicion of her sex.[64]

It was precisely the forbidden, smoky saloons filled with raucous laughter and heavy with the spice of male comradeship that enticed women to pass as men. In disguise they could enjoy the most boisterous aspects of male culture free from the ever-present fear of sexual harassment. When Elsa Jane Guerin — who lived undetected for 13 years as 'Mountain Charley,' an American prospector, soldier and cabin boy — came home to visit her children she reverted to female garb. But she was soon bored with female life and 'could not wholly eradicate many of the tastes which I had acquired during my life as one of the stronger sex.' Elsa simply put on her trousers again and, as Charley, wandered around St. Louis, Missouri, 'in any and all places that my curiosity led me.'[65] But when she compared male and female clothes she found, 'the change from the cumbersome, unhealthy attire of woman to the more convenient, healthful habiliments of a man, was in itself almost sufficient to compensate for its unwomanly character.'[66]

For some women, the lure of the breeches was an enticing combination of a financially-rewarding occupation, a more exciting social world, and an escape from the tyranny of a husband or father. A black British sailor, 'William Brown,' left her husband for the sea and became as famous for her agility in climbing the rigging as she did for her 'partiality for prize-money and grog.'[67] Her skill earned her a position as captain of the foretop and also quashed rumours about her true identity during 11 years at sea with the British Royal Navy. Her sex was only discovered in 1815 when the *Queen Charlotte*'s crew was paid off and her estranged husband stepped forward to claim part of her earnings. While William Brown secured her position on the foretop, Hannah Snell, one of Britain's best-known eighteenth-century female sailors, distinguished herself aboard the *Swallow* by her domestic skills. Even though she began her career as cabin boy she 'rendered herself so conspicuous both by her skill and intrepidity that she was allowed to be a very useful hand on board.'[68]

According to her biographer, Hannah became such a skilled sailor that she dealt with suspicions by challenging any man who made accusations about her femininity to beat her at some task. When she was teased about her lack of beard 'with the disagreeable title of Miss Molly Gray' (she served as James Gray) she returned the insult with a smile, an oath and a challenge. She worked 'to prove herself as good a man as any of them on board for any wager to be deposited in her master's hands.'[69] This combination of tough-guy persona and intrepid sailor worked to fend off possible discovery.

In quite different circumstances Dr. James Barry, a woman who cross-dressed to graduate from the University of Edinburgh's medical school in 1812, may have developed a rather fierce personality to mask fears of detection. James Barry was always remembered as arrogant and temperamental and, like the Baltimore cattleman, she seemed to swagger in her male role, acting a near caricature. 'At balls it was always noted that [she] flirted with all the best-looking women in the room.'[70] On a similar note Barry would make caustic remarks about women 'he' found unattractive to 'his' employer, Lord Charles Somerset, Governor of the Cape Colony. Barry's stinging remarks about and flirtations with other women served to further distance 'him' from the female world. In the stories of cross-dressing women, however, this attitude is part of a larger wholesale adoption of what are seen as male values.

Other disguised women, once confident in their new role, often forgot their self-consciousness and played their 'part' with great flair. Loreta Janeta Velasquez commented that living as Lieutenant Harry T. Buford she 'became accustomed to male attire and to appearing before anybody and everybody in it,' and she 'lost all fear of being found out and learned to act, talk and almost to think as a man.'[71] Valerie Arkell-Smith in her guise as Colonel Barker was surprised at how easily she convinced people of her new identity.' As the weeks slipped by I began to experience a sense of exhiliaration at the knowledge I was getting away with it,' she wrote in 1956. 'As time went on I became more and more daring.'[72] Sailor Mary Anne Arnold, who worked, undetected, aboard a British East Indiaman ship in 1838, described her experience as 'performing the character of a man.'[73]

Even for those female soldiers who were not attempting to 'pass' as men, there was often a theatrical element to their hard-won acceptance as a male comrade. Flora Sandes rose to the challenge to conform to masculine behaviour when she would attempt to excuse herself from a night on the town with her mates. According to her autobiography, 'the men always squashed [my excuses] by telling me "to be a man". . . It always seemed to me that men took life much more easily and straightforwardly than women.' Although Sandes had acquired the status of a brother in arms, she still felt that her authority and experience could be challenged. While lecturing to British troops about conditions in Serbia at YMCA huts in France, she struck up a friendship with three dejected English soldiers. It was evening and they had been waiting all day for a train to take them back to their regiment after their leave had been cut short. Sandes, who was a striking figure in her grey Serb uniform and cropped white hair, told them she was a soldier and while they listened politely, she knew they did not believe her. But when she returned with four bottles of beer they exclaimed: '*Now* we know you are a *real soldier*.'[74]

Flora's exposure to the world that had been closed to her until the war gave her an elevated status among the men she encountered at home and in Serbia. But her new identity was always set in contrast to her former life; she proved her 'manhood' by stressing how different she was from other women. She was proud that she knew, for example, that Serb soldiers convalescing in hospital preferred a chunk of bread and a bunch of spring onions as a get-well gift far more than a cake.

> "Our sergeant knows what we like," Flora's admiring soldiers told her. "The French ladies come and visit us sometimes and bring us cakes. Cakes!" — scornfully — "food for women and children, not soldiers."[75]

Since Flora was a soldier like them and thus an honorary man she could be counted on to act appropriately.

Flora Sandes was seriously wounded on 15 November 1916 during the Serbian army's recapture of Monastir and spent six months recuperating. She was hit by a Bulgar bomb, knocked unconscious and dragged from the battlefield under fire. The Serbs believed that brandy was better than water for the wounded so an ambulance attendant poured half a bottle down her throat and stuck a cigarette between her lips. Flora waited in agony for transportation to the hospital and when she arrived blood was dripping through the stretcher. As the doctor probed for shards of the bomb, Sandes dug her head into his broad chest and for the first time howled in pain. Her arm was smashed and she had more than a dozen wounds on her back and down her right side.

But the doctor stopped this sudden outpouring of torment and pure emotion by admonishing Flora Sandes to 'shut up and remember that [she] was a soldier' which 'did far more good than any amount of petting would have done.'[76] Flora was told by the division commandant Colonel Milic that after her recovery she would be placed with the divisional staff, away from the front. She smiled but silently prayed that he would forget his promise; 'I should lose all caste with the men if I chose a soft billet instead of roughing it with them.'[77] The soft, safe, idealized female world epitomized everything a real soldier, male or female, was not. Her story at once contradicted and confirmed the polarity of the sexes; the question remained, if a woman is everything a man is not, how could a woman become a man?

When, for example, Marina Yurlova's comrades teased her about looking like a girl, she responded: 'A babba indeed! I could not have been more grossly insulted. Wasn't I a soldier? The dirty devils!'[78] On another occasion when an officer treated Marina like a domestic servant by asking her to clean his room, she was angered because, 'I did not want to be thought a girl — I was a soldier.'[79] As her Cossack regiment headed towards Mount Ararat in the Ottoman Empire to fight the Turks, singing volubly of slaughter, she thought, 'All I hoped was that they wouldn't think me a soft-hearted babba; and I vowed I wouldn't give them a chance.'[80] Loreta Velasquez was determined to show her fellow officers that Harry T. Buford was 'as good a man as any of them and was able to face the enemy as valiantly.'[81]

At every step of her transformation the female soldier rejected parts of her former self and developed a way of coping with the seeming contradiction of living as both woman and soldier. Zoya Smirnova and her high school friends who fought with the Tsar's army on the eastern front in 1916 not only traversed Galicia and scaled the Carpathian mountains uncomplaining, but never shirked their duties. They shared all the soldier's privations and over time their experience forged a new identity. 'The girls almost forgot their past, they hardly responded to their feminine names, for each of them had received a masculine surname and completely mingled with the men.'[82] Like the contemporary Foreign Legionnaires the women shed all traces of their former life in embracing their political cause.[83]

Conversely, violence, physical stoicism and courage were so equated with the masculinity of soldiering that any behaviour which fell short of this ideal was deemed feminine. A soldier of the White Army, Lul Gardo, was deeply moved while watching a small girl play with a toy next to the body of her mother killed during a bombardment. Struck with emotion she suddenly thought, 'all at once I was a woman again.' When a woman soldier fighting in Lul Gardo's regiment got separated from the troops and committed suicide, Lul was prompted to consider whether she would have done the same. But she concluded, 'it would have branded me as a coward. My friends would shake their heads and say, "she was only a woman after all."'[84] The female soldier was constantly on the alert to prevent slipping back into her feminine self.

Once in battle Lul Gardo felt herself transformed. 'I was to myself no longer a woman,' she wrote. 'I was a soldier first and last and always a soldier with a rifle for my pathway and victory for my goal.'[85] While fighting in White general Kornilov's army, she interrogated a captured Red Army soldier and, in a reversal of roles, forced him to undress before her. With a vindictive glee she told him: 'You had a woman once, I suppose and now a woman has you! A different game, eh? . . . But this is war and sex does not count.'[86] It is only in male guise that Lul Gardo believed she could take such an aggressive, hostile stance. Yet her revenge is in itself a contradiction. If war really obliterated sexual difference the interrogation by a woman could not have the impact she assumed it did.

Warfare is often presented in the female warrior's story as an essentially masculine experience. But biological concepts of sexual difference also give way to an understanding of gender as something fluid, interchangeable and dynamic. The San Francisco journalist, Bessie Beattie, discovered this when she asked Nina, 'the comedy member of the [Russian women's] battalion' whether she liked her hair cut short. Nina replied that she liked long hair for a girl but not a soldier. 'It was a key note,' wrote Beattie:

> Nina spoke for the whole battalion. Soldiers and women were, for them, things apart. When they cut off their long braids and soft curls, and pledged themselves to fight for their country, they put aside all superficial feminities.'[87]

Among the female soldiers of the Red Army there was a similar equation of masculinity with military prowess. Women who fought during the civil war of 1917 resented any allegations of femininity and male resistance to female soldiers was successfully opposed. 'When a young female combatant, equipped with oversized papakha, leather coat and Browning was detected by her comrades as a "little girl" [devchina] she proudly replied, "I am not a little girl now, I am a soldier of the Revolution."'[88]

The female soldiers also demonstrate their male identification clearly when they come into contact with their female contemporaries. Bochkareva admonished the women of her battalion to remember that they were mere surrogates for recalcitrant males. 'Woman is naturally light-hearted. But if she can purge herself for sacrifice, then through a caressing word, a loving heart and an example of heroism she can save the Motherland,' Bochkareva exhorted her troops from the Petrograd cathedral. 'We are physically weak but if we can be strong morally and spiritually we will accomplish more than a large force.'[89] If 'women' were light-hearted and weak, Bochkareva was not. Her deliberate use of these images helped to justify the all-female battalion since they evoked the ideals of sexual purity and maternal self-sacrifice.

They also, however, served to divorce Bochkareva from association with her own gender.

Sexual activity, however, remained the great divide between the masculine and feminine military experience. The women of the Russian battalion all took a vow of chastity for 'the duration' and any woman suspected of striking up a friendship with a male contemporary was dismissed.[90] There was often a discrepancy between the reality of the female soldier's sexual experience and what she chose to divulge publicly about it. Emma Edmonds' story suggests the disguised female soldier may have been sexually active but this experience is either invisible or made explicitly erotic in public representations of these women. Despite their acceptance among their fellow soldiers or the success of their disguise all female combatants lived in fear that they could be dismissed as prostitutes.

When Flora Sandes' Serbian regiment reached Corfu after the long retreat through Albania in the autumn of 1915, she met a few of the English officers with the Salonica Force. Surprised by an English woman in soldier's uniform they assumed Sandes was 'a kind of camp follower.' Flora refused to confront these suspicions head-on and let her Serbian comrades quash them for her.[91] Rumours resurfaced, however, when she was wounded in 1916 and admitted to a British military hospital in Salonika. Flora was put in a tent by herself rather than with the men who, 'looking upon me as they did as quite one of themselves' urged her to join them. Some of the nursing sisters were even annoyed that Sandes was visited by soldiers and 'in consequence were rather sarcastic about my supposed wish to be moved into the men's tent.'[92] The implication was, of course, that Flora Sandes was enjoying a more than platonic relationship with her comrades.

Marina Yurlova's motives were also subject to scrutiny while she recovered from a leg wound in hospital. She had travelled with her regiment from the Armenian plains slowly retreating towards Erivan and the Araks river. During the first action against the Turks Marina was wounded on a dangerous expedition blasting bridges to block the enemy advance. Her mentor Kosel was killed by enemy fire so for her 'everything that meant gentleness and understanding was gone.'[93] Marina arrived at the Red Cross hospital in Baku, a Caspian seaside town, deeply depressed, with a grossly swollen leg and spent several weeks convalescing. Word about a female soldier quickly got round and Marina became an attraction 'like a caged animal whom people poke with umbrellas and walking sticks.' The visitors all probed about her army life, suspicious that she was a 'bad girl.'[94] When she was wounded again in 1916 Marina encountered a disbelieving nurse who, '[found] it hard to forgive me for being of the same sex.'

Rumours about prostitutes who bought nurses uniforms on the black market in Germany and Russia to work at the front may explain the hostile reaction Marina often received. Widely circulated were newspaper stories about incidents such as the German capture of a Russian detachment near the Naroc Sea where, among the prisoners, was a 19-year-old female nurse in 'male costume.' When the woman was asked why she was fighting with the men instead of serving as a nurse she replied that in Russia 'the nurses had a very evil reputation' so she preferred to wear a soldier's uniform.[95] Whether these stories were true, they reinforced a belief that any woman working at the front among men — whether soldier or nurse — was sexually available. Maria Bochkareva 'prayed to God to hallow' the women of her battalion with chastity while instructing them to live 'as saintly women.'[96] Ironically the nurse who attempted to seduce Prince Djamal Dadeshkeliani prompted Kati to write, 'on this occasion and on others . . . I confess that I blushed for my sex and congratulated myself on the uniform that ranked me with the other.' Her moral outrage was a guarantee of deflecting reader's concerns about her own character and motives for joining the ranks.[97]

In her writing, Dorothy Lawrence stressed the propriety of her motives in going to the Western front. Only when she returned unceremoniously to London in 1915 did she learn the full meaning of the term camp follower — the accusation hurled at her by dismayed British officers upon her discovery in their ranks. 'Though I had often heard the term, I supposed it referred to wagons that carried provisions,' she wrote. 'Not once had our soldiers removed this idea.' She did, however, keep a heavy knife concealed in her uniform but 'no call came for its use.'[98]

Some female soldiers were even promoted as the ideal of women's sexual purity if they retained their virtue amongst an all-male regiment. Hannah Snell's biographer demanded 'not only respect but admiration' for her preservation of virtue. The frontispiece to her 1750 biography urged female readers to emulate her propriety but not her military career.[99] Deborah Sampson assured readers of her memoirs first published in 1797, that she 'preserved her chastity inviolate by the most artful concealment of her sex.'[100]

According to their biographers, Hannah Snell enlisted to find her husband and Deborah Sampson left home to support her country's cause against the British. While neither explanation was fully accurate, both conformed to traditional interpretations of women's desire to breach convention by donning male clothes.

In reality, in societies where a woman's survival was limited to her value in marriage, in co-habitation or as a prostitute, 'going for a soldier' presented an enticing alternative. In 1803 a young girl dressed in male clothes appeared before a London magistrate as a 'common prostitute' and upon hearing her sentence 'with the utmost calm and indifference said she wished to go to sea.'[101] In 1843 former sailor Margaret Johnson was reduced to soliciting when she was forced to retire from the sea.[102]

The following year the fifth edition of *The Life and Sufferings of Miss Emma Cole* recounted the adventures of a young domestic servant who was accidentally lured into a Boston brothel. Emma Cole fended off her first customer with a knife and fled by selling her hair to a barber, buying a sailor's outfit and signing aboard the *Juba* bound for New Orleans.[103] Another Bostonian who possibly inspired the Emma Cole story was Louisa Baker who escaped from a home of 'naughty ladies' to enlist as a marine in the American navy during the War of 1812 aboard the *Constitution*. Her record of adventures was published under the pseudonym, 'Lucy Brewer', to protect her family's reputation since she had worked as a prostitute before adopting a male guise. She was inspired to leave by a young officer who told her about soldier Deborah Sampson and Brewer wrote:

> From this moment I became dissatisfied with my situation in life . . . I felt now no other disposition than in disguise to visit other parts of the country and to pursue a course of life less immoral and destructive to my peace and happiness in this life.[104]

Ironically, it was not Deborah Sampson's chastity but her ability to transcend the boundaries of her sex that inspired other women to emulate her. It also suggests that men and women may have read the female warrior's story very differently as the example of two university students' interpretation of Deborah Sampson's memoirs illustrates.

When Harvard student John C. Lee gave Theodore Keating a copy of *The Female Review* on 12 July 1820, he wrote on the inside cover: 'Dark are the ways of Providence nor knows man to *interpret* them.' Keating felt no such qualms about interpretation however, and when he donated Sampson's book to his BFM Fraternity of Bachelors in 1835, his interest in the female soldier's sexual status was explicit. 'A history of extraordinary celibacy among females which lasted the whole American Revolutionary War,' he wrote. 'But it was at length conquered by the joint powers of Cupid and Hymen and Peace — "Frailty thy name is woman."' Keating's sarcasm belittled Deborah Sampson's achievements by emphasizing her presumed sexual ambiguity that also reflected the threat that her independence posed.

Since any woman attached to the military was suspected of working as a prostitute, the emphasis on the female soldier's sexual innocence is vital. Comparisons with Joan of Arc were used in English accounts of female soldiers to legitimate their adventure and confirm their asexuality. Flora Sandes was dubbed the 'Serbian Joan of Arc incarnate' by the Australian and English press in 1920 — the year of Joan's canonization. Like St Joan, Maria Bochkareva was 'the symbol of her country' and 'a striking incarnation.'[105] Madame Kokovtseva, commander of the 6th Ural Cossack Regiment, was labelled 'the Muscovite militant — a Russian Joan of Arc' by the London *Graphic* in 1915. As Frank Mundell wrote of Joan in 1898: 'She was above sex and yielded to no one in courage or military virtues.'[106] To be 'above sex' meant to be involved with greater concerns than earthly passions. But such sentiments also helped to evade a vastly troubling question of the single — and therefore sexually suspect — woman serving, undisguised or not, in an all-male regiment. Only a heroine, stripped of her sexuality, could be portrayed sympathetically and her transgression of the male-female duality made understandable.

However saint-like her portrait, throughout her long history of popular representation in ballads, life-histories and in the press, the warrior heroine continued to defy expectations about women. But was her consequent assumption of 'manhood' ever complete? Some of the female combatants were well-aware of the strictures inherent in this process of imitation. When Flora Sandes remembered the long march from Monastir to Belgrade in 1918, she often repeated Rudyard Kipling's poem 'If' to herself to revive her flagging spirits. '[I] must force [my] heart and nerve and sinew to serve their turn long after they are done' she would chant in a whisper, forcing each step forward. But, she remarked: 'Often though I have repeated those lines to myself . . . they did not result in making a man of me.'[107]

If being a man meant excelling at the epitome of masculine activity — the art of warfare — then the process of imitation was a success. Women proved at every level they were as competent, as skilled, as aggressive, as deadly and as courageous as their male counterparts. But once sexually active, their entire identity was placed in jeopardy, as Emma Edmonds' story illustrates. Their adoption of masculinity was successful but ultimately limited; entering the military meant conforming to a masculine, hierarchical world. The combatants did not claim their equality as newly-appropriate for women. Rather they divorced themselves from association with other women, often mocking and denigrating them to ensure their own status amongst their male comrades.

As individuals they could assume the role of mascot or an exception who proved the rules. They simultaneously challenged understandings of gender — they were biologically women after all — and reinforced them. They were seen not as courageous *women* but brave soldiers, their military identity subsuming every other name, face and experience. The female warrior enjoyed a temporary passage into the male world, made acceptable only because of extraordinary historical circumstances and to be revoked when she was no longer needed or found out. Whether the radical potential of her experience and the tantalizing contradictions she embodied really changed historical understandings of sexual difference remained a moot question.

4

The Denouement

Ever since the days of Queen Thalestris, there have been ladies who
aspired to be gentlemen and despised their own position . . .
Metaphorically speaking, and in the sense of wishing to rule, thus it has
ever been and is with all her sisterhood, as every married man is well
aware, but the actual inducement of the garments in question
is comparatively rare.
Chambers's Journal, 30 May 1863

DOROTHY LAWRENCE, DISGUISED as Private Denis Smith joined a
British Expeditionary Force tunnelling company at the Western Front
in 1915. After ten days of unpleasantness — she was plagued by
rheumatism, chills and in great discomfort from her tight swaddling —
Sapper Smith could take her masquerade no longer and requested to speak
with 'his' immediate superior. The Sergeant in charge merely smiled and
patted her on the back when her sex was revealed to him. With a sigh of
relief Dorothy Lawrence turned to the mine fuses she was preparing with her
pal Tommy Dunn. A few minutes later she felt two meaty hands grab her by
both arms as burly military policemen hauled her from the trench.

Dorothy Lawrence was furious at the Sergeant who had betrayed her and
scowled as she passed him. 'You are the biggest blackguard I have ever met,'
she shouted, 'If I *were* really a man I'd knock you down here and now.'[2]
Dorothy naively believed that the Sergeant would or could keep her secret
because she had confided in him. Instead she was quickly marched to British
Third Army headquarters and presented to the astonished commanding
Colonel as a possible spy and promptly made a prisoner of war.

Despite the grave charge, the absurdity of her position prompted
Dorothy to burst into laughter when seated before a crush of Secret

Intelligence officers. 'So utterly ludicrous appeared this betrousered little female, marshaled solemnly by three soldiers and desposited before 20 embarrassed men,' she wrote years later. 'On arrival I heard, "Oh-o-o! (groan) it is a woman. Certainly we shall never get even with a woman if she wishes to deceive us."'[3] News of her arrest spread quickly through the area and several young officers dropped into her interrogation room to have a look. One exclaimed angrily that the 'episode' would soon pass like rapid-fire along the front line and in the background ran a murmur of 'what would they say back home.'

Her private letters were fetched from the abandoned cottage fellow sapper Tommy Dunn had housed her in and scrutinized by the Secret Intelligence Corps' officers. Dorothy Lawrence had formed a friendship with this Lancashire miner when she reached the Western Front and he had smuggled her into his tunnelling company. Now that it was all over, seated at a makeshift wooden table watching the men, Dorothy Lawrence 'lapsed into feminine attitudes despite [her] little khaki uniform, concealment no longer being necessary.'[4] Her 'lapse' back into femininity was also partly to appear as unthreatening and 'lady-like' as possible. Finally, the commanding Colonel dismissed his prisoner for the night and told the guards: 'Whatever you do take her away from here! I don't know what to do with her.'

On horseback Dorothy Lawrence was shuttled across the French countryside in a desperate search for 'suitable accommodation.' When her escorts reached Calais, Major-General Sir Henry Seymour Rawlinson commanded coldly, 'find some decent clothes for her and get her out of here.' The next stop was Senlis and then back to Third Army headquarters in St. Omer where she was re-examined. Added to Dorothy Lawrence's misery, after her questioning she was thrown into a guard room policed by eight soldiers who had strict instructions to refuse all visitors. She remained there for three nights, her guards, she claimed, growing increasingly ashamed of the treatment she received.[5]

When her interrogation resumed Dorothy Lawrence was seated before three British generals, including Sir Charles Munro, 20 staff officers and other military officials. Throughout the gruelling investigation she swung between amused irony and anger at the officers' unwillingness to believe her story. A sympathetic officer told her: 'They simply don't know what to make of you. . . . One thinks that you are a spy and another says you must be a camp-follower and everyone has his own views on the subject.'[6] If Dorothy Lawrence were a spy or a prostitute, her motives would have been clear. But since she denied both these charges and any claim to fervent patriotism, she placed herself beyond the comforting tradition of a Joan of Arc and any other female warrior heroine. Distressed that her confession elicited only further confusion, Dorothy Lawrence fumed: 'Our higher command surely lacked imagination and proper perspective otherwise this trivial escapade never could have assumed such proportions.'[7] But she also knew why her appearance at the front generated such commotion.

While being held for cross-examination, uncomfortable before her audience of officers, Dorothy Lawrence blurted out: 'If masculinity, as nature's endowment, had fallen to [my] lot, probably [I] would have tried to be in the navy, if not a member of the law.'[8] Her masquerade at the front represented not only a critical breach of the security system but raised growing fears about women taking over male occupations during the war. The officer's confusion about Dorothy's motives stemmed from an inability to understand her desire for male power. Unwilling to accept 'the consequences of nature' that failed to endow her with masculinity, she improvised. And if she could, then why not any woman? The British military's strict adherence to order and authority was lampooned by Dorothy's adventure and her announcement to her interrogators 'that virtually *you* rest in *my* hands not I in yours.'[9]

While still in her captor's hands, however, the 'adventurous girl' was driven to the nearby Convent de Bon Pasteur. The strict Romanist order — no nuns left the convent precincts — housed Dorothy for two weeks while the military officials decided her fate. It became part of a process to reform Dorothy into a proper young lady (and perhaps more importantly to make any immediate news about action at the front that she might try to sell to English newspapers hopelessly outdated by the time she reached London). The official's need to place Dorothy into safe, female hands and in an appropriately domestic role is a consistent theme in the woman warrior's story. It marked a resoundingly clear end to a temporary abberation.

But the end of Dorothy Lawrence's story also points to an important contradiction in public reactions to the discovery of a female soldier. While she caused much consternation among the British Expeditionary Force officers assigned to her case because of the security threat she posed, elsewhere Dorothy Lawrence and her counterparts were met with admiration. The convent residents quizzed her about her time at the front and affectionately labelled her the 'female desperado,' as they were 'utterly enthralled at the adventures of a woman who had got out to the big world . . .' Lawrence declared proudly, 'I eventually became quite a popular heroine.'[10] Out of respect and curiosity all the off-duty soldiers in St. Omer came to shake Dorothy's hand before she left for England. As she sped away from the small crowd her ears rang with a compliment bestowed upon her by an English Tommy: 'Most of us would have come, only authorities have kept rather quiet about it; not all the men know.'

Her status as an exception rather than the forerunner of a trend, ensured that a heroine unmasked (and safely despatched to the domestic realm) could become a celebrity and her feats exaggerated. The more courage, skill and intrepid daring her adventure required the further it was placed beyond emulation. As a preternatural, fictionalized character, like Fanny Campbell the female pirate captain, the warrior inspired rebellion and resistance to a passive acceptance of the female role. But since she remained unique, imbued with fantastic qualities or infantalized, assuming the role of mascot, the radical potential of her actions was undercut.

Two years after Dorothy Lawrence's return to London, an American woman posed a similar threat to military security when she was caught as a stowaway aboard a US army transport ship bound for France. She was taken to a local police station where she awaited news of possible charges. But while she fidgeted nervously in a New Jersey jail, the sting was taken out of her success in outwitting the military's efficiency. In press reports her ingenuity and motives were trivialized and turned into an amusing story without a hint of female subversion. Hazel Carter had deceived both the US army and her officer-husband, Corporal John Carter, who had no idea his wife was sitting in the last carriage when his troop train pulled out of the station at Douglas, Arizona. She had stolen a uniform, cropped her black hair short and with a service cap pulled low over her eyes avoided detection for two days. A suspicious officer put her off at a remote station where the train was switching tracks. But the indefatigable Hazel Carter simply hopped back on among a crush of soldiers when the 'all aboard' call came after a half-hour break.

The regiment reached Hoboken, New Jersey the following day and Hazel was easily lost in the teeming crowd of soldiers waiting on the dock. She found her husband's ship and quietly slipped into the baggage hold where she stayed for several days. She was eventually discovered when her squad was paraded onto the after-deck for a medical examination after a rumour circulated that a woman was aboard. According to Hazel she had enlisted after the Red Cross rejected her application and 'because I was born on a ranch and was used to riding and looking after myself since I was a child . . . I decided to disguise myself as a soldier and go [to France] anyway.'[11] She identified independence and courage as qualities that would enable her to carry out her mission.

While she waited for the federal authorities to decide her fate — possible charges of impersonating a soldier and stowing away on an army transport ship were later dropped — the local town of Hoboken, New Jersey took an interest in her. Hazel Carter pleaded with Mayor Patrick Griffin to allow her to stay as a war worker but he flatly refused. Instead he provided her with money from the 'poor fund' to buy clothes for her journey back to Douglas. The police officers did their bit by saying 'she was the handsomest and smartest-looking soldier they had seen in Hoboken since the war started, which cheered the corporal's wife considerably.'[12] But once her disguise was revealed Hazel Carter was rapidly reformed into a proper young, lady. Griffin outfitted her appropriately so that she could return home, against her wishes, 'under her own personality.' In the police officers' eyes, she rapidly changed from an androgynous figure with 'somewhat masculine features' that made it difficult to detect her true sex into a 'corporal's wife.' Once safely identified and properly clothed, she was packed off home. Though the men revealed a lingering admiration for the 'pseudo US infantryman' any threat she posed was easily dismissed and the contradiction resolved.

The praise female combatants received as heroines was often little compensation for the humiliating financial and social loss they and other cross-dressing women experienced upon discovery. Elsa Jane Guerin left a well-paid job as a brakeman on the Illinois Central Railroad after more than eight months when her boss began to suspect her true sex.[13] English sailor Margaret Johnson's fortunes plunged when she decided to give up her life at sea. She shipped out from Liverpool bound for St. John, New Brunswick aboard the *Thetis* in 1843 in search of her husband and successfully avoided detection for five months. A valued seaman, she only resumed women's clothes upon reaching Liverpool. But without financial support — her husband was never found — she gradually fell 'from the path of rectitude into a vicious course of life' and appeared in court for assaulting her landlord. When the magistrate told the court of her exploits as a sailor, 'she cast her eyes on the ground and faintly smiled.'[14] It was an accomplishment of which she knew she could be proud.

Rather than turning to prostitution to support herself, former sailor and railway porter Mary Walker was reduced to begging after her sex was revealed and she lost her job working as a barman under the name Thomas in 1867. Her male occupations had included two years as a ship's steward, an errand boy and a light porter at a cheesemongers in London. Once deprived of the only occupations she knew for the six years since she left her native village, Mary became destitute and was picked up for begging in man's attire in Whitechapel on 30 March 1868. According to an account of her trial, 'she has long been known to the police , not so much as a bad as an eccentric character.'[15]

Many women dreaded the return to domesticity as much as the loss of their newly acquired and mightily enjoyed male power. Even though they proved themselves highly skilled workers, once revealed, their female identity was grounds for instant dismissal. After almost four years spent working as an able-bodied seaman Mary Anne Arnold was found out by her captain aboard an English ship, the *Robert Small*. He became suspicious of his 14-year-old sailor during a ritual tarring and shaving of crew members when the ship crossed the equator in 1839. According to Arnold's testimony, when Captain Scott began to question her 'there was no use denying it once I was suspected so his clerk took down all I said in answer to his questions.'[16]

Scott wrote to London that upon discovery, Mary Anne was sent to live in a ship's cabin where 'the lady passengers have given her lots of presents; her hair is already getting long and I suppose she will soon think of ringlets.'[17] But despite this attempt to reshape Mary Anne, her skill at sea was unquestionable. Before she joined the *Robert Small* she had worked successfully below decks and aloft for two years as a cabin-boy aboard a Sutherland collier with no complaints from the six captains under whom she served. In 1838 after a shipwreck off the Irish coast she worked as cabin-boy in the *Choice* bound for London with stores for the *Robert Small*, Scott's ship. 'I have seen Miss Arnold among the first aloft to reef the mizen-top-gallant sail during a heavy gale in the Bay of Biscayne,' he wrote. 'She has well done her work as a strong active boy in this ship.'[18] According to Mary Anne, along with her last month's wages Scott paid her the compliment of saying 'that I was his best man and that he was very sorry to part with me.'[19] Even Mary Anne's brothers — a boatswain of the *Royal Adelaide* and the other a carpenter aboard the *Britannia* stationed at Portsmouth — approved and knew about her career as cabin-boy.

Despite the approval she received from her brothers, fellow workers and her employer, it was impossible for her to continue working as a seaman. Scott may have feared for his reputation if Mary Anne was not immediately separated from the men once she was detected. When she begun to display all the accoutrements of a young lady — growing out her cropped haircut and wearing dresses — it was safe for Captain Scott to sing her praises. It was equally important for Scott to prove that Mary Anne was not living aboard ship as his mistress and that his relationship with her was entirely platonic and paternal.

Though Mary Anne could confidently 'unfurl the main, fore and mizen' by herself, was completely fearless and 'as good as any man on board,' she was in search of a more appropriate career. The Lord Mayor of London offered Mary Anne financial support because she was an orphan who 'was herself wholly unacquainted with feminine arts.'[20] Deprived of the only occupation she knew, a female guardian was appointed to teach Mary Anne the art of sewing and nursing children, to prepare her for a domestic role. Her own ambitions were more in keeping with her occupation as cabin-boy. 'She thought she could be of service to ladies who travelled for she was never sea sick in her life and was not afraid of anything.'[21] Ironically, despite her domestic education she continued to seek some place where her talents might not be wasted. A lady's companion, however, would have none of the status, financial or social rewards she enjoyed as a sailor — a position she would have fulfilled had she not been discovered.

To a young woman locked into a future of unending domestic toil, going to sea held an almost unparalleled appeal. Ellen Watts, an orphan, disguised herself as Charles Watts and went to sea in 1838 to escape from her apprenticeship as an outdoor servant. 'Before her term expired she determined to leave the plough to plough the deep,' because there 'she could enjoy more freedom than in domestic service.' For more than three years she worked aboard ship and enjoyed a reputation for such courage and recklessness that

'her exertions caused a degree of envy among the other lads.' She was discovered only when a tailor attempted to interfere with two lady friends she
was entertaining in an orchard while on shore leave. A fight ensued and
Ellen Watts was forced to leave her trawl ship in Brixham.[22] But like Mary
Ann Arnold she swore that exposure was the only thing that stopped her
work at sea.

Some women vigorously fought against a return to feminine domestica-
tion after their discovery because of its devastating implications. George
Wilson, an unfortunate female sailor who languished for several years in a
Baltimore jail for horse-stealing, was severely punished for her refusal to
accept the transition without a fight. As a young teenager she left England to
cross the Atlantic several times before she was tried and sentenced for theft
in 1836. According to a Baltimore newspaper, George Wilson was repeatedly
flogged for her intransigence in jail and 'she, of course, knows nothing of
women's work; she can handle a needle with no further dexterity than will
enable her to sew a button on her pantaloons.'[23] The report implied that
George Wilson was punished with solitary confinement, lashings, and a diet
of bread and water for refusing to perform tasks that would mark her re-
entry into the female world. Dressed in trousers, answering only to a male
name, the story of the tall woman, 'as muscular as a pugilist' is a stark example
of the pressure exerted on cross-dressing women to resume a 'feminine' role.

Trading men's for women's work was a social and economic demotion
and often an enormous source of resentment. The women soldiers hard-won
and continual battle to prove themselves to their comrades could be rendered useless when those in command found out. Though a woman might
unofficially be protected and allowed to remain once she had performed
some heroic act, military or company officers often felt impelled to turn her
in. If a woman enlisted as an ordinary soldier she benefitted from the class
or ethnic solidarity she shared with her comrades. As an exception, but one
of their own, she was treated as a mascot or as a flattering attempt at male
imitation. To those in positions of power, however, she more often represented an annoying or unsettling breach of authority.

Isabelle Gunn, a young Orkney woman, lived for two years as John
Fubister, a skilled labourer with the Hudson's Bay Company. In an institution organized along quasi-military lines in North America, she survived
with the help of her fellow Orcadians. Before the dramatic revelation of her

true identity, she canoed 1,800 miles along an inland waterway when she was several months pregnant. At the Pembina fur trading post on the Red River during the Christmas of 1807, John Fubister was among a group of HBC men celebrating at a Northwest Company Officer, Alexander Henry's, house. Fubister, feeling unwell, asked to lie down somewhere and Henry made the following entry in his journal of 29 December:

> I was suprised at the fellow's demand; however, I told him to sit down and warm himself. I returned to my own room, where I had not been long before he sent one of my people, requesting the favour of speaking with me. Accordingly I stepped down to him and was much surprised to find him extended on the hearth, uttering dreadful lamentations; he stretched out his hands toward me, and in piteous tones begged me to be kind to a poor, help-less, abandoned wretch, who was not of the sex I had supposed but an unfortunate Orkney girl, pregnant and actually in childbirth. . . . In about an hour she was safely delivered of a fine boy.[24]

By the spring thaw Isabelle Gunn and her son, the first white child born in what became the Canadian west, were in a canoe headed for Albany fort on James Bay and then home. (The father was John Scarth, an experienced Hudson's Bay Company man, who had gone out from Orkney at the same time as Isabelle but would not claim his child.)

Trapper Peter Fidler heard about Isabelle's story as she travelled along the Red River that spring. In a diary crammed with topograhical notes, weather reports and navigational degrees, Fidler recorded on 1 May 1808 that three days before, Isabelle Gunn, who 'worked at anything and well like the rest of the men,' had passed through.[25] Once stationed back at Albany Isabelle was put to work washing for her former mates and minding the 11 Hudson's Bay Company officers' children at the fort. That she resented her position is clear from a letter sent home from Albany by Orcadian schoolteacher William Harper. He wrote that his compatriot was living 'with her child and her chief employment is washing for all hands which indeed she is no witch at as far as I think she has been washing for me . . . she seems not inclined to go home.'[26] Although she was never again employed in the demanding work of transporting loads of furs and supplies by canoe, Isabelle Gunn managed to stay an additional year and was sent home on 20 September 1809.

But whether or not a woman was actually deprived of her former occupation, in popular history the discovery of her sex marked the inevitable re-emergence of her femininity. An English journalist recorded the Russian volunteer, Zoya Smirnova's decision to quit after she was seriously wounded on the eastern front in 1915. She spent a month recovering at a base hospital and was unable to find her regiment again. 'The girl lost her presence of mind and for the first time during the entire campaign began to weep, thus betraying her sex and age,' wrote a *Times* correspondent. 'Her unfamiliar country-men gazed with amazement upon the strange young NCO with the Cross of St. George medal on her breast who resembled a stripling and finally proved to be a girl.'[27]

According to contemporary story-tellers, thin, girlish voices, tears, a consistent refusal to participate in male comraderie and any confession of physical weakness amounted to evidence that a woman was in the ranks. In hindsight, narrators of the warrior heroine's story dropped clues to their readers that despite her valiant and even highly successful masculine imitation, the properties of her true sex might lurk beneath the surface. Ann Jane Thornton, who served aboard English and American ships in 1835, suffered much ridicule and aroused suspicion in her mates 'for not being able to drink her full allowance of grog.'[28] Although she had proved herself as an expert sailor, once her ship reached London and she resumed female clothing, she was so menacingly jeered by her former mates that she burst into tears.

The female combatant was often portrayed taking great risks to protect her identity, even attempting to heal her own wounds rather than chance possible detection. Her stoicism in biting the bullet at once proved her 'manly' courage and ensured her continued occupation. In popular stories, the female warrior was either elevated to a position of impossible heroism or discovered by a sudden show of female weakness. The hardiest often endured an agonizing recovery from battle injuries, suffered in silence. Mary Anne Talbot in the guise of drummer-boy John Taylor was obliged to keep up a continuous roll to drown out the cries and confusion on the battlefield even when she was injured during the British capture of Valenciennes on 28 July 1793. She carefully concealed her wounds with liniment and bandages 'from the dread of [the men] discovering my sex.' A year later Talbot was assigned to the *Brunswick* under Captain John Harvey where she worked as his principal cabin-boy and powder-monkey. During a naval battle with the

French on 1 June 1794 the female tar was hit with a grape-shot just above her left ankle. Mary Anne was lucky since the *Brunswick* sank with more than half her crew on board; 44 were killed including Harvey and 114 of the survivors were wounded. This time her injury posed little danger of detection and she safely spent four months recovering in Haslar Hospital, Gosport before she returned to sea.[29]

The female combatant's silent courage contributed to a legend of her exceptional heroism. The stories of her almost supernatural feats served to place her increasingly beyond the realm of a female reader's day-to-day reality. But it also strengthened the woman warrior's image as an independent, autonomous creature hewn from the finest stuff of human courage. Eighteenth- and nineteenth-century readers were prepared to believe that sailor Hannah Snell could sustain a dozen bullet wounds during the British seige of Pondicherry, India in 1748 but hid the tell-tale shots that riddled her hips.[30] When she was taken to a naval hospital she convinced the doctors that only her legs were injured and with the help of a black woman, Hannah Snell extracted the bullets from her own groin. According to her biography, three months later she was fit enough to sail.

Sailors Mary Anne Talbot and Hannah Snell avoided detection for a variety of pragmatic and understandable reasons. But upon discovery, the female combatant knew she would be forced from the centre-stage of action into a minor, supporting role. She all but lost the equality that she fought so hard to gain and enjoyed so easily. Her acquired male status would be stripped away rendering her vulnerable to abuse or to preserving her value only as a patriotic emblem. If she was allowed to stay on as a military wife, her position would often change drastically as Christian Davies' story illustrates. Once revealed, she was forced to justify herself by acquiring either the properties of patriotic glory, devoted love or superwoman.

The devotees of love — those who went in search of or with a husband or lover — were sometimes remarried in an elaborate ceremony that not only reunited the couple but reaffirmed their appropriate roles. Christian Davies was finally forced to give up her disguise when wounded at the battle of Ramelies in 1705. Though she was in agony because of a fractured skull, the anxiety of possible discovery by the surgeons was worse than the physical pain. Two years earlier she had successfully escaped when wounded in the hip at the battle of Donauwerth. She never fully recovered but managed to nurse herself back to reasonable health. Her second injury, however, was so serious that it was impossible to continue the deception and the surgeons immediately informed Lord John Hay, commander of the 2nd Dragoons, Scots Grey, that his 'pretty dragoon' was, in fact, a woman.[31]

Later, Richard and Christian Welsh were wed a second time in a ceremony before the assembled company and lavished by Lord Hay with a pouch of gold. It marked Christian's explicit transition from soldier into woman, as Lord Hay insisted that she resume marital relations with her husband. Fearing that pregnancy would expose her disguise, Christian had refused to sleep with Richard until the end of the campaign but now she promised Hay she 'had no objections to . . . the duty of an honest wife.'[32] That night she conceived a child and only resumed her soldier's uniform for her own protection or on foraging expeditions.

But she continued to play an ambigious role within the camp, often speaking as the voice of conscience to the soldiers and demanding respect as a former combatant. Christian criticized soldiers as 'unmanly who treat a woman ill,' especially if they seduced her with a promise of marriage — 'a practice too customary with our cloth.'[33] Her opinion on military tactics was also considered and when returning from a foraging expedition where she ran into French soldiers, she chastized the Duke of Marlborough's officers for playing chess while the enemy was about. When Lord Kerr dismissed her as a 'foolish, drunken woman,' the Duke replied that he would as soon take her advice as any brigadier in the army.[34] However, even Christian's unique status did not protect her from sexual harassment by other officers. When an officer attempted to rape her in his tent, she stated that it was a situation she would have avoided 'by telling him I would send him the prettiest girl in the camp to give his lordship a fall.' She left him and ran into Dolly Saunders, 'a very pretty girl' and directed her to the officer's tent where he would give her a dozen shirts to make, thus leaving Dolly to fend for herself.[35]

Whether a woman could gain a form of official sanction for her presence in the ranks — fulfilling a particular function — often became the deciding factor in whether she was allowed to remain. In some highly public cases, such as that of Mary Anne Arnold, despite her value as a skilled seaman, this permission was impossible to obtain. If a woman became identified as the property of a man already in the ranks — such as Isabelle Gunn with

John Scarth and Christian Davies with her husband Richard — continuing in a male role was unacceptable because she was needed elsewhere. But some women, even after disclosure to an officer, were aided in their desire to carry on the good fight because they could be used as powerful symbols of a nationalist spirit.

A celebrated female combatant of the Napoleonic wars, Angélique Brulon, was successively daughter, sister and wife of soldiers who died on active service with the French forces in Italy. In 1792 at age 21 she joined her father's 42nd Regiment of Foot in which her husband had died. According to contemporary accounts her exemplary military performance immediately attracted attention and despite the revelation of her identity 'her conduct . . . was so honourable that she was permitted to remain in the service notwithstanding her sex.'[36] Brulon worked her way up from fusilier to corporal, lance-corporal and sergeant-major and only retired after she was badly wounded by a shell splinter at the seige of Calvi in 1799.

Brulon fell into the category of romantic heroine and patriot because of her portrait as a woman following her husband into battle, thus sanctioning her presence. Lady Charlotte Guest, a literary editor and wife of Welsh iron-master Sir Josiah John Guest, who visited Paris from Wales in April 1851, was disappointed that she did not meet the famous Madame Brulon. According to Guest's account, Brulon was best-known for snatching up her dead husband's regimental flag and carrying it through the action at Marengo in 1800 where the French defeated the Austrians.[37] Though Brulon actually executed all the actions of an officer and soldier, she was remembered for a supportive gesture that she did not perform but made her contradictory position more acceptable.

Several years earlier two daughters of an Alsatian philosopher also made a place for themselves in the ranks because of their family connections and powerful symbolic value. Félicité and Théophile de Fernig 'felt their warlike ardour stirring' when their father Louis Joseph de Fernig was appointed commandant of a Garde Nationale detachment during the 1789 revolution. One evening the women dressed in uniform and surreptitiously joined their father's troops, helped by their new comrades. The sisters were found out after a few nights when the commander of a neighbouring detachment and a friend of their father's noticed their studied attempts to avoid his glance. Puzzled by this behaviour General de Beurnonville asked de Fernig to call the volunteers forward. The ranks parted to let the women through although they were unrecognizable in their uniforms, their faces smeared with smoke and their lips blackened by bullet cartridges torn open with their teeth:

> M. de Fernig could not understand how it was he did not know these two members of his little army.
>
> "Who are you?" he sternly demanded.
>
> At these words the whole company began to exchange smiles and whispers.
>
> Théophile and Félicité realising their secret was out, fell on their knees, blushed and burst into tears, acknowledging their misdeeds, and flinging their arms around their father's knees, implored him to forgive the deceit they had practiced upon him.[38]

Fernig, of course, accepted his daughters apologies with tears coursing down his cheeks at their 'marvellous display of love and self-sacrifice.'

When a woman claimed to have undertaken her masquerade for patriotic or romantic reasons her acceptance in the ranks was much easier to tolerate upon discovery. Fernig's daughters rose rather than fell in his eyes for their obvious emulation of him and devotion to the cause which quickly cancelled out their violation of his parental authority. They continued to serve as soldiers and became known as 'two Joans of Arc,' 'dauntless heroines of liberty' and 'miraculous apparitions of tutelary spirits' in their military careers.[39] The religious allusions made them at once familiar and their motives more sympathetic, but also placed them well-beyond the capabilities of other women. Their story as told by the nineteenth-century historian, O.P. Gilbert, ends on the comforting note that after retirement the sisters enthusiastically resumed feminine behaviour, 'throwing themselves into the part with zest, displayed no small talent for coquetry, took great interest in the upbringing of children as well as in the making of preserves.'[40] The message was clear — the women had not been unduly changed by their foray into the masculine world.

As an orphan, wife, daughter, lover or zealous defender of the faith, the female soldier assumed a non-threatening position in which she depended upon male approval for survival. Other women, without male relations, lovers or friends to support their disguise, took on the role of patriot to protect themselves. They feared that their desire for masculine power, that was the ticket to independence and action, would most likely be misunderstood or dismissed. Deborah Sampson, who served in the Continental Army during the War of Independence, escaped detection by circumventing orders to be vaccinated for small pox along with her regiment in 1782. Since she believed that an unmasking was equivalent to the end of her active life, Sampson preferred to risk contracting the disease. The following summer, however, she fell ill during an epidemic and an army surgeon, Dr. Binney, discovered that she was a woman. Impressed by her courage and nationalist spirit, Binney agreed to keep her secret and saluted her — 'you have been true to the cause of freedom.'[41]

Sampson originally joined a Massachusetts regiment at the age of 20 because she was 'fond of adventure and had a great deal of energy'; this bold, fearless woman felt 'the sphere in which she moved too quiet and too narrow for her enterprising temperament.' Enlisting broadened her very narrow set of choices by enabling her to travel and to experience the world through male eyes. But Sampson was careful to equip herself with an acceptable motive by presenting herself as an enthusiastic patriot. As her biographer noted, 'her example in enlisting as a soldier is certainly not to be commended to the imitation of our fair countrywomen; but her inflexible resolution and firm self-control after she enlisted are deserving of high praise.'[42] It was those individualists, like Dorothy Lawrence, who refused to mouth such sentiments about self-sacrifice, wider patriotic concerns or romantic devotion who posed the greatest dilemma.

There were occasionally other, more pragmatic reasons for allowing a woman to remain in the ranks or aboard ship after discovery. During the Napoleonic wars when the Royal Naval press gangs were particularly active and able-bodied men scarce, a female sailor discovered among the recruits might be overlooked. When Elizabeth Bowden, a female tar with the British navy, appeared in court as a witness in trial against Lt William Berry in October 1807, no comment was made about her eight months at sea. Bowden gave testimony against Berry, charged with performing 'an unnatural act' with Thomas Gibbs, a boy who worked on her ship the *Hazard*.[43] Given the sensitive and grave nature of the crime — Berry was found guilty and hanged — the lack of comment seems remarkable. During the American Civil War, reports of female soldiers, according to one contemporary account, became so frequent that they were mentioned without explanation.

The *Witness* published in Plattville, Wisconsin merely noted on 16 March 1864 'the return from the army of Miss Georgianna Peterman,' who had been a drummer with the 7th Wisconsin for two years.[44] In his diary on 26 May 1864, a musician of the 104th New York Infantry, Henry Besancon, noted that it was raining, that someone had stolen his overcoat and that 'a female dressed in Rebel uniform was taken this morning.'[45] On 29 May 1864 A. Jackson Crossly, a soldier in Company C of the US Engineers, wrote to his friend Samuel Bradbury from federal army headquarters of the same incident. He said that a woman dressed in man's clothes was among the prisoners taken five days before: 'She was mounted just like a man and belonged to cavalry though she was taken as a spy.'[46] During periods of protracted war female combatants were found to unofficially fill pressing labour demands.

In Holland, army and naval recruiters, fishermen and even farmers advised impoverished young women to take to the sea or to pass as men in other occupations in a long-established tradition of female cross-dressing. An innkeeper advised Francina Gunnigh, travelling alone through France in 1811, to sell her clothes and buy a man's suit for protection. Unfortunately she was caught a few days later without any identification, arrested by a French gendarme as a deserter and quickly enrolled in the French army corps at Cherbourg.[47] As Gunnigh's story illustrates recruiters worried less about a man's capacity for duty than rounding up required numbers. During periods of manpower shortages, if a young tar was adequately performing 'his' duties, dismissal on the basis of gender might create more problems than it solved.[48]

Whatever the circumstances of a woman's presence in an all-male regiment or crew, the grand contradiction of living in a female body as a social male remained irresolvable. However they managed their masquerade, they were continually pulled by the tensions inherent in their position. Some strove awkwardly to maintain a sense of female self and to secure their position through taking up a domestic role while vigorously preserving their male status. Others adamantly refused this connection, shunning childcare, mending, washing or other duties deemed women's work. But nursing was usually the arena most highly loaded with expectations and where this tension was felt most keenly.

Although the Georgian Princess, Kati Dadeshkeliani, successfully disguised herself as Prince Djamal in the Tsar's Army with the help of her fellow officers, she preferred the hospital to the trench. Unable to fully embrace a masculine identity she joined the regimental ambulance where she 'never had the same feeling of uselessness, of powerlessness, or failing in duty' that she had in the trenches. Humiliated by these feelings of inadequacy, she felt more comfortable nursing because in this capacity she enjoyed 'abundant scope for my womanly faculties, for my energy and my will-power.'[49] Away from the intimate contact of the dug-out, she was free to bathe, once again comfortable with her female body because she no longer feared accidental discovery.

After almost nine months living as Confederate officer Harry T. Buford, Loreta Velasquez began to forget that she was actually disguised and became careless about maintaining her identity. 'I scarcely presented as credible a manly appearance,' she claimed. 'I had too by this time become so accustomed to male attire that I ceased to bear in mind constantly the absolute necessity for preserving certain appearances.'[50] On leave in New Orleans Loreta Velasquez's apparatus that gave her a more masculine figure went 'badly out of order' and she was arrested on suspicion of being a woman. She was fined the hefty sum of $10 and confined to prison for ten days.[51] Although Kati Dadeshkeliani feared sexual harassment, ridicule and dismissal rather than imprisonment if her sex was discovered, she was keenly aware of the need to keep up her masculine appearance.

Both Flora Sandes and Maria Bochkareva, while highly conscious of the value of their comrades' approval, continued to work as *de facto* nurses. They proved their 'manhood' on the field by adamantly refusing to take the soft option in any situation and by participating in all facets of male culture. Since they were known to be women, they lived without the tension of possible detection and they took on the role of care-giver. While fighting on the eastern front with the Tsar's army against the Germans during 1917, Bochkareva was often called upon to give medical attention to women in the villages wherever she was stationed.[52] In a letter written home from a trench on 10 November 1916 Flora Sandes mentioned that although the Red Cross still supplied first aid to her Serbian regiment, 'when the men near me get wounded they generally get me to do them up.'[53] She also noted that all the Red Cross workers went 'armed to the teeth' in Serbia suggesting that her position was not much different from theirs.[54]

At several other points in her career with the Serbian army, Flora Sandes was called upon to organize medical operations and supplies. In 1918 a flu epidemic struck Chuprija and Sandes, after recovering from a bout, took over from the sole doctor at a temporary army hospital. In a repeat of her experience during the typhus epidemic in Valjevo, she arrived to find things 'in a fearful state.' French and Serbian soldiers lay shivering in their filthy clothes without blankets or sheets, 'dying like flies of flu and pneumonia.' Throwing military discipline to the winds, the English quasi-ambassadoress simply took over. 'So, as Fate seemed to have landed me there,' wrote Sandes, 'I took charge, and the responsibility and hard work soon completed my own cure.'[55]

Her combined status as Serbian officer and English nurse gave Sandes considerable power. But her organizational role helped to legitimate her position in an all-male environment and to strengthen her unique position. Once Flora Sandes had exercised her dual authorities as nurse and officer, the French soldiers began to bring their troubles to her and orderlies called upon her to soothe delirious patients. She became a contradictory but comforting emblem of maternal care doled out in a military uniform.

Unlike her fellow soldiers Flora Sandes also refused to leave the wounded Bulgarians she encountered on the battle field and administered what first aid she could. Her willingness to nurse the enemy, often young boys, earned her both her commanding officer's wrath and her comrades' amusement. 'They think quite a lot of my opinion,' wrote Sandes in a letter to her sister Sophie, 'and would even let me keep a pet Bulgar . . . if I wanted to.'[56] Despite Flora's position as comrade, once her responsibilities were connected with the female sphere of nurturing, she was gently chided and her motives infantalized. Such episodes worked to ensure, however tenuously, a connection with her femininity without threatening her officer's status.

When Russian soldier Zoya Smirnova's identity was discovered after her discharge from hospital while wounded at the eastern front in 1916, she was persuaded to turn from soldier into nurse. Hazel Carter also told the American press when she was caught as a stowaway that she had planned to sign on with the Red Cross as soon she reached Paris. Before she decided to try her luck at the Western front Dorothy Lawrence claimed she was turned down by the British war office 12 times in her attempt to get a first aid posting. However accurately these women described their own desires, their inclination to nurse made their stories more acceptable and understandable.

While some of the female combatants who entered the military undisguised felt great pressure to turn a feminine face to the public by stressing their nurturing role, others rejected its associations. The Dutch philanthropist and soldier, Jenny Merkus, pointedly corrected contemporary journalists' reports that she became involved in the 1876 Serbian revolt against the Ottoman Empire in a domestic capacity. 'I did not wish to nurse wounded soldiers,' she wrote, 'but to help liberate Christian people, and also Christ's land from the sovereignty of the Turks.'[57] Her role was clearly political and though she risked ostracism in her home country for her outspoken views and unorthodox approach, she refused to be conveniently categorized.

Her disassociation with the feminine sphere is reminiscent of Christian Davies' unwillingness, once back in skirts, to take on a maternal role. During an arduous march Christian rescued a soldier's small child struggling in the mud. She carried the girl until the regiment broke camp, warmed and fed her and filled her apron with food for the next day's journey. But even though the girl's father was wracked with malarial fever, Christian refused to assume further responsibility for the child and returned her to him because, 'he would [gladly] have had me taken care of her but I would not undertake the charge.'[58] Her later military career involved work as a sutler (providing food for the troops), and cook but her duties never extended beyond this commercial sphere.

The happiest situation occurred when the female warrior could choose her own moment of disclosure and freely return to her true sex. Some used their male disguise to accomplish a goal — to travel, to earn a better living, to find someone — that once realized, rendered their masquerade unnecessary. Although Mary Anne Talbot was originally forced into her role as cabin-boy by the villainous Captain Bowen, when he was killed during the battle of Valenciennes in July 1793 she continued to work as a sailor. Upon Bowen's death she learned that her original guardian Mr. Sucker had swindled her out of a fortune and she resolved to get her revenge. She successfully hid her identity while working for Captain John Harvey as a powder-monkey, aboard a privateer, on Lord Howe's battleship the *Queen Charlotte* and while imprisoned in Dunkirk. But after her return to London she revealed her disguise when a press-gang in Wapping seized her in 1797.

Mary Anne Talbot continued to dress in male clothes even after this incident and it served her well when she finally confronted the odious Mr.
Sucker. A mysterious young man, wrapped in a thick black cloak turned up
on Sucker's doorstep one day and requested to speak with him. When
Sucker entered the drawing room the man turned and asked him if he knew
a Miss Talbot. Sucker replied that unfortunately his charge had died at sea in
1793. Without pausing for breath Mary Anne drew a sword from underneath her cloak and announced that she was the long-lost Miss Talbot. When
she demanded that Sucker relinquish her inheritance, he pleaded that it was
spent. Three days later he died 'without any previous appearance of illness'
because of the shock her appearance had provoked.[59] In Mary Anne's show-
down with Sucker, her trousers, cloak and masculine carriage fortified her as
much as the sword she brandished.

It was important for a female combatant to choose the right moment to
reveal her identity. Hannah Snell, still in the guise of James Gray, made sure
that she had collected her pay, that she had sold the two suits of clothing
owed her from her regiment and that she had a gallery of witnesses, before
she retired her alias. Seated before her messmates at John Winter's pub in
Downing Street, Westminister, she disclosed her secret before an audience
who would, 'at any time afterwards be ready to testify to the truths of all her
merry adventures.'[60] She realized that her story would probably be ques-
ioned and looked upon as 'little better than a romance.' Turning to the
man who shared her bed, she announced: 'Had you known, Master Moody,
who you had between a pair of sheets with you, you would have come to
closer quarters. In a word gentlemen, I am as much a woman as my mother
ever was and my name is Hannah Snell.'[61] Once Moody recovered from his
shock he loudly praised her merits and proposed to her. Hannah Snell, however, refused since she had developed an aversion to matrimony because of
the 'hardheartedness and inhumanity' of her first husband. She was praised
by her comrades who sensibly drew up a petition detailing her military
experience and was granted a pension for life.

Although Hannah Snell chose to divulge her secret to her comrades to
ensure their support, other former combatant's feared the return to a position of social, financial and political inferiority. It would be wrong to claim
that all women continued to yearn for what they experienced as men. Some were
relieved when the tension of living under an assumed identity was lifted.

Others looked forward to resuming or beginning motherhood, female friendships and a place in the world of women. No one who had witnessed the carnage of war yearned for its return and some clearly articulated their battle fatigue and a growing revulsion of violence. But the female soldier uniquely experienced the tension of withholding emotions from her comrades who, however sympathetic, could not completely understand the strain under which she lived. The female combatant, disguised or living in a regiment of men, could not always keep these feelings of intense isolation at bay. However much she lived as a social male there were limits to her friendship with her fellow soldiers. She was either forced to keep some distance to ensure her secret or lived with the knowlege that the war only provided her temporary passage into her companion's world. Although women only expressed this fear and unquenchable loneliness in rare moments this was the other side of acquiring male privilege .

It was sometimes in another woman's presence that these emotions arose most poignantly. During the Serbian offensive of October 1918 near Crna Vrk [Black Peak] on the Bulgarian border Flora Sandes was introduced to the women in a Turkish harem. Describing them 'as hideous, old hags,' Sandes said when she entered the women 'screeched' and covered their faces and 'it took a long time before I could persuade them that I was a woman.' A few days later Sandes' regiment reached Nish in Northern Serbia and encamped. The women were equally curious about the English lady in the uniform of a Serbian officer and Sandes quickly found herself surrounded by a wide-eyed group. She was 'carried off' to a cottage, seated on a three-legged stool and bombarded with questions. Her discomfort is evident in her description of this meeting written in 1927:

> Though I could understand the men perfectly I could not understand half the women said. They talked too fast, and their voices were very shrill, unlike the men who have rather soft voices. I was beginning to feel rather dazed, so was relieved when a couple of the men came in, laughing and saying they had been hunting for me everywhere and had come to "take care of me."[62]

Sandes experienced Serbia through male eyes and from her privileged perspective as an English woman. It is unsurprising that she felt so little affinity for these women who appeared to her rough, uneducated and somehow menacing. Perhaps Flora Sandes was made uneasy when reminded that, after the war, she would once again be banished to the female world and cut off from her male friends. She would never lose her English status that socially placed her above the village women she met, but upon demobilization in 1922, the circumstances that allowed her to befriend her Serbian comrades as equals, changed beyond recognition.

Perhaps Flora Sandes did not long for female friendship because of the steady stream of British nurses she encountered in Serbia. But many female combatants wrote that they keenly missed their women friends and their emotional support. When Marina Yurlova was wounded in 1915 and learned that her friend and protector Kosel was dead, she longed for female companionship. Lying on a stretcher, waiting for transport to the hospital in Baku, she thought 'the world was full of torn and broken men, and male voices cursing and crying out for water; and no woman there at all, not even a nurse. . . . I began to cry for my own nurse.'[63] After American civil war soldier Emma Edmonds returned to civilian life she wrote enthusiastically to her friend Jerome Robbins: 'Oh Jerome it is pleasant to have a lady friend once more and I know one in the person of Miss Lizzie H. to whom I could trust the inner-most secret of my heart.'[64]

Although in reality Emma Edmonds missed the comforts of female friendship during her service with the Army of the Potomac, in the autobiography of her wartime experience she invented a companion. One evening, passing along a row of patients languishing in hospital beds, Emma's attention was attracted by 'the pale, sweet face of a youthful soldier who was severly wounded in the neck.' There was nothing to be done to help the soldier but to comfort him with brandy and water, wrote Emma. The boy motioned her towards him as if imparting an important message. 'The little trembling hand beckoned me closer, and I knelt down beside him and bent my head until it touched the golden locks on the pale brow before me.'[65]

The soldier then whispered into Emma's patient ear, 'I am not what I seem, but am a female. I enlisted from the purest motives and have remained undiscovered and unsuspected.' After she received the chaplain's blessing the young woman died by Emma's side. Since Emma Edmonds makes no mention of this incident elsewhere and since she later freely admitted to fictionalizing her autobiography, it possibly never happened. But the lone female soldier who only in death receives the comfort of another woman seems a powerful image of how Emma Edmonds saw her isolated and difficult position. Despite the strong solidarity the female soldiers developed with their mates, some still yearned for the warmth and ease that a woman friend might have offered them.

Trapper, prospector and soldier, 'Mountain Charley' also harboured an aching desire for this friendship. On a journey to California in the spring of 1855 she yearned to comfort a mother with two children who had just discovered her husband's dead body along a mountain trail. But dressed as a man 'Mountain Charley' could offer little emotional support. 'I longed to disclose to her my sex and minister to her in that manner in which only one woman can to another,' she wrote. 'Yet I did not dare to and I was forced to give her only that rough consolation which befitted my assumed character.'[66] As the mother of a young son and daughter Charley's frustrated desire to help the young widow added to her own sense of loneliness.

While sitting in a St. Louis saloon before her departure to the West, Charley grew philosophical about her life as a man. She missed her children's company and felt her masquerade forced her 'to wonder an outcast from the companionship and sympathy of my own sex [and] to labour as a menial for the pittance which stood between myself and starvation.'[67] Although she gained advantages from her masculine occupations, the relationships she enjoyed as a woman were set apart from her male identity. The pleasures of each disparate sphere were completely incompatible and fostered the growth of a divided self.

A return to the world of women was a return to peace but it implied agonizing contradictions. Some female combatants described feeling most alive during the war. Flora Sandes noted during the Serbian army's 1916 campaign, 'incessant fighting weariness indescribable but hand-in-hand with romance, adventure and comradeship which more than made up for everything.'[68] Within the ranks she found an acceptance that she had experienced nowhere else and wrote to her sister on 14 October 1916, 'for anyone to say they are proud of anything I do is such a novel experience — it's generally so much the other way — that it had quite bucked me up.'[69] But she added in a postscript written a week later after a close friend was killed, that she had renounced her earlier descriptions of war as a form of sport and said, 'I've changed my mind . . . and loathe war and everything to do with it with all my heart, but if I wrote particulars the Censor would not pass it.'[70]

Wounded a second time in 1916, Marina Yurlova regained consciousness in the heat of battle which was 'a waking nightmare' that 'bruised' her mind and for months afterwards jolted her awake with visions of dead men, 'lying with their eyes staring up at God.'[71] After three years living as a soldier she began the long, slow process of recovering from the violence she had endured and trying to piece her life together again. The adventure that had lain just ahead of her in 1914 when she resolved, 'to find my place . . . to do things,' had worn thin.[72] And what price had she paid for her search? She had lost her home, her family, and finally, her identity. Women did not uniquely experience the terror of war but once they retired from active service many could not even acknowledge their part in an armed struggle. Once back in a skirts and dresses, married and perhaps raising children, she could claim little of the male solidarity that characterized her war years. Along with her uniform she shed the privileged position she held as a man among men.

Inevitably there were women whose military service and use as a political or patriotic symbol made her a valuable celebrity even after her retirement. Some even managed to exploit their wartime experience, and turned their own adventures into a script for the stage, worked as a publican, published their memoirs or demanded financial and social recognition of her 'masculine' exploits. Others, unable to make the transition back to womanhood, foundered alone, penniless, confused and broken. They inhabited neither a male or female world and were shunned by both. But whatever life thrust upon them they were inevitably and permanently changed by their leap into the masculine void. Some returned home to find that their reputations preceeded them and they were already immortalized in ballads or stories Whatever future they made for themselves the world remained fascinated by their extraordinary lives and the mocking inversion their adventure represented. For some, the discovery of their real identity marked the beginning rather than the end of a life split in two. Once they have lived as men, their female self took on a profoundly different meaning.

5

When the World Looked On

❧

*A fighting woman is by long odds fiercer than a fighting man. If women
had the physical strength and could be disciplined they would
dominate the earth. . . . The tiger is in every woman; it's
only a question of what's going to bring it out.*
Dr. Graeme M. Hammond, 'When Women Fight,'
New York Times Magazine, 2 September 1917

EARLY ONE MORNING on a cool day in June 1920, when the
Melbourne Express pulled into Sydney's Central Station, a murmur
ran through the crowd of excited Serbian expatriates, curious
onlookers, journalists and local dignitaries gathered on the gritty platform.
As the engine's smoke drifted upward, Lieutenant Flora Sandes of the
Serbian Army appeared at the carriage door like an apparition. She drank
in the throng clamouring for the attention of 'probably the only woman of
military rank ever to visit Australia.'[1] A cheer rose as she waved quickly,
swung her officer's cane, and with her customary ironic grin, descended
from the train.

State commandant Colonel Bruche and Colonel Dowse, chief staff officer
of the Australian forces, rushed forward with outstretched hands to greet
their guest who saluted smartly. From amidst the crush, a bold chorus of
'Zivila! Zivila! Zivila!' [alive, alive, alive] rose from Serbian lips in welcome.
Buoyed by the customary greeting, Sandes shook a flutter of hands and
swapped hasty kisses as the Serbs crowded round her. An enormous bouquet was thrust into her arms by Mrs. Jovanovich on behalf of Sydney's
Serbian community while her husband George proclaimed in Serbo-Croat:

We offer to heaven our heartfelt thanks for your safe arrival after the many
hardships you have endured. . . . The name of Flora Sandes is engraved on
every Serbian heart and will live imperishably on the scroll of fame as the
reincarnation of "Joan of Arc."[2]

After a brief reply Sandes 'was allowed to make her way from the platform
to the motor' and sped away to a reception at the Hotel Australia.

At the hotel another group of Serbs dressed in national costume, waited
'in a most excited state over their modern Joan of Arc.'[3] But comparison
with the newly-canonized saint was not the only praise lavished upon
Lieutenant Sandes, further proclaimed as 'the saviour of our country,' 'our
brave warrior' and 'our hero.' Wrapped in a Union Jack and a Yugoslavian
flag, Flora Sandes posed for publicity photos on an enormous high-backed
chair surrounded by bouquets that her appreciative audience had presented to her. But while Sandes modestly accepted the effusive com-
pliments, she remained keenly aware that her year-long world tour was a
vital political mission.

In Melbourne Lieutenant Sandes met Governor-General Ronald Munro-
Ferguson and Prime Minister W.M. Hughes and in Sydney she spoke to the
state Premier, John Storey, and the Federal Defence Minister, Senator Pearce,
as an official envoy of the Serbian army. To these politicians she pressed
Yugoslavia's request for stronger trade ties between the nations to help
rebuild their war-shattered economy. The New South Wales Governor, Sir
Walter Davidson, enthused to a packed house before Sandes' first slide-
lantern show at Sydney's King's Hall: 'I have not heard of anything finer, or
brighter, or more natural, or more modest, or braver or more skillful than
the work of Lieutenant Flora Sandes.'[4] She urged Australians to lend financial assistance to replenish the devastating agricultural losses the Serbs had
experienced during the war; one night in Sydney alone she received £300
from her audience. However, the press found Flora Sandes more intriguing
as a contemporary Amazon than as a politician pleading recognition for
'what Serbia has done and . . . the necessity of coming to her aid.'[5]

Flora Sandes was acutely aware of the difficulties she faced despite her
large audiences. A Melbourne newspaper commented on her speech to the
Sydney Millions Club: 'Miss Sandes is, of course, welcome as any woman
would be who had given such exceptional service to an allied nation . . . but

we are not sure of Serbia and our hands are very full of our own needs.' Next to the cutting in her scrap book of the tour she wrote in a firm hand, 'this hurts!'[6] Although the English press appeared more accepting of this 'unofficial ambassador' of the British Empire, Australia appeared less willing to take Sandes' political message seriously and focussed on the ambiguity she represented.[7] 'The Lieutenant is neither Amazonian nor petite,' claimed a *Morning Herald* reporter the day after her colourful welcome to Sydney. 'She is suited admirably by the Serbian uniform [and] with it go boots, spurs and leggings, and the officer's cane, all perfectly congruous with the wearer's self-possessed military bearing.'[8] Even in Australia's most cosmopolitan city, a middle-aged woman with cropped hair, dressed in an officer's uniform, smoking casually in public and, on occasion, sporting a lengthy sabre, aroused a feverish interest. She was 'an outstanding figure in the history of her sex,' 'a real heroine' who possessed 'the spirit of Florence Nightingale.'[9] The press also struggled with the contradiction Flora Sandes embodied; she was heralded as the 'new woman' but compared to St. Joan and her secular counterpart, Florence Nightingale.

To Australians in 1920, Lieutenant Sandes appeared as the product of a break-down in the rigid pre-war concept that a woman's role should be confined to the domestic sphere. Her experiences, however, were painted in vivid, heroic colours, to place her far beyond other women's emulation. Her exceptional qualities were used to question but ultimately to reinforce accepted male and female roles since Flora Sandes would remain as the only exception to the rule. Despite this reassurance in the press she provided a tantalizing speculation about what the newly-liberated women of the post-war era might become. If Australian women were not literally about to swap skirts for trousers and take up arms, they might still adopt some of Flora Sandes' more radical behaviour. When she appeared on Sydney's Central Station in her trim, smart but very masculine uniform and boyish haircut, one reporter commented, 'the short hair creates no surprise and makes one wonder how much longer women in general will continue to this ornament in the present fashion.'[10]

Flora Sandes' male costume carried the added weight of military credibility and she commanded respect, however grudging, as the war hero of an allied nation. As a Brisbane article illustrated, there were concerns that her bold, public assertion of male power might have profound implications.

Some of our lesser garments — known for convention's sake as a skirt — may only need a very little alteration — say with a pair of scissors and a couple of pins to make them pantalettes. But, hardy as the less-controlled sex is, it gazes at Flora Sandes with something like respect and a vision of Futuristic Life in its eye. Hitherto, the female who had the temerity to appear in trousers(!) has usually been so skittish that a sportsman would say, "they should have their oars docked." Flora Sandes in the trim, smart uniform of the Serbian army has a calm, well-controlled dignity, a slim figure, fetching grey hair clipped short, an inscrutable but kindly eye — but hang it all girls — if you saw her first . . . what sex would you dub her?[11]

This article was typical in its equivocal description contrasting women, the 'less-controlled sex,' with officer Sandes who possessed 'a calm, well-controlled dignity' rather than the 'skittish' menace of the earlier betrousered viragos. Yet, despite the author's tentative approval, Flora Sandes' sexual ambiguity implied a chaotic disruption of roles that could shake the foundations on which gender divisions were firmly based. If Australian women cast Flora Sandes as 'a futuristic vision' they too might demand the male power that this latter day St. Joan so clearly enjoyed. The highly charged symbols of masculine authority Sandes adopted — her officer's uniform, public smoking, her confident and authoritative air, her political power, her military gestures and weapon — were thus no longer the exclusive perogative of men. Reporters struggled to make sense of it all.

The Australian Bystander focussed on whether Flora Sandes' long years in a masculine environment had left her femininity intact. An article following her King's Hall speech declared:

Flora Sandes is not unsexed. In gaining one sex she has not lost the other. She evidently likes to have it both ways — and she gets it too. This is the greatest triumph of her career. She has a man's force of character but her greatest strength is her woman's weakness.[12]

During her lecture Flora Sandes admitted to only one instance where she used her feminine wiles. Her regiment arrived, exhausted and starving at Corfu camp in February 1916 after the torturous retreat through Albania, only to discover there were no rations. Even though the Serbian soldiers were accustomed to going without food for a day or so, the regiment had no money to buy whatever supplies were available. Flora Sandes decided to take action and hitched a lift into town in the pouring winter rain to plead her regiment's case to the British, French and Italian authorities to no avail. At the end of a frustrating day, Flora returned to the French Military Commandant who had a bakery stacked with bread.

At that moment, drenched with rain, hungry and exasperated Flora 'managed to pitch them such a pitiful tale of woe about the suffering of the men and the awful time I was having trying to get them something to eat, that I quite softened their hearts.'[13] Moved by her plight the French gave her two big sacks of bread, a sack of bully beef and a barrel of wine but cautioned her 'not to make a precedent of this unofficial way of doing business.' For her Australian audience, Flora Sandes exaggerated her conscious decision to make her appeal as a woman. She claimed that she decided to 'give up being a Corporal for the time being and be a woman again.' In this version of the story, she took out her hanky and 'made the biggest bluff at crying I could screw up on the spur of the moment.'[14] The Australian press picked up on this sign that Flora Sandes was, after all, like any other woman who used her emotions to 'soften up' unco-operative men. The newspapers failed, however, to add that Flora was determined to prove her worth to her regiment and when she returned, her commanding officer clapped her on the back and complimented her, '[you've] been a pretty good Corporal.' A month later she was promoted to Sergeant.

Confusion still arose. If Flora Sandes could 'have it both ways,' then any woman could. Newspapers and public commentators attempted to quash this disturbing idea by emphasizing the Lieutenant's earlier nursing career over her role as a combatant. In Brisbane, Thomas Welsby lectured to the Royal Queensland Yacht Club on the tradition of the war nurse comparing Florence Nightingale with her latest incarnation, Flora Sandes 'to whom he wished long life and retention of her "manhood."'[15] This popular theme was repeated in *The PFA Magazine* where a writer said of Flora Sandes, 'the spirit of Florence Nightingale is by her side now until the day when she too, will look for the lamp in the coming darkness.'[16] Elsewhere press reports and publicity materials about Flora Sandes re-invented her history to assert that she took up soldiering only out of necessity.

By the time Flora Sandes arrived in Australia she was a veteran fundraiser who could anticipate the interest her unconventional appearance would arouse. After her first nursing post in Serbia in 1914 she regularly returned to Britain to raise money and gather supplies for her adopted country. As an official military representative fresh from the Eastern front, Flora Sandes became known as 'Britain's promise to Serbia' that their Balkan ally was not forgotten. In March 1918 she toured YMCA huts in France with her slide-lantern show to lecture British Expeditionary Force, Australia and New Zealand Army Corps, Canadian and American troops about Serbia. But despite the enthusiastic welcome she usually received, Sandes never took her acceptance among men for granted.

In France the soldiers and officers crowded the YMCA huts every night, 'even the doorways, and with men sitting on all the window-sills' to listen to her illustrated lecture on Serbia. Flora Sandes modestly believed the warm reception was based on the soldier's sufferance that, 'like themselves I was soon going to the Front again.'[17] To criticize Flora Sandes' bravery in action, however, would have impugned the soldiers' military identity and her flattering imitation of masculinity. The Tommys usually gave her a reception they reserved only for 'one of their own.' To a woman who was keenly aware of her fight to prove her 'manhood' it was welcome praise indeed.

Sandes, however, could never be sure how her male audiences would respond. While in France, waiting to begin her lecture, a British captain approached her. He began asking her casually about the numbers in the Serbian army, and fearing the captain might be the local censor, her answers remained evasive. But, he exclaimed with sarcasm, 'Don't you know how many there are in your own Army? And you are supposed to be a sergeant-major?' The captain was a censor and Sandes passed his test with flying colours. However, when invited to dine with an English general a few days later, she remained equally vague about the Serbian army. '"Huff-puff," spluttered the general, crimson in the face with rage, "do you take me for a damned spy?"' he bellowed at his guest. 'I apologized', wrote Sandes, 'but he refused to be mollified, or to talk to me any more and I felt that he at least had no further use for women soldiers.'[18]

The female soldier often had little control over the reaction she generated. Some, like Sandes, had difficulty using the public platform their fame offered them to make any serious statement. Jenny Merkus, a Dutch social reformer who supported the Herzegovinian revolt against the Turks in 1875 and joined the Serbian army a year later, used her notoriety to express her religious views. But despite her desire to help 'liberate Christian people' her real mission played a poor second, in contemporary accounts, to the novelty of a woman in trousers. As the Serbian writer Geza Kon described her appearance in Belgrade:

> She was a young, rich, but far from beautiful Dutch woman . . . As she dressed like a man and rode horseback, she was known as the amazon of the Herzegovina uprising. All Belgrade seemed to go mad about this female revolutionary. The poet Jura Jaksic sang, "Our Joan, not the one from Orleans, yet her equal, as pure as an angel." On the evening of Palm Sunday a torchlight procession was organized in her honour. Jenny appeared on the balcony with a Montenegran cap on a large mop of blond hair, and this feminine figure with a man's cap . . . caused more enthusiasm than if Peko Pavlovic [leader of the revolt] had turned up in person.[19]

If Jenny Merkus chose that occasion to make a speech about the revolutionary cause, according to Kon, her words were overshadowed by her powerful image as an exotic, blonde angel. Even though Merkus was considered a heroine of the revolt — a cause she financed and fought for — she was best remembered for cutting a striking figure.

The subsequent revision of the female warrior's history to conform more closely to prevailing understandings of sexual difference is a remarkably consistent theme. The martial acts she performed, her motives for enlisting and her reflections on military life were usually purged from historical and contemporary accounts. Passing women soldiers were so quickly mythologized, forgotten or discredited that St. Joan often survived as the only credible account of a woman in battle. The religious overtones associated with Joan's temporary acquisition of male power also served to soften any real threat the contemporary soldier might pose.

Since the Amazon's story was the stuff of fantasy, the discovered female combatant could arrive home to find herself already immortalized. The female tar, Mary Anne Arnold, read with interest Captain Scott's letter about her discovery aboard the *Robert Small* in 1839 when it was reprinted from the *Times* in an Indian newspaper. When she reached London a few months later, she capitalized on her fame by asking the Lord Mayor for financial assistance while she awaited her return to Asia.[20] Her story added to a growing litany of ballads about women who took to the seas, making her experience more believable and understandable.

Four years earlier City Police Inspector McLean had been despatched by the Lord Mayor to make inquiries 'in order that assistance might be rendered if required' after reading about sailor Anne Jane Thornton in the London press. Under the heading, 'a romantic adventure' it was reported that a female tar had arrived at London's Fresh Wharf aboard the *Sarah* just returned from St. John, New Brunswick in February 1835. After Anne Jane Thornton's appearance at Mansion House a book immortalized her years at sea but contradicted earlier reports that she was 'exposed to much annoyance from the jeers and obscene language of the sailors and labourers on the wharf.'[21] In this version, perhaps to prove her expertise to any doubting readers, the ship's captain allegedly invited 'some gentlemen to see his phenomenon fly up the shrouds.'[22]

Anne Jane Thornton's adventures, however, so grasped the popular imagination that her story was reprinted in a Providence, Rhode Island pamphlet accompanied by a ballad entitled, 'The Female Sailor.'[23] An introduction which summarized Thornton's story, assured readers that 'the following song is founded on fact, however romantick [sic] it may appear.' The ballad later resurfaced as 'The Female Sailor Bold' and in other versions of 'The Female Sailor.' In 1840 a book describing the experiences of Ellen Stephens, 'the cabin-boy wife,' and the 'surprising adventures of Almira Paul,' a Canadian sailor, used Thornton's story to verify their heroines' nautical endeavours in male disguise.[24] But since these Amazons were so frequently mentioned in popular literature, audiences needed little convincing of their existence.

Sometimes these stories were reshaped beyond recognition to conform to cultural expectations. While there is apparently no trace of a song about Isabelle Gunn, who spent two years disguised as John Fubister with the Hudson's Bay Company, a ballad entitled, 'Canada-I-O' appeared a year after her return to Orkney. First published in 1810, it describes a woman who masquerades as a man to follow her lover to Canada. When her lover discovers her aboard his ship, he threatens to drown her. But the captain intervenes, falls in love with the stowaway and 'she's now a captain's lady in Canada, heigh-o.'[25] It is possible that Isabelle Gunn left Orkney to accompany a lover but the happy reunion in the ballad is certainly fictional.

The heroine of 'Canada-I-O' was safely married off, but in reality Isabelle Gunn reappeared in Orkney, larger than life, with an illegitimate child and a bold explanation. She never married but eked out an existence knitting stockings and died alone in 1861, her death certificate signed by the inspector of the poor.[26] Although the story survived over two centuries and two continents by little more than word-of-mouth, Isabelle Gunn's own telling of the dramatic events in the Northwest can only be guessed at. As a fictive character she was far more important than she was as a real woman.

The story of Isabelle Gunn was widely known amongst the Scottish Selkirk settlers who arrived in Red River, Manitoba in 1812. According to Donald Murray, who knew John Scarth, the father of Gunn's child, 'she was sent home to Orkney and . . . became, with her daughter, public characters, and were known as vagrants under the name of the "Nor-westers."'[27] As a boy in Orkney, Murray was told this 'tale of the countryside' which became embroidered over the years. By 1934, the story was still in circulation but Orcadians now believed that Isabelle Gunn, 'was locally regarded as a witch selling love-philters and charms to the young men and maidens of the country-side.' Others said she was the daughter of Bessie Millie — the witch made famous by Sir Walter Scott in his novel *The Pirate* — who sold good winds to sailors.[28] More contemporary versions cast doubt as to whether Isabelle Gunn had, as trapper Peter Fidler recorded in 1808, 'worked at anything and well like the rest of the men.'

Later generations, who lived in a world where sexual differences were more clearly entrenched and publicly celebrated transgressions far fewer, found this female heroine too fantastic. That she became identified with supernatural or even malevolent forces, reinforced her role as a social outcast and the disruption her assumption of male power represented. As a witch, she was recast in a female role as a means of further divorcing her from the masculine world. According to local accounts, she became a pathetic rather than romantic figure.

Not all the Amazons had such little influence over their public personae. Some found opportunities to cash-in on the fame that surrounded them upon their discovery, even if they never again knew the financial security they had enjoyed as men. Mrs. Cola, who served aboard a British man-o-war, retired from the sea in 1782 when she inherited a property and opened a sailor's pub in London's East End.[29] Trading on her reputation as a former soldier with the Duke of Marlborough's army, Christian Davies ran a pub in Paddington while she waited for her soldier husband's discharge. Before

Hannah Snell opened 'a Widow in masquerade' — her London public house — she became well-known for her stage performance at Sadler's Wells in 1750 where she 'went through a number of military exercises in her regimentals.'[30] A female soldier during the American revolution, Deborah Sampson conducted a tour through New England in 1802, recounting her war experience and performing military exercises with her musket.[31] But despite this fame, for many the stage proved to be a fickle occupation. At the turn of the eighteenth century, sailor Mary Anne Talbot worked with London's Tottenham Court Road Thespian society and at a Drury Lane theatre playing both male and female roles; after serving only a few months, however, she was confined to a term in Newgate prison for her debts.[32]

The live appearance of a former combatant was often merely an added attraction on a bill. After all, street songs about the Amazons had been sung in ballad operas, at concerts, in musicals and plays and in 'pleasure gardens' throughout the eighteenth and nineteenth centuries. In 1803 London saw the first performance of 'the British Amazons or Army without Reserve' which ended with 'female volunteers in scarlet doing military exercises accompanied by patriotic songs praising the loyalty of all British countries and a vision of Bonaparte in the temple of British victories.'[33] The 'Invincible Brigade or Female Cavalry' featuring 'ladies of the establishment' in uniform performing exercises with the lance and sabre, was a favourite at the Royal Ampitheatre in August 1828.[34] These acts were used to bolster nationalist sentiments while at the same time providing audiences with the titillating image of women in male costume or handling weapons, imitating men.

On a less public level, this unconventional warrior remained a popular dramatic fantasy, ensuring an audience for theatrical performances and Amazonian biographies. But as the writer A.J. Munby discovered, women acted out this desire at open masked balls that flourished in London's working-class neighbourhoods in the mid-nineteenth century. In Camberwell, London in 1862, Munby found among the women in male clothes a volunteer in uniform whom he took for a man until someone called her Jenny.[35] On an evening walk to Walworth by the Blackfriar's road he passed the Surrey Gardens where he noted of the 150 shopmen, milliners and 'loose-women' gathered there, the best dressed woman wore a jacket, trousers and a cap.[36] At a Derby Day ball in June Munby observed that more than half the women 'were in male clothing — as sailors, highlanders or swells.' Dressed as men they felt free to swear and 'to be slapped around and pulled about in unfeminine ways.' Munby spoke to a woman, who he found drinking at the tavern bar among the men, sporting a sailor's outfit of white shirt, trousers, (naval) hat and smoking a cigar. She told Munby that she was a bonnet maker but, 'I often come to these bals masques and always in men's clothes because it's a greater spree. I come in a different character every time. I like smoking very well, but don't smoke when I'm in women's clothes — oh no!'[37] Here young working-class women and artisans could rent a costume at the door for three half-crowns, drink, smoke, dance and escape life's drudgeries while enacting their secret dreams. Female cross-dressing was, to Munby, a harmless, even innocent preoccupation, but he made careful note that the women in the gardens were not working as prostitutes in their disguise.

The practice of female cross-dressing also extended to more conventional spheres and, while walking back from Clapham on a Saturday evening, he turned into a South London music hall to watch a tall, finely made young woman, named Miss Stuart, 'dancing a Highland fling in full male costume, kilt and bare legs.'[38] Madeline Sinclair, another Highlander dancer of Munby's acquaintance danced on Oxford Street accompanied by an Italian organ-grinder. She appeared as 'a tall, young man in full Highland costume; wearing a Glengarry bonnet, a scarlet jacket, a sporan and tartan kilt and stockings, his legs bare from the knee to the calf.' A crowd looked on, debating whether she was a man or a woman since, 'her tall strong figure became her male dress so well that opinions were equally divided about her sex.'[39]

Whatever dangerous connotations that a person of indeterminate sex in male clothes might excite could be ignored in the theatre and popular literature by imbuing the warrior heroine with romantic or innocent motives. She continued to prosper. By 1903 women performing in military uniform could still attract a crowd to an Edinburgh performance of 'the Belle of Cairo' at the Royal Theatre. Audiences watched an adventurous young woman escape the unwelcome attentions of a Greek slave merchant by disguising herself as a butler and making her way to the front in the Sudan, where she meets an English officer, who falls in love with her.[40] Although the Amazon was concurrently mocked in music hall parodies of the earlier romantic ballads such as 'William Taylor,' [now sung with a Cockney accent as 'Billy Taylor'], her fascination endured.[41]

It was this potential to cast off the strictures of womanhood that had long held a particular fascination for female audiences. Nineteenth-century ballads such as the 'She-He Barman of Southwark,' based on the real-life history of Mary Walker — a sailor, a stoker on a Cunard boat, a porter on the Great Western railway and a publican — acknowledged women's restlessness with their position. The song exhorted:

> The ladies like the trousers,
> Of that there is no doubt.
> Many would be a barman,
> But fear they'd be found out.[42]

When she first appeared in court in 1867, the court 'was densely crowded outside and in, with roughs, male and female' to hear the plea of a woman who 'standing there, with broad shoulders squared and stout arms folded on the dock rail . . . seemed just such a fellow as one may see drawing beer at an alehouse or lounging about any seaport town.'[43] Fictionalized accounts of these women who 'put on the Gurnsey and chucked away her shift' nurtured this most secret desire. They became so popular that by 1863 a magazine article entitled 'modern Amazons' could urge readers that women more commonly enlisted as soldiers despite 'the rapid naval promotion of the female sailor with which we are all familiar through ballad.'[44]

Women privately dreamed of the liberation these real and unreal characters seemed to offer. Emma Edmonds was inspired by the heroine of Murray's novel, *Fanny Campbell or the Female Pirate Captain*; Christian Davies claimed to emulate a female Captain Bodeaux who spent a night at her family's home and died during the English siege of Limerick where her sex was discovered. While the preface to Deborah Sampson's account of her service in the Continental Army professed not 'to encourage the like paradigm of female enterprise,' a substantial number of women were among *The Female Review*'s original subscribers. Her book inspired sailor Louisa Baker to enlist as a sailor with the American navy during the war of 1812 and Mississippi cabin-boy Ellen Stephens cited the *Review* to add credibility to her story.[45]

Her constant popularity often acted as an incentive for the 'real-life' combatant to write her own biography or to seek out a sympathetic writer and

*Portrait of Sergeant Flora Sandes wearing the Kara George Star for non-commissioned officers, Bizerta, Tunis, 1917. (*Flora Sandes Collection, Sudbourne, Suffolk.*)

*Flora Sandes with friends from the Second Regiment of the Serbian Army on active duty, circa 1917. (*Flora Sandes Collection, Sudbourne, Suffolk.*)

*English soldier and sailor, Hannah Snell, in portrait by J. Faber, 1750. (*National Army Museum.*)

*This etching by Alfred Crowquill illustrates the sexual ambiguity that stories of cross-dressing female soldiers suggested; Crowquill's caption reads, 'What do you think of my protector Captain Maria?' (*Mansell Collection.*)

*Loreta Janeta Velasquez disguised as Confederate scout Harry T. Buford during the American Civil War. (*The British Library*.)

*Deborah Sampson, who fought during the American Revolution disguised as Robert Shurtleff. (*The British Library*.)

*Dr. James Miranda Barry cross-dressed to graduate from an Edinburgh medical school in 1812 and lived as a man until her death. (*BBC Hulton Picture Library.*)

*Flora Sandes in the trenches with her comrades from the Second Regiment, circa 1916. (*Flora Sandes Collection, Sudbourne, Suffolk.*)

*Above Russian Women's Battalion
of Death, formed by the provisional
government and led by former-
Tsarist soldier, Maria Bochkareva,
1917. New recruits are shown
training in Petrograd. (*Trustees of
the Imperial War Museum.*)

*Suffragette Elsie Howie dressed for
a 'Votes for Women' parade as Joan
of Arc, 1909, in a procession to
celebrate Mrs. Pethwick-
Lawrence's release from jail.
(*Communist Party Picture Library.*)

*Dorothy Lawrence, a would-be journalist who disguised herself as an engineer and spent 10 days working at the West front in France, 1915. (*The British Library*.)

Below Forts of the Hudson's Bay and North West Companies at Pembina on the Red River where Isabelle Gunn gave birth to her son in December 1807, by Peter Rindisbacher, c. 1822. (*The National Archives of Canada, Ottawa, Ontario*.)

*Angélique Brulon, served in Napoleon's infantry between 1792 and 1799 through seven campaigns under the nom de guerre, Liberté.

*_Below_ Princess Kati Dadeshkeliani's record of service, 1915–1916.

RECORD OF SERVICE

e 4th, 1916. Served in the
nd Field Ambulance under
untess E. N. Vorontsov Dash-
v, unofficially in charge of
ores and rations from May
th, 1915, till June 1st, 1916.

e 10th, 1916. Appointed by
e Chief of the Red Cross on
e South-West Front in charge
stores and rations of the unit
om June 1st, 1916.

e 10th, 1916. By an order of
e 2nd Cavalry Corps dated
ovember 26th, 1915, was award-
the silver medal with legend
or bravery" on the ribbon of
. George, No. 112630.

y 13th,* 1916. Whilst carrying
ounded between Gorodenko and
leshchiki received a kick from
horse on the left leg, which
used a fracture of both bones.
acuated to the Pokrovski
spital in Kiev on August 9th,
16.

eturned to duty on November
, 1916.

Dr. KARABEKOV
Officer Commanding

his date was incorrectly
entered.—K.D.

Прохожденіе службы.

Прохожденіе службы.

*Sergeant Flora Sandes, at an outdoor café, circa 1917. (*Flora Sandes Collection, Sudbourne, Suffolk.*)

*Flora Sandes, seated on left, second from end, front row, with officers and men of her company, taken on the eve of the Serbian army's big offensive, 1918. (*Flora Sandes Collection, Sudbourne, Suffolk.*)

publisher. Since British and North American audiences had been fed on a steady diet of conventionalized romantic adventures, women often participated in creating their own legends. The former combatants colluded in this process, re-inventing their own histories to dismiss possible suspicion about their motives for enlisting or their conduct in an all-male environment. Others used their experience as propaganda, publishing their accounts while the war still raged. Few, it seems, could write unselfconsciously of their foray into the male world. Selling her story also became a time-tested method of generating an often desperately needed income and some had little control over or interest in the results.

After Mary Anne Talbot was rescued from the debtor's prison in Newgate she found refuge as a domestic servant in publisher Robert S. Kirby's house in St. Paul's churchyard. Kirby recorded her story in his magazine of colourful characters entitled the 'Wonderful Museum' along with an appeal for financial assistance from charitable donors. But ill-health due to her war injuries forced Talbot to retire from Kirby's service after three years. Christian Davies was also impoverished in her old age ending her life at the Chelsea Pensioners' Hospital where her husband was a guard. She may have sold her story — it appeared soon after her death in 1739 — to supplement a meagre income. It didn't make her wealthy but it was highly successful with a reprint in 1741 that featured a lengthy appendix and it appeared as the work of J. Wilson, former surgeon in the army, in 1742. Perhaps playing on this popularity, actress Peg Woffington, who became famous for her adoption of male roles, made her breeches debut in *The Female Officer* in Dublin in 1740. She performed this role at London's Covent Garden and gave it 'by desire' at Drury Lane several times in the following years.[46]

Once the female warrior's story was sold, writers, balladeers, playwrights and story tellers in each society and historical period drew upon related cultural references to explain the female soldier. In Serbia, although comparisons were never made between their role within the Serbian army and the Balkan tradition of the 'Albanian virgins' — girls who swore sexual abstinence in return for male social and even property rights — this custom may have made Flora Sandes and Jenny Merkus more acceptable. The 'dedicated girls' of northern Albania and Montenegra wore men's clothes, assumed a masculine name and enjoyed all male social rights if a family was bereft of a son or if a girl refused to marry the husband chosen for her. These women headed households and could even exercise political power within their village.[47] To Flora Sandes' comrades who knew of this custom her motives were consistent with the desire for autonomy and the physical freedom of male clothing that prompted the Balkan women to change their identity.

Accounts from other women travellers in this period also suggest that the tradition of sworn virgins reflected a social rather than biological understanding of sexual difference. American journalist Rose Wilder Lane who visited Northern Albania in 1921 wrote that she was taken for a 'dedicated girl' because she was unmarried in middle-age and wore short hair. 'In these mountains when a girl is old enough to marry the man to whom she has been promised, she may escape the marriage by swearing before the chiefs of the two tribes an oath of life-long virginity,' a Shala tribal chief, Lulash, explained to Lane. 'She takes a man's place in the tribe. Naturally, when they see you, at your age, with short hair, they think that is what you did.'[48] On the way to Seltze-Kilmeni when English traveller and writer Edith Durham met 'a lean, wiry, active woman of forty-seven' clad in male clothes who mocked her married sisters, she wrote of their meeting:

> [The woman] had dressed as a boy, she said, ever since she was quite a child because she had wanted to, and her father had let her. . . . She treated me with the contempt she appeared to think all petticoats deserved — turned her back on me and exchanged cigarettes with the men, with whom she was a hail-fellow-well-met.[49]

Both accounts strike a familiar cord. Flora Sandes was 39 years old when she enlisted in the Second Regiment and Jenny Merkus fought in Herzegovinia at the age of 36. The female combatant's alienation from other women that Durham noted in this 'hail-fellow-well met' was an almost universal experience. Dressed in their uniforms with regulation hair cuts these single, middle-aged women were perhaps more easily assimilated into the Serbian army because of this custom. A woman who traded her sexuality for male social privilege was not only understood but seen to be acting out of pragmatism. The Balkan soldiers responded sympathetically to the desire to escape the stifling confines of bourgeois spinsterhood that inspired both Flora Sandes and Jenny Merkus to flee their home countries. More importantly they played a dual role as foreigners willing to take up the Serbian cause ensuring their legendary status. Flora's involvement grew to such proportions that by the mid-1970s she was remembered by one man in Yugoslavia as the English woman who 'could haul a canon uphill that even seven strong Serbs could not manage.'[50]

While the warrior heroine was popular in Britain and European culture over centuries, in each historical period current versions of her story reflected particular social realities. Eighteenth-century heroines were later used to illustrate how far Victorian ladies had progressed because, as a contemporary writer, Menié Muriel Dowie, claimed, they could go about their adventures 'in the cold seriousness of skirts.'[51] Equality between the sexes rendered a male disguise unnecessary according to Dowie who said of her own foreign travels: 'I am not a woman's rights woman in the aggressive sense. . . . I do not rejoice in ugly clothes and . . . I am not desirous of reforming the world or doing anything subversive.'[52] Dowie edited her collection of female adventure stories recognizing that the playful sexual ambiguity of a character like Christian Davies was far too unsettling for a Victorian audience.

The female soldier was a stock figure that underwent a significant transformation in the nineteenth century. In 1819 James Caulfield published a two volume set of 'remarkable persons' that included, along with famous murderers, conjurers and thieves, the life histories of several Amazons. Christian Davies, Hannah Snell, British sailor Anne Mills, pirates Mary Read and Anne Bonny all featured as women who 'pleaded the tender passion as an apology for assuming masculine pursuits and habits.'[53] According to Caulfield even Anne Mills, once famous for decapitating a French sailor and then carrying off her opponent's head as a trophy, was induced by 'some love affair to follow the fortune of a favourite lover who had gone to sea.'[54] Romantic love was a conventional motive for the female combatant but the heroine's behaviour (in this collection) still spoke volumes more about her love for adventure.

A few years later, *The Soldier's Companion* recast the female warrior in a much more feminine light. Christian Davies' story appeared under the chapter heading 'Female Courage' emphasizing her role as sutler rather than soldier. 'Courage' the author assumed, was a male characteristic that only exceptional women might demonstrate in rare instances. Gone was Christian Davies' autonomy over her husband and her boisterous self-confidence. Rather, this collection featured exemplary wives and mothers who were praised for their individual valour when in reality women still played a vital role in the British military, many serving in hazardous situations. The stories documented women's presence in the British army and navy, but posed a striking contrast to the earlier warrior heroines.

The bureaucratization of the British military marked a turning point for women's involvement while popular histories told of heroines who were part of this disappearing world. By the middle of the century, organizational changes within the British army directly affected the lives of military women and were reflected in the female heroines' stories. Women who had been a vital part of the military world for at least four centuries were shut out. They were increasingly segregated from camp life and their 'official duties' were gradually narrowed as soldiers' sexual and marital relations were brought under direct military control for the first time.[55] As James Parton wrote of Florence Nightingale's organization of services during the Crimean war, 'the loss of the history of army women made the rise of military nursing and the opening of restricted careers for uniformed women's auxiliaries, appear to be something new.'[56] Those who had performed a variety of service functions, moving in and out of the military environment, found themselves permanently excluded.[57]

Among those military wives singled out for honour in popular literature was 'Frederica of Waterloo' who accompanied her husband on to the battlefield and, 'whilst employed in the offices of mercy to a wounded comrade received a wound in the leg.'[58] This nurse was known for her bravery — she sustained a leg wound during Waterloo — and for giving birth to a daughter named Frederica by the Duchess of York upon her return to England. These stories became increasingly popular as alternatives to the masquerading warriors. Even the term 'Amazon' was broadened to include any 'military maid' in the sphere of war.

An account of a soldier's wife who distinguished herself during the British attack on St Vincent in June 1796 related by Major-General Stewart of the Royal Highlanders followed this new tradition of military heroines. In Thomas Carter's *Curiosities of War* the anonymous soldier's wife was directed to remain in charge of the company's knapsacks but she pushed forward in the assault to urge the men forward. 'Well done my Highland lads!' she exclaimed. 'See how the brigands scamper, like so many deer! Come, let us drive them from yonder hill.' Intrigued by his 'Amazonian friend,' Stewart discovered that she urged the men forward in the thick of battle and assisted the surgeons with the wounded.[59] The new heroine posed little threat since nursing could be seen as an extension of the domestic realm and because the soldier's wife confined her military cheerleading to the sidelines.[60]

The story of Mrs. Retson, a sergeant's wife, also conformed more closely to the increasingly 'feminine' image of the war heroine who displaced the female soldier. At the battle of Busaco in September 1810 Mrs. Retson took over a drummer boy's duties when he became paralysed with fear. Quoting from Sir William Napier's account of this Napoleonic battle, Carter wrote, 'it is difficult to state whether [her action] was most feminine or heroic.' Presumably moved by maternal concern, Mrs. Retson replaced the drummer boy thus equating her low status with his. However, despite the feminine context in which these exemplary wives and mothers operated, they were still seen to be encroaching on male territory. Where then could women make themselves useful? Thomas Carter provided an answer: 'It was left to the nineteenth century to exemplify woman's true sphere of duty on the battle-field — this was shown by Florence Nightingale and her devoted sisterhood.'[61]

Yet only three years before the Crimean War, Queen Victoria issued a directive that anyone, 'without any reservation as to sex,' who was present during the naval actions of the Napoleonic wars was entitled to a gold medal.[62] Sir Byam Martin, appointed by the Naval and Military Admiralty to consider applications, wrote that Jane Townsend, aboard the *Defiance* at the battle of Trafalgar in 1805 was entitled to an award since she produced, 'strong and highly satisfactory certificates of her useful services during the action.' However, Martin added, 'upon further consideration, this cannot be allowed. There were too many people in the fleet equally useful and it will leave the army exposed to *innumerable* applications of the same nature.'[63] Two further claims from Ann Hopping and Mary Ann Riley who participated in the battle of the Nile, were promptly refused. Just as the female soldiers were viewed with scepticism, women who served in other capacities outside military authority were officially ignored

While an increasingly domesticated military maid grew in popularity during the late nineteenth century, feminists began to use the female combatants to challenge prevailing notions about women's innate physical and mental weakness. They reappeared in a collection by suffragette Ellen Clayton entitled *Female Warriors* as an argument for women's right to political participation. The Amazon, she wrote, would counter her opponents' claim that women had historically played no part in warfare and were thus ill-equipped to govern the state:

> Popular prejudice, having decided that woman is a poor weak creature, credulous, easily influenced, holds that she is of necessity timid; that if she were allowed as much as a voice in government in her native country, she would stand appalled if war were even hinted at.[64]

Clayton criticized the notion that any woman who refused an identity as a passive and subservient female was 'masculine' and therefore unnatural. The masculine and feminine, social commentators argued, could not co-exist in the same body. The Amazons threatened to disrupt this equation and Clayton claimed that during the eighteenth century nearly every European army boasted one or more female soldiers who preferred the dangers and hardships of a foreign campaign to the deprivations that accompanied separation. Women managed to enlist without detection because no physical exams were required but 'more especially because the female soldiers behaved themselves quite as *manly* as their comrades.'[65]

The new military woman was expected to conform to moral as well as physical ideals and Clayton noted that the earlier female warriors were out of fashion because their hard, muscular bodies and rough faces greatly deviated from the Victorian concept of beauty. Sir John Carr's description of the Maid of Saragossa, reprinted in Carter, made the contrast clear. Unlike descriptions of Hannah Snell and Christian Davies, Augustina Saragossa was 'perfectly feminine' and saw no need to disguise her identity during the French siege of Sargossa in 1809. Since she was neither wife nor mother, but a beautiful young woman, Carr's description of her was explicitly sexual. Augustina was known for her action during battle when she snatched a burning match from a dead artillery man's hand and fired off a 26-pound cannon. When Carr met her, this Amazon was 'drinking her coffee when the evening gun was fired; its discharge seemed to electrify her with delight; she sprang out of the cabin upon the deck and alternatively listened to its sound.'[66] Quashing any conscious attempt at titillation, Carr assured his readers that, 'The sailors it may be supposed were uncommonly pleased with [Augustina]. . . . Some were heard to say with a hearty oath, "I hope they will do something for her; she ought to have plenty of prize money; she is of the right sort."'[67] To ensure no mistake was made about her sexual identity he added that when Augustina chose to wear her uniform she modestly preserved her petticoat and virtue. Any potential attackers were threatened with her sword. Augustina was set apart from the earlier warrior heroines by her eroticism; she carried a sabre but still wore a petticoat.

She came to public attention when granted a pension and the pay of an artilleryman for her part in the siege of 1808 from the Spanish government. However, even this very feminine heroine was not universally praised and Carr noted that Sargossa's citizens criticized Augustina for setting a dangerous example. 'There were many . . . who coldly called this young heroine the artillery woman,' wrote Carr. '[They] observed that they should soon have nothing but battalions of women in the field instead of attending to their domestic concerns if every romantic female was rewarded and commissioned as Augustina had been.'[68]

Clayton's opponents also acknowledged interest in the warrior heroine and argued that her disappearance measured the progress of British women. Since Florence Nightingale had carved out an appropriate niche for 'ladies' as nurses in the masculine sphere of war, female cross-dressing, they argued, was anachronistic and unnecessary. Menié Muriel Dowie, in her collection of female soldier stories, argued that Victorian women could now undertake courageous and adventurous exploits as *ladies*. But while she acknowledged the existence of more genteel, modern viragos, she dismissed the female soldiers' claims of military prowess as highly exaggerated. 'It is difficult to take them seriously, these ladies of the sabre,' she wrote. 'They are to me something of a classic jest: their day is done, their histories forgotten, their devotion dead, and they have left us no genuine descendants.'[69] Reported cases of passing women in male occupations and even female soldiers from this period were still common enough that Dowie's statement that 'no descendants' existed raised an intriguing question. What of the modern women who still entered masculine occupations in male guise rather than toil at lower paying and less interesting jobs? A contemporary article by A. J. Munby provided at least 16 examples of modern equivalents and 'scores' of women who worked in male clothing as bricklayers, grooms, navvies and at other occupations.[70] Munby's essays on cross-dressing women were based on newspaper items he received from the Romeike and Curtice Press Cutting and Info Agency where he kept an account throughout the 1880s and 1890s.[71]

Munby's contemporary examples and Dowie's refusal to recognize their existence reflected the parallel importance of class to ideals of sexual difference. The chapbooks and popular life-histories that Dowie edited were drawn from literature firmly rooted in the life of the labouring poor who read and enjoyed them. Women who passed as men, these stories revealed, refused to accept the restrictions of their gender and took a direct route to independence and financial security. The earlier women warriors celebrated working-class life in a way that was no longer acceptable or even believable. Women today, claimed Dowie, 'do well to keep to their own clothes. An air of masculinity, however slight, goes against the woman who would be successful in the public eye.'[72] This statement, presumably directed at middle- and upper-class women, further implied that any deviation from the feminine ideal smacked of class inferiority.

Interest in the warrior heroine had not waned but took on a new significance. A journal of popular literature in 1872 featured an article entitled 'what can women do?' using examples of female soldiers to demonstrate their versatility. But in contrast to the intrepid women travellers and adventurous governesses who swept the British empire, contemporary cases were usually cited in 'primitive' cultures. 'Some of the African potentates have Amazonian armies and Mrs. [Anna] Lenonowens, in her recent interesting account of her governess-experience at the Court of Siam makes frequent mention of the body-guard of Amazons at the Palace.'[73] In her book, Anna Lenonowens also linked the women who cross-dressed within the Maha Phrasat, where all court ceremonies were performed, with those who sought refuge there for 'the most disgusting, the most appalling, and the most unnatural [crimes] that the heart of man has conceived.'[74] The English traveller, Richard Burton, produced an influential book on the 'Amazonian' guards of the West African King of Dahomey and John Duncan's *Travels in Western Africa* included 'pictures' of these unusual women. A. J. Munby wrote about attending an exhibition at Crystal Palace in 1893 of 37 female soldiers, taken prisoner by the French in Dahomey.[75] The reality of other cultural roles for women in foreign lands was erased by interest in female warriors so that any woman with a weapon was dubbed an Amazon.[76] The black and Asian women in these accounts evoked an earlier age when gender boundaries were much more amorphous and reflected a renewed British fascination with the 'deviation' they represented.

But since these contemporary Amazons belonged to exotic cultures, far removed from Europe, their existence was rarely questioned. However, during this period the exploits of British and American female combatants came under close and cynical scrutiny. As her story was rewritten, doubts were raised that any woman could actually undertake the adventures that increasingly became the perogative of men. Leslie Stephen, editor of the Dictionary of National Biography, sneered about the 1740 version of Christian Davies' story in 1888: 'the book is uniformly disfigured by the revolting details of many unseemly and brutal acts, related in a tone of self-glorification which is suggestive of nothing so much as an unsexed woman.'[77] The historian, George Trevelyan, also noted in his copy of Wilson's 1744 version: 'There are many next to incredible things in the narrative and the Dictionary of National Biography holds it as untrue — in everything except that she *was* a female soldier and died in 1739 of which there is external evidence.'[78]

Antiquarian booksellers continued to swap details of chapbook heroines and the faded news cuttings which inspired them. William J. Thomas, an expert on centegenarians, replied to a reader of *Notes and Queries* literary magazine in 1873 with inquiries about the eighteenth-century female soldier, Phoebe Hessel, that he had 'often been addressed privately' about her life. The correspondence that ensued, however, was intended only to verify whether she had died at the age of 108.[79] Following a *Daily Telegraph* article in 1892 about Hannah Snell a debate ensued about the veracity of her story and one reader claimed she was 'an impostor [who] never was in either the army or the navy.'[80] Stories of women that filtered back from America during the civil war were also given little credibility in England where Munby commented on his indifference to the subject: 'Politeness forbids me to answer.'[81] But although the female soldiers came under public scrutiny and the consistency of their life-histories was found wanting, fascination with their exploits had not diminished. Interest even turned to the martial heroines of the Civil War who were plentiful and often highly successful vehicles of propaganda.

The Civil War nurse and soldier, Emma Edmonds, claimed that she donated the proceeds of her first book *Nurse and Spy* which, according to a Texas publisher sold more than 175, 000 copies, to the Sanitary Commission, the Civil War's equivalent to the Red Cross.[82] *Pauline of the Potomac*, an account of a spy for the Grand Army of the Republic (GAR), Pauline

Cushman, that Emma Edmonds pronounced 'a low quality of fiction,' was published in 1862. In the same year Madeline Moore's 'perilous adventures and hair-breadth escapes' as a GAR soldier featured in *The Lady Lieutenant* was widely-read, while Loreta Janeta Velasquez waited until 1876 to publish her book about fighting with the Confederates, *The Woman in Battle*. These stories were popular because of their timely subject but also because they moved heroines into the sphere of action where most were forbidden to go. Through the adventures of Pauline Cushman, Emma Edmonds or Madeline Moore women waiting for their husband's return or restless with a desire for an exciting life could live out their fantasy. Imbued with patriotic rhetoric, the books were, however, considered suitable reading.

Although the heroine of this literature always passed as a man, either to follow her lover to war, to seek revenge for his death, or to escape domestic confines, their authors were often careful not to flaunt their male masquerade. Edmonds self-consciously concealed her disguise until halfway through the book presumably to lend the Union cause credibility. Describing the battle of Bull Run where the Army of the Potomac met the Confederate forces for the first time, she wrote, 'Col. R's wife . . . , Mrs. B. and myself were, I think, the only three females.' This was only one example of her attempt to diminish the deception her adoption of a male identity involved and nowhere is her earlier incarnation as bookseller Frank Thompson mentioned. To reinforce this sleight-of-hand, Emma Edmonds described Mrs. B. as her constant companion even though she wrote to her friend Jerome Robbins after the war how much she missed female company while in the army. But however carefully she attempted to hide her male identity, Emma Edmonds felt compelled to defend her decision to enlist as Frank Thompson.

In her introduction to *Nurse and Spy* Emma Edmonds claimed that 'patriotism was the grand secret' of her success and asserted that:

> it makes little difference what costume [a woman] assumes while in the discharge of her duties — perhaps she should have the privilege of choosing for herself whatever may be the surest protection from insult and inconvenience in her blessed, self-sacrificing work.[83]

Costume, however, made an enormous difference to a woman's 'blessed' work. Years later Emma Edmonds, no longer concerned about rallying her public to the Union cause, acknowledged the 'freedom and glorious independence of masculinity' that trousers afforded her.[84] In her book Edmonds advocated that women send their lovers skirts and crinolines with a note suggesting that until they enlisted this was their appropriate costume. Attached to the crinoline would be the following poem:

> We send you the buttonless garments of women!
> Cover your face lest it freckle or tan!
> Muster the apron-string guards on the common
> That is the corps of the sweet little man.[85]

(Underlying Edmonds' advice was a burning resentment towards men who refused to use the power their masculinity conferred upon them.) For if skirts were powerful symbols of feminine weakness, an insult to be flung in the face of a cowardly man, then according to this logic, a woman's desire for buttoned garments was understandable. Beneath the patriotic rhetoric, the subversive qualities of the female warrior's story often shone through or were used to open debates about sexual difference. Emma Edmonds' account of the American Civil War, which she confessed in 1883 was 'not strictly authentic,' promoted the Union while inadvertently revealing the contradictions between her words and actions. She argued that a woman's nature made her inherently more suitable for nursing — an extension of the domestic sphere — but also celebrated her joy at venturing into the masculine world.

Flora Sandes wrote her first autobiography in 1916 to raise funds and to promote the Serbian cause, but it also spawned discussion about women's military role. To British reporters she was 'the modern girl' who 'has solved the riddle often put, "should women be soldiers?" and has answered it so far as she is personally concerned.'[86] Maria Bochkareva, commander of the Russian Women's Battalion in 1917, was dubbed by the American press 'the twice-wounded girl officer who initiated the woman suffrage soldier organization.'[87] The female soldier's propaganda value became inextricably linked with the questions she raised about the propriety of her role.

Maria Bochkareva recognized this when she convinced Alexander Kerensky to approve a Women's Battalion in May 1917 'to shame the men' who were quickly deserting the Eastern front. When she spoke at the Marynsky Theatre's benefit for an invalid's home, she appeared after Mrs. Kerensky with an appeal to the largely female audience. 'Our mother is perishing,' she cried. 'Our mother is Russia. I want to help save her. I want women whose hearts are crystal, whose souls are pure, whose impulses are lofty.'[88] Her stirring speech prompted 1,500 women to enlist that evening, to venture into battle in place of the men. Bochkareva's efforts at marshalling a force of female martyrs became an international symbol for the war's social disruption. Her efforts at maintaining sexual purity and a rigid military code were unflinching; giggling was strictly forbidden; in two days more than 80 women were dismissed for too much laughing and for frivolity; the women were always confined to barracks and minor breeches of discipline punished with slaps across their face.

In Russia and in Britain, women's movements were internally divided in their support for the war and so held opposing views on the Women's Battalion. While some Russian feminists were enraptured with Bochkareva, the socialist-feminist journal, *Rabotnitsa*, appealed to mothers of women enrolled in the battalion, 'have we become so small that mercy means nothing to us, that love and sympathy for those dear to us no longer prevail and have given way to an obscene and sordid thirst for blood alone?' The Petrograd Committee of Peasant Deputies was more forthright in its condemnation calling the battalion, 'an inadmissible and inappropriate vaudeville show,' while a correspondent of the *Women's Cause* argued that women had a right to fight for their country if they chose.[89]

Emmeline Pankhurst of the Women's Social and Political Union made meeting Bochkareva a priority when she visited Petrograd with Jessie Kenny in June 1917. Suffragette Anna Shabanova entertained her English guests at the Astoria Hotel, where they met Bochkareva, were escorted to the Women's Battalion barracks and then to various patriotic fundraising rallies. Mrs. Pankhurst witnessed the blessing of the battalion's colours at St. Isaac's Cathedral, inspected the troops and frequently visited the barracks where she was saluted as 'the eminent visitor who had done so much for women and her country.' Later Bochkareva remarked, 'we became very much attached to each other.'[90]

After Mrs. Pankhurst's visit, the illusory connection between female soldiers and the struggle for women's suffrage was firmly fixed in the public mind. Although her trip was intended to help bolster Russia's flagging war effort, the women in uniform were a bigger attraction. They epitomized the height of female sacrifice but were also portrayed as a conduit through which Russia's women could directly address their allied counterparts. In an open letter the Russian soldiers implored them to 'have patience for a time, for if Russian men betrayed the common cause, the Russian women will save it.'[91] Although they appeared in international press photos with heads shaved clean, wearing coarse uniforms, and shouldering heavy guns, their rhetoric — pleas for 'Mother Russia' and self-sacrifice — never strayed from the domestic realm.

But the modern Amazon's perplexing contradictions remained unresolved. One English journalist provided the following explanation for Russia's anomaly:

> There appears to be no sex-antagonism in Russia. Indeed the line of sex cleavage is of the very faintest. Men and women do not lead separate lives. They work side by side normally, whether in the fields or as students of medicine, politics and the like in universities. And, as every one knows, there are (or were before the war changed everything) as many women Anarchists as men. It is only natural that the iron-hearted and adventurous should desire to share in the great adventure.[92]

This vision of Russia as a country where the sexes were equal rather than divided into separate spheres, intrigued feminists who were invited to believe that the Women's Battalion was the most dramatic outgrowth of this egalitarianism. But whatever the reality, the women soldiers, as journalist Louise Bryant observed, 'caught the public fancy like no other feature of the great war.'[93]

English and American audiences viewed the Russian soldiers as a test case of whether women were fit to enter the ultimate male occupation. An interview with the eminent American neurologist, Dr. Graeme M. Hammond, addressed whether the Women's Battalion was ushering in a new generation of female fighters who would no longer be satisfied with their domestic lot after the war. 'Is the women's regiment simply a super-advertising device of the Russian patriots who hope to stir through the sense of shame the slacking martial spirit of the men?' asked journalist George MacAdam. 'Or has the woman soldier really arrived? Is she a new element of topsy-turvydom in a world that during the last year or so has been turned topsy-turvy in so many ways?'[94] When Hammond stated that women were physically and emotionally capable of fighting like men, MacAdam asked, 'But if women were to be taken into our armies . . . what is to become of our ideals, of chivalry and of all that has grown out of them?'[95] Whether women were disguised as men or fighting *as women* they posed the same threat; once they had conquered this most exclusively masculine environment all boundaries between the sexes would be rendered obsolete. Thus the female soldier came to epitomize women's entry into male occupations and was seen as the ultimate sign of egalitarianism.

The San Francisco journalist, Bessie Beatty, after spending several days with Bochkareva's battalion concluded that:

> Women can fight. Women have the courage, the endurance and even the strength for fighting. [The Russians] have demonstrated that and, if necessary, all the other women in the world can demonstrate it.[96]

When Elihu Root, a member of the American Mission to Russia returned to Chicago in early August 1917, he expressed a similar sentiment: 'the Russian women are doing a wonderful job of shaming the men into fighting and where necessary I hope American women will follow their example.'[97] Rheta Childe Dorr, a feminist and journalist whose reports from Russia were syndicated in more than 20 American newspapers, believed that the Women's Battalion proved their right to equality. 'I was a feminist finding in these women the realization . . . that women are not a class governed by limited impulses and emotions,' she wrote. 'They belong to the race.'[98] According to some commentators, however, it was not enough for women to take up arms, these contemporary Amazons needed to exhibit superhuman resistance to the slaughter around them to prove their case.

The battalion was also used to argue against women's active participation in combat. The 'deep impression' the female soldiers initially made on Florence Farmborough, an English Red Cross nurse stationed at the Galician front in 1917, melted away at news that the women had expressed terror on the battle field. She noted in her diary that when someone read aloud a Moscow newspaper report about Maria Bochkareva around a camp-fire near a Romanian village, 'we sisters, of course, were thrilled to the core.' When she nursed some of the wounded female soldiers two weeks later, Florence Farmborough was disappointed to learn that a few had cowered in the trenches, 'fainting and hysterical' or crawled back into the rear. 'Bochkareva retreated with her decimated battalion,' she wrote. 'She was wrathful, brokenhearted but she had learnt a great truth. Women were quite unfit to be soldiers.'[99]

Despite the eventual defeat that the battalion suffered at the final Russian offensive — six were killed and 30 wounded — it was constantly used as a symbol of female resistance. An American woman working at a Red Cross night canteen in Beauvois in 1918 fantasized about forming her own women's battalion. 'Oh [war's] a wretched business,' she wrote, 'but my fighting blood is up and I'd give anything if I could be a man.' The women in her camp smoothly ran a lorry depot for six months until the Red Cross administration sent a string of inexperienced and incompetent male officers to supervise their operations. 'I wish I could form a "Legion of Death,"' she sighed in frustration.[100] It was assumed by fascinated onlookers that the Russian female soldiers had been granted the equality that continually eluded women who worked in auxiliary services.

In reality the Women's Battalion, heralded as feminine virtue personified, was mocked and jeered rather than welcomed by its male counterpart. Even those female soldiers who entered regular regiments in disguise, held the battalion in contempt. Four days after she nursed some of its soldiers, Florence Farmborough attended a female combatant with a badly contused leg at a Red Cross station in Illisheysti. 'She did not belong to the Women's Battalion of Death,' wrote Farmborough. 'She had, however, heard of them and from her curt remarks one could understand that she held them with little respect.'[101] Given that the lone female soldier in an all-male regiment worked hard to distinguish herself as unique, the comments from Farmborough's patient are hardly surprising. As if recognizing the advantage of being the sole exception, Flora Sandes commented on the Women's Battalion: 'I'd very much like to see it but I don't think I'd like to be in it.'[102]

Contemporary commentators largely agreed that the battalion failed because it operated separately and because it proved unable to cope with the class struggle that permeated everything at the dawn of Russia's revolution. Louise Bryant, who interviewed several former battalion members predicted that, 'there will always be fighting women in Russia but they will fight side by side with men and not as a sex.'[103] The number of individual enlistments of female combatants rose rapidly throughout the summer of 1917 even though women's battalions sprung up in Moscow, Perim, Odessa and Ekaterinodar.[104] The equality, comradeship and social acceptance the lone Amazon experienced, still appeared as a greater motivation to enlist than patriotism or nationalistic fervour.

Lifting the veil of propaganda Louise Bryant found that even the women of the battalion themselves regarded their venture as a failure. Some felt they had been seduced by Bochkareva's appeals to enlist for the wrong cause. Anna Shub, a 17-year-old from Moghilev, left home where the Bolsheviks took power at the beginning of December 1917 because she thought, 'the poor soldiers of Russia were tired after fighting so many years and . . . we ought to help them.' But she felt she should 'die of shame' when she realized the women's battalion was intended to embarrass the soldiers into fighting.[105] Another woman lamented that she had joined, 'moved by a high resolve to die for the revolution,' but found that the women were misunderstood. 'We expected to be treated as heroes, but always we were treated with scorn . . . The soldiers thought we were militarists and enemies of the revolution.'[106] Undeterred by their previous experience, the women Bryant interviewed resolved to fight for the new Soviet government — in male battalions.

The growing number of disguised Russian female soldiers reported by the Western press in England and North America sparked an interest that lasted beyond the Great War. Writers drew on all the time-honoured conventions of the earlier female warriors, depicting women bravely enlisting to find their lovers or from a deeply held conviction about the justice of the cause. They reawakened interest in this ancient heroine, providing her with a modern context. In this climate women turned to the real-life soldiers for inspiration as the boundaries between the male and female world began to crumble.

Among the British nurses who encountered Flora Sandes in Serbia, she emerged as an indomitable figure. Isobel Ross, working with the Scottish Women's Hospitals, wrote of her first meeting with Sandes at Ostrovo in September 1916: 'We [nurses] felt so proud of her and her bravery.'[107] The *Nursing Times* commented on Sandes' enlistment, 'we have always thought women would do invaluable work in the Army Service Corps. This proves it.'[108] When Red Cross nurse Elsie Corbett was having a difficult time setting up a hospital in Leskovatz in October 1918, she 'kept on wondering what Florence Nightingale or Flora Sandes would have done.'[109] That Sandes had grasped a rare opportunity to act out a life-long fantasy of working as a man amongst men, seemed heroic and even enviable to the women who watched her from afar.

Perhaps it was this same admiration that brought women to hear Sandes while on her Australian tour in 1920. She was often feted by charitable women's groups such as the Soldier and Sailors' Mothers and Wives Association, the Red Cross and local sewing circles. In Coffs Harbour, New South Wales, Sandes inspected a local hospital, had her photo taken by admiring nurses and attended a dinner held in her honour by 'the lady war workers.'[110] A largely female audience gathered to hear the 'lady sergeant' when she spoke in Sydney and in Brisbane, newspapers advertised her talk in the 'Women's Realm' and 'Women's World' sections.[111] As philanthropic fund raiser Sandes fitted neatly into an acceptable role for a middle-class lady despite the incongruity of her other function as military attaché to the Serbian army. Her female audience could identify with and even emulate the radical potential of her utterly unconventional image.

While the fantasy lived on, the retired female soldier or sailor found her re-entry into womanhood an extremely difficult process. Some never found their way again in a world where their achievements could be so easily forgotten, dismissed or exploited by others. With their retirement came the loss of a world that had temporarily relieved them of their oppression as women even if it yoked them into the military's hierarchy. But how they coped with the painful transition back, giving up the power and male acceptance they had temporarily enjoyed, was not the stuff of stories. These quiet and miserable reflections that were visible only in glimpses in public records — in court reports, in requests for military pensions and occasionally, in memoirs — form the final chapter of this story.

6

Wounds That Would Not Heal

And dost thou ask what fairy had inspired
A NYMPH to be with martial glory fired?
Or what from art, or yet from nature's laws,
Has join'd a FEMALE to her country's cause?
Why on great Mars's theatre she drew
Her FEMALE pourtrait though in soldier's hue?
Deborah Gannett, an address, Boston, 22 March 1802

A T THE AGE of 42, the highly-respected Mrs. Benjamin Gannett, neé Deborah Sampson, was proud that she could still pass for a lad of 18 in the uniform of a Continental Army soldier. On a public speaking tour through New England and New York in 1802, she entertained theatre audiences with her stories of fighting in the American War of Independence. But while Deborah Gannett billed herself as a living symbol of 'Liberty and Peace' she subtly played upon her ambiguous position. Her diary entry for May 5, Providence, Rhode Island, noted: 'When I entered the hall I must say I was much pleased at the appearance of the audience. It appeared from almost every countenance that they were full of unbelief — I mean that in regard to my being the person that served in the Revolutionary Army.'[1]

Deborah Gannett sat quietly in her chair, eavesdropping on those who 'swore that I was a lad of not more than 18 years of age,' before she rose to give her speech. Rather than delivering a rousing action-packed tale of battling against the British, she was full of apology for the 'uncouth' actions of her masquerade. Yet even as she justified her 'good intentions of a bad deed' Deborah Gannett acknowledged the subversion it implied. 'I burst the tyrant bonds which held my sex in awe and clandestinely or by stealth, grasped an opportunity which custom and the world seemed to deny, as a natural privilege,' she told her audiences.[2] It was more than soldiering that Deborah Gannett claimed as her 'natural privilege' because wearing breeches, she openly admitted, entitled her to a freedom she had never before experienced.

'A new world now opened to my view,' she declared, 'the objects of which seemed as important as the transition before seemed unnatural.'[3] This was the world of politics, of honourable actions and important deeds that had propelled her 'to elope from the soft sphere' of womanhood. As her friend, the Honourable Peter Force of Washington D.C. wrote of her, 'she conversed with such ease on the subject of theology, on political subjects and military tactics that her manner would seem masculine.'[4] Deborah Gannett's humble apologies anticipated her audience's criticism of her 'demonstrative, illustrative style' and were employed to arouse her listener's sympathy. Like many other female soldiers who publicly declared their motives for enlisting, Deborah Gannett glossed over her early experiments in male clothes thus tailoring her history for audience consumption. In reality the young unmarried Deborah Sampson had first enlisted, 'to have a little frolic and to see how it would seem to put on a man's clothing but chiefly for the purpose of procuring a more ample supply of money.'[5]

While staying with Captain Leonard's family in Middlesborough, Massachusetts in 1782 Deborah borrowed his son Samuel's clothes and enlisted as Timothy Thayer. With the bounty money in hand, Deborah went to a tavern in nearby Four Corners, 'called for spirituous liquors, got excited and behaved herself in a noisy and indecent manner.'[6] Deborah managed to get home safely and the next morning, 'returned to her female employments as if nothing had happened.' However, when spring arrived and Middlesborough's newly enlisted soldiers joined their regiment, Timothy Thayer was missing. Evidence pointed to Deborah as the culprit and she was forced to repay the enlistment money. But she soon left Middlesborough for Bellingham to enlist in the 4th Massachusetts Regiment for three years as Robert Shurtleff. Her many successful exploits in male clothes and her appreciation of trousers which she realized were so much more convenient than dresses, gave her the needed confidence to embark on her venture.

She had an inkling of the public disapproval she might arouse when the First Baptist Church of Middlesborough, hearing of her exploits in the Four

Corners tavern, took action. On 3 September 1782 the congregation considered Deborah Sampson's case and found, 'although she was not convicted, [she] was strongly suspected of being guilty and for some time before behaved very loose and unchristian like.'[7] The church agreed to consider her excommunicated until she returned to Middlesborough to make amends by asking forgiveness for her actions.

Framing her lecture as an apology for 'error and presumption' Deborah avoided accusations that she had proved either morally or physically unfit in the Continental Army. She wore her uniform proudly because she was convinced that her audience would approve her unconventional actions. To the women she expressed, 'my most sincere declaration of friendship for that sex . . . which neither in adversity or prosperity could I ever learn to forget or degrade.'[8] It was a ploy to reassure them that as Robert Shurtleff she had neither exploited her power with other women nor sacrificed her virtue to her fellow soldiers. Deborah Gannett cleverly ended by declaring that 'our Masters' and our Lords' proper spheres are the field and cabinet' and the 'Mistress and Lady' belongs in the kitchen and the parlour.[9]

She watched with great interest the women who came to hear her speak, perhaps aware that she might receive the most violent reactions from those who perceived a challenge to their own identity as wife and mother. In her diary of the 1802 tour she noted: 'I think I may with much candour applaud the people for their serious attention and peculiar respect, especially the ladies.'[10] Her address appealed directly to her female audience with a claim that 'it is only one of my own sex, exposed to the storm, who can conceive of my situation.'[11] She presented her desire to throw off the bonds of domesticity as a universal female experience so that her apology was not for harbouring this desire but for acting upon it.

Her claims to embrace hearth and home, however, belied the circumstances of her own life. Deborah Gannett left her husband Benjamin and three children to look after themselves while she organized the business details of her highly profitable tour. The lectures were a valuable source of income and gave her a public profile that supported her request for an increased military pension. While journeying through New England and New York the minor celebrity visited her former officers including Captain George Webb in Holden and General John Paterson in Lisle. Paterson had become a Judge and served as a federal congress member from 1803 to 1805.

It seems highly probable that her 1802 visit provided an opportunity for Deborah Gannett to request a petition for a pension. When it was eventually granted in 1805 payment was retroactive to 1803, which represented Paterson's first opportunity to submit a request on Gannett's behalf.[12] Despite her protestations to the contrary, this Mistress and Lady had pragmatically ventured from the kitchen and parlour from great necessity and with much skill.

The struggle for financial recognition of her role during the war had begun several years earlier when Deborah petitioned the Massachusetts Legislature. In January 1792 she asked to 'receive pay for her service in the army but being female and not knowing the proper steps to be taken . . . has hitherto not received one farthing.'[13] Her claim was passed to the House of Representatives who granted her $34 stating that:

> Deborah Sampson exhibited an extraordinary instance of female heroism by discharging the duties of a faithful, gallant soldier and at the same time preserving the virtue and chastity of her sex unsuspected and unblemished and was discharged from the service with a fair and honourable character.[14]

On 11 March 1805 she received an additional $4 per month from the Washington, D.C. pension office which was increased to $6.40 per month in 1816.

But Deborah Gannett swore another oath in Washington two years later, relinquishing her invalid pension to receive benefit of a Congressional Act passed March 18, 1818. Increasing her monthly payment to $8, it provided 'for certain persons engaged in the land and naval service of the U.S. in the Revolutionary War.' In 1820 she applied but was denied further aid giving her a retroactive pension between the war's end and January 1803. After her death in 1831 the pensions office again struggled with the peculiarities of Deborah Gannett's case when considering the payment to her heirs. A special act of Congress directed the Treasury to pay $466.66 to her surviving relatives because, 'as there cannot be a parallel case in all time to come the committee do not hesitate to grant relief.'[15] It was much easier for a government to recognize and reward an anomaly rather than the precursor of a trend and the female combatants often exploited this realization.

Records exist of other female soldiers who fought in the American War of Independence including Sally St. Clair who died at the battle of Savannah;

Margaret Corbin, killed at the battle of Fort Washington in November, 1776 and a woman known only as Samuel Gay who served as a corporal in the 1st Massachusetts Regiment and was discharged in August, 1777, 'being a woman dressed in mens clothes.'[16] Since none of these women received a pension they suggest that it was Deborah Gannett's fight for financial recognition rather than her military service that made her unique. By presenting herself as an exception to the 'softer sphere' she succeeded in gaining support, humbly submitting to open discussion of her sexual chastity. She did not advise other women to emulate her but advocated they embrace the domestic confines she had fled. Despite her breeches and musket, Deborah Gannett repented of her erroneous ways while privately savouring her audience's shocked response to her 'male' endeavours.

Her struggle for financial and public recognition never attacked the oppressive social structures that first motivated her to adopt a masculine identity. However, Deborah Gannett's speaking tour in 1802 was laden with the contradictions faced by most retired female combatants. They apologized for their 'unnatural' existence as soldiers, but it was their very sexual ambiguity that attracted audiences and became the platform upon which they based their claim for financial recompense for their military service. Favourable publicity was crucial to their request for a pension since governments and officials were quick to dispute their claims but eager to support a popular heroine. The former combatant balanced the need to convince the world she was both masculine enough to have fought and feminine enough to have no further thoughts of such subversion.

A generation later, Civil War soldier Emma Edmonds who fought in the Grand Army of the Republic, furthered her campaign for financial support by appealing to her former comrades. Although she was unable to attend an 1883 reunion of her 2nd Michigan Infantry Regiment, she complained rather bitterly to her friend Albert E. Cowles that:

> I have thought, of late, since my health has failed me that perhaps it would be no more than right if Uncle Sam should pension one female soldier who has actually served two years, or nearly so — faithful, hard service when he has pensioned so many male effeminates who never smelt powder on a battlefield.[17]

Like Deborah Gannett, Emma realized the importance of presenting herself as a woman who had made a unique contribution to the Republican cause and so she stressed the importance of her *active* service. Ironically, she held those men who did not see direct action, in great contempt, condemning them as 'male effeminates,' and demanded as much recognition for her manly behaviour as for her individual courage.

Her comrades' testimony proved invaluable and Byron M. Cutcheon, a Michigan congressman and former officer, successfully cleared her alias 'Frank Thompson' of a desertion charge that threatened her petition's success. In her autobiography, *Nurse and Spy*, Emma claimed that, wracked with malarial fevers, she left the army with a doctor's certificate of disability. She later confessed that when her request for a medical discharge was denied she simply left rather than risk detection.[18] Her comrades corroborated this by testifying that she served in the 2nd Michigan Infantry regiment for two years without discovery. Although this second statement was patently untrue, as Jerome Robbins' account of his friendship with Frank Thompson revealed [see chapter 3], it was crucial to Emma's credibility. In 1884 Captain William R. Morse supported her claim by stating that, 'She followed through hard-fought battles, never flinched from duty, and was never suspected of being else than what she seemed. . . . The beardless boy was a universal favourite.'[19] General Orlando M. Poe wrote that, 'her sex was not suspected by me or anyone else in the regiment' even though he resigned along with Emma's alleged lover Inspector Reid in April 1863.[20] She recognized the importance of maintaining that her disguise was never disclosed in a letter to her friend Richard Halstead. As her health began to deteriorate Emma used Halstead's testimony to support her request for an increased pension only after he had edited his original claim. 'Just after the statement, "She was my bunk mate considerable of the time" please just add — But I *never knew* she was a woman,' wrote Emma. 'Our lamented General O. M. Poe put those words in his testimony and they turned the scale for my pension.'[21] On November 15, 1897 Halstead received Emma's thanks for the 'correction.'

After her appearance at the 2nd Michigan Regiment's reunion in Flint, Emma became aware that, although now respectably married to carpenter Linus Seelye and a mother of two children, she was still subject to moral scrutiny. Colonel Frederick Schneider noted that even though 'the slender and wiry Frank Thompson of 1863 now appeared as a woman of above medium height and had grown rather stout and fleshy,' rumours about her

possible sexual misconduct in the army still abounded.[22] She wrote to
Halstead from Fort Scott, Kansas on 27 January 1885:

> I was properly punished for going to the reunion — God forgive me for
> going. It has always been the pride of my life that I had ever been a member
> of the beloved 2nd Michigan but I discovered while at Flint that the honour of
> membership has cost me more than I am willing to pay — that of slurs against
> my character.[23]

Whatever 'slurs' Emma had to endure from a suspicious public, the 'unani-
mously and highly eulogistic' testimony of her comrades secured her a pension of $12 per month from 5 July 1884.

Emma Edmonds' first instinct after her retirement from the 2nd Michigan
regiment was to leave her adopted country by working abroad for a foreign
mission. She was perhaps aware that the American people might not understand the years she lived as Frank. She wrote to her friend Jerome Robbins
on May 10, 1863: 'My intention is to go at once into the missionary work,
notwithstanding the protestations of my friends to the contrary. . . . Miss
Lizzie H. wants to go with me on a foreign mission but I must not encourage
her for she is not strong enough.'[24] Emma eventually decided to seek
avenues for her philanthropic work at home that might help to mitigate her
earlier deviance. After the death of her son Linus in 1872, Emma and her
husband were asked to manage an orphanage in Oberlin, Ohio. They stayed
for a few months before moving to Lateche, St. Mary's parish, Louisiana
where they ran 'a coloured orphans' home under the auspices of the
Freedman's Aid society.[25] They remained in Louisiana for three years until
Emma became ill again and the family moved to Fort Scott, Kansas. Her
next venture was to build a home for retired civil war soldiers who were
currently living in county poor houses. The building was to be financed out
of Emma's pension and the scheme was perhaps undertaken in another
attempt to clear her name of any impropriety. However, when her petition
for an increase was several hundred dollars less than expected, she became
disheartened and forgot the project. Her work was characterized by her bold
unconventionality in her search for self-fulfilment and her need for public
approval. She spent the last months of her life rewriting her autobiography
but she died before its completion.

Efforts to generate publicity served the dual function of clearing the former combatant of any improper charges and, since many women were incapacitated by war-related injuries and illness, providing an often vital source of income. Loreta Janeta Velasquez, who served as Confederate Lieutenant Harry T. Buford during the Civil War, supported herself and her son from the proceeds of her memoirs published in 1876.[26] Her story, *Woman in Battle*, was controversial. Jubal Early, a sceptical Southern general, charged that Velasquez's account was full of 'inconsistencies, absurdities and impossibilities,' which he substantiated with compelling evidence. He noted, for example, the impossibility of her claim that in June 1861 she took 'the train bound north' from Columbia, South Carolina to Richmond, Virginia, 'thus filling up the gap in the railroad from Gainsboro, North Carolina to Lynchburg, Virginia.'[27]

Yet more than 40 Southern members of Congress who saw in Velasquez a post-war heroine who still trumpeted the Confederate cause endorsed her story. Early wrote to Southern Congress member, W. F. Slemons, detailing his doubts about its authenticity as a caution against supporting her. Early, who never took an oath of allegiance to the United States of America, believed that Velasquez had fabricated her story but he also objected to its moral tone. If her book was written as fiction, he argued '[it] ought not to be patronized by Southern men or women for it is a libel on both.'[28] He found descriptions of Confederate officers as 'drunken marauding brutes whose mouths are filled with obscene language,' and Velasquez's assertion that women threw themselves into Harry T. Buford's arms 'without waiting to be asked' deeply offensive.[29] Early felt that it was his duty to voice these criticisms of Velasquez since she was 'no true type of Southern woman.' Fearing that Early was 'endeavouring to injure me and my book,' Velasquez defended it as a realistic account of her experiences, although she admitted to writing it from memory 'having lost many of my notes.'[30] Moreover she countered Early's indignation stating that the officer's behaviour was painfully realistic.

That the book had become important to Velasquez was reflected by her refutation of Early's charges. He first heard about the book on a visit to New Orleans from a 'gentleman from Virginia' who had recently travelled with Velasquez. Early skimmed through the volume and pronounced it a fake to the Virginian. When she heard of Early's dismissal of her work, Velasquez turned up in his hotel lobby and demanded to speak with him. 'I subsequently had a brief interview with Madame Velasquez,' he wrote, 'and I thus became satisfied that she had not written the book of which she purported to be the author or that it had been very much changed and influenced in style by her editor.'[31] Velasquez claimed that Early was threatening her livelihood and reputation.

The controversy revealed how vulnerable the female soldier was to criticism but also the substantial rewards that might be reaped by successful promotion. Endorsement by more than 40 Southern politicians undoubtedly aided sales of Velasquez's book and the subsequent 'correspondence with the press' that became her livelihood. Her claims to have served in the Confederate Army were further substantiated by retired officers like James Longstreet, a former Lieutenant-General, who willingly came forward to verify 'that there was a woman in the ranks with us who became Lieutenant and called her name Buford.'[32] Early missed the point in his criticism of *Woman in Battle*; its readers approached it not as an accurate historical documentation of the Civil War but as the adventures of an unusual female. As a result his accusations against Velasquez did little to curb her popularity or to discredit her claims. Menié Muriel Dowie reprinted it in her 1893 collected edition of female adventure stories praising its 'air of truthfulness which comes . . . with very great refreshment to a connoisseur of the elaborated adventure of the average adventurer.'[33] Whatever the official pronouncement of her authenticity, the warrior heroine appealed to an audience willing to believe in her.

Public opinion of the former combatant only became an issue for those women whose identity was disclosed during or after their service. A few pensions were quietly awarded to women under male names. Despite assurances that Emma Edmonds was the only woman to serve in the Grand Army of the Republic, Jennie Hodgers of the 95th Illinois Volunteer Infantry was also awarded a soldier's pension under the name Albert Cashier. Irish-born Hodgers assumed her male identity to enlist during the American Civil War at Belvidere, Illinois on August 6, 1862 and retired from active service three years later. Without her real identity being disclosed she was granted a pension of $70 per month and accumulated an estate of $500. But when adjudged insane in Illinois in 1913, a conservator was appointed to handle her financial affairs. With no known living relatives, several purported heirs came forward but none could be validated.[34] Since Albert Cashier maintained a male identity for the remainder of her life there was no complication in granting her pension. Her guise made her anonymity as important as fame was to her 'feminine' counterparts.

Ironically British sailor and soldier Mary Anne Talbot managed to increase her military pension only by resuming her alias as John Taylor. She too understood the importance of publicizing her cause and in later years depended, 'on the liberality of many noble and generous persons to whom I was necessitated to make my case known.'[35] The tale of her struggle to eke out an existence after her retirement from sea was recorded by her employer and publisher, R. S. Kirby, in 1804. In the introduction to Mary Anne Talbot's account of her adventures, Kirby urged that 'public knowledge of the hardships she had undergone may induce a feeling and liberal public to undertake something for her benefit.'[36] Subscriptions for her relief were sent directly to his house at St. Paul's, London where she worked as a domestic servant.

After a trip to New York aboard an American ship with Captain Field, Mary Anne in her guise as John Taylor, returned to Rotherhithe, on 20 November 1796. She went ashore with her mate John Jones in plain seaman's dress, since the residents of Wapping considered officers 'little better than spies,' but their boat was seized by a press-gang. Mary Anne had left her papers aboard ship, so was forced to reveal her true identity to avoid service. She returned to Captain Field and told him about the discovery. After leaving Rotherhithe, Mary Anne immediately made several applications at the Naval pay office, Somerset House for money due for service in the British navy. It was only after a long and private discussion with naval officials that she was granted a subscription of 12 shillings per week.[37]

Mary Anne's unusual history moved the pay office to find a suitable home for her where the landlady Mrs. Jones was given strict instructions, 'if possible to break me of the masculine habit I was so much used to.' But since Mary Anne insisted frequently on donning her seaman's clothes, Mrs. Jones complained that her charge, 'was bound to masculine propensities more than what became a female such as smoking, drinking grog, etc.'[38] Assuming her male identity was, however, the only way Mary Anne could join her former mess-mates for a drink and protected her from a newly discovered sexual vulnerability. To her, cross-dressing remained a necessity.

Her stay at Shoe Lane was short-lived and she spent the next few years changing addresses that included several months at St. Bartholomew's hospital. The chest and back wounds she suffered during the siege of Valenciennes had reopened because of 'too free use of spiritous liquors.' When her wounds refused to heal she petitioned the Duke of York for a supplement to her pension and several months later Mary Anne received a 'quantity of female apparel' from the Duchess. The clothing may have been a subtle reprimand since she continued to wear her sailor's clothes even in the women's hospital ward, a practice that often shocked visitors to St. Bartholemew's. She insisted that 'having been used to male dress in the defence of my country I thought I was sufficiently entitled to wear the same whenever I thought proper.'[39]

After another seven months in convalescence Mary Anne finally received 'a very handsome present' from the Duke of Norfolk. She applied for funds to Lord Spencer, first Lord of the British Admiralty who gave her a guinea, and served her breakfast at his home.[40] Mary Anne existed on the charity of well-connected friends — neither a stable nor adequate income. Her life was beset by chronic illness and the poverty that plagued most single, working-class women of late eighteenth-century London. Unlike them, however, Mary Anne enjoyed a high public profile and family connections that she could exploit. Its value became evident when she was summoned to call in at Bow Street's Magistrate's court in 1799. A woman, dressed in the uniform of a Light Horseman, stood before the court on a vagrancy charge because she had been presenting herself as Mary Anne's alias John Taylor to solicit wealthy Londoners for money. Justice Bond sentenced the impostor to three months in the House of Correction.[41] The incident revealed the extent of Mary Anne's popularity and the efforts made to protect her. Soon after this episode Lord Morton requested John Taylor's appearance at the War Office to settle the matter of a pension. A half-year's payment of Her Majesty's bounty was handed over to Mary Anne in her sailor's dress.

Even the meagre charity she did receive was influenced by her background. Mary Anne was the illegitimate daughter of the late Lord William Talbot, steward of Her Majesty's household and Colonel of the Glamorganshire Militia. The nobility she solicited may have felt duty-bound to help Talbot's daughter who was cheated out of her inheritance by her corrupt guardian Mr. Sucker and was reduced to working at menial, low-paying jobs. To ensure sympathy for her position she ended her plea for support that Kirby published in 1804 with an apology reminiscent of Deborah Gannett. 'Nothing but troubles and misfortunes for the last two years of my life have occurred,' she wrote, 'I have only to apologize to my readers for any deviation from the paths of propriety.'[42] But just as Deborah Gannett wore her uniform and revelled in her audience's discomfort, Mary Anne too was unapologetic about her forays in male dress.

She worked for Kirby for the next three years until her health forced her to resign. An acquaintance offered her a home in Shropshire in December 1807 where she died two months later on 4 February 1808, at the age of 30. The following year Kirby reprinted her story adding a postscript to assure readers that beneath her sailor's clothes beat a very female heart:

> It has been remarked that females who have assumed the male character have in general renounced with their sex the virtues which distinguish it, and with the dress and manners of the others, have adopted only its vices. . . . In the subject of these pages, if long habits of association had blighted the delicacy and modesty which are such ornaments to a female she had nevertheless contracted (if however, she did not possess from nature) all that blunt generosity of spirit and good nature peculiar to British seamen. . . . She retained notwithstanding her long metamorphosis, much of the sensibility of her sex; and to a friend or acquaintance she was ever willing when able to render either pecuniary assistance or personal service.[43]

There are contradictions in Kirby's testimony to his long acquaintance with Mary Anne. The courage of her 'metamorphosis' could only be applauded if her 'feminine' characteristics of duty and service were made equally evident to readers. And along with a generation of sailors who fought during the Napoleonic wars, Mary Anne's real sacrifice — her health, youth and identity — were never fully rewarded or acknowledged. Her gender added another, vastly complicating dimension to the retired seaman's struggle for survival since better-paying male jobs remained closed to her and she refused marriage, cohabitation or prostitution as an economic alternative.

Without the advantage of Mary Anne's noble connections, some former combatants were compelled to press their claims more forcefully. Christian Davies used a variety of means to solicit money from officers when she returned to London at the end of Marlborough's campaigns in 1712. She visited the Duke to persuade him to provide compensation for her as a widow of two soldiers and for her own military service, but was refused. However, when she informed him that was she was living in a 'house of civil conversation' — a brothel — he invited her to dinner. According to Wilson's original account of Christian Davies' story, after an evening where they 'ripped up old stories and were as merry as so many new-paid-off sailors,' she left Marlborough's house with a petition drawn up for Queen Anne, swearing to her twelve year's service in Orkney's regiment.[44]

In her best clothes, Christian Davies knelt before the Queen to present her petition. She received it 'with a smile and helping me up said it should be up to her to provide for me and perceiving me with child added, "if you are delivered of a boy I will give him a commission as soon as he is born."'[45] Although Christian gave birth to a daughter she was granted £50 and a shilling a day for life. She further supplemented this income by gently reminding other members of the English nobility of her part in Marlborough's campaigns. While guarding the King's tent at an army encampment in Hyde Park, she collected several guineas from officers she solicited for funds. Without this she 'must have either perished or gone upon the parish.'[46] In her later years Christian Davies set up a public house in Paddington but still counted on the support of well-placed friends. Unlike her male counterparts she faced the added burden of having to justify her right to financial recognition for her military service. Two ex-soldiers that Christian met *en route* to the Chelsea College Board reacted violently when they learned she was requesting an increased pension. One of them shouted that she had 'never done anything for the government' thus provoking a fight in which she deftly cracked a wooden plank over her attacker's head.[47]

The last 25 years of her life were plagued by poverty, obscurity and illness. The Dublin pub that she left in 1692 to pursue her husband had been taken over by a stranger and Christian could not afford a lawyer to reclaim her property. When she returned in 1712 she also learned that her eldest child had died and the youngest was in a workhouse. In Ireland she set up a pub and pie house where she met and married a soldier named Davies. She bought his discharge but two days later after a drinking binge, he re-enlisted and she returned to England to wait for him. Christian then used her influence to have her husband admitted to the Pensioners' College at Chelsea as a guard. She lived there with him, suffering from dropsy, rheumatism, scurvy, and various other ailments before she caught a fever and died on 7 July 1739.[48] As she was lowered into the Chelsea Burying Ground three grand volleys were fired over her grave.

If neither family nor upper-class friends could be called upon for help, any assistance a former combatant received depended entirely upon circumstance. Phoebe Hessel, who served as a private soldier in the English Third Regiment of Foot in the War of Austrian Succession (1740-48), was only granted a pension when she attracted the attention of George IV, then Prince Regent, on a Royal visit to Brighton in 1817. The Prince noticed her selling fruit and gingerbread on the steps of a lodging house near the main road. When he learned that she had fought the Spanish during the British siege of Gibraltar and at Montserrat, the Prince awarded her a half guinea a week and more if she needed it.[49] According to a contemporary account, Phoebe Hessel was assisted by the parish in 1792, 1797, 1806 and was 'admitted into the workhouse but her spirit was uneasy in such a situation.'[50] The small pension enabled her to continue living independently until she lost the use of her legs and in the confines of her bed relived her days as a man, impatiently awaiting death. When she recalled her years spent as a soldier, she echoed a familiar refrain lamenting, 'the error of her former ways.'[51]

There was often a yawning discrepancy between the popular perception of the warrior heroines and the mean reality of their later lives, as Christian Davies' and Phoebe Hessel's stories testify. Along with Mary Anne Talbot, Hannah Snell enjoyed initial recognition as a public figure. She performed on the stage at Sadlers Wells; her portrait was painted by J. Faber, R. Phelps and J. Wardell in 1750 and by J. Johnson and J. Young in 1789; her biography, published by Richard Walker in 1750 was sold on the streets of Amsterdam and only a few days after her retirement from the British Navy she was granted a pension of £30 per year for life.[52] Although Hannah Snell exploited her rapid rise to fame by opening a successful public house in Wapping, little was known about her death in 1792.

She had originally gone to sea in 1745 to search for her husband, a Dutch sailor named James Summs, who abandoned Hannah when she was six months pregnant. While working aboard a British naval sloop of war, the

Swallow, under Captain Rosier in the East Indies, she learned from another sailor that John Summs had been hanged for murder on a Dutch vessel. The first publication of her story in 1750 informed readers that after her unhappy marriage she was 'resolutely bent to be lord and master of herself and never more to entertain the least thoughts of having a husband to rule and govern her and make her truckle to his wayward humour.'[53] However, Hannah married carpenter Samuel Eyles in November 1759 at Newbury, Berkshire and had a son by him. According to Reverend Daniel Lyson's *Environs of London* she continued to have some public following since, 'a lady of fortune who admired the heroism and eccentricity of her conduct, having honoured her with particular notice, became godmother to her son and contributed liberally to his education.'[54]

After Samuel Eyles' death Hannah wed a third husband, Richard Habgood, at Welford in 1772 and 14 years later her pension was raised by a special grant to a shilling a day. She became insane and was admitted to Bethlehem hospital in 1789 where she died three years later.[55] A desire for the economic security that always eluded Mary Anne Talbot may have provoked her to remarry after her initial declaration of independence. Did any connection exist between Hannah Snell's insanity and her retirement from the British navy forty years earlier? Certainly her transition back to womanhood was not a peaceful one. Many former female combatants and women who cross-dressed in other male occupations, never accepted the lowered status that accompanied their resumption of female dress. Some led a dual life, venturing forth in their breeches armed with a male name to maintain their connection with the masculine world. But for others, old age or illness made the maintenance of another identity impossible and they were forced back into a social position abandoned so long ago.

The consequences could be devastating. After former infantryman Albert Cashier was admitted to the East Maline State Hospital in Watertown, Illinois and coerced into wearing dresses, her condition deteriorated rapidly. After three years active military service she continued to live as Albert, working as a gardener and handyman in Livingston County even after a doctor discovered her identity in 1911. When she became seriously ill Albert was taken to the Soldier and Sailor's home in Quincy where the physicians and administrators agreed to keep her secret. However, she became increasingly mentally disturbed and was transferred to Watertown where, for the first time in more than 42 years, she was forced to wear women's clothes. She died six months later on 10 October 1915.[56]

Like all old soldiers, many of the women who fought in the dubious battle for King and Country soon faded from public sight. But unlike their male contemporaries, once they resumed a female identity, these women were barred from the male society that could have eased their transition back to civilian life. Coming home to the 'softer sphere of womanhood' could be the most brutally isolating experience because there was often no comforting companionship and little public recognition beyond their value as curiosities. Even the intense friendships formed with fellow soldiers in the heat of battle vanished when the larger world intruded and men suddenly became conscious that their mate was not, after all, one of them. When Flora Sandes left the Serbian Army after its demobilization in 1922, her painful metamorphosis back into womanhood unalterably changed her relationships. '[It] lost me all my old pals,' she wrote in 1927:

> Though still quite friendly they were now quite different. Never again could it be quite the same. As long as I had occasion to notice, men are never quite so naturally themselves where there are women present, as when among themselves. Formerly they had been so used to me that I did not count.[57]

It was not that Flora Sandes had not counted, but that her 'femininity' had been unobtrusive. Without her uniform, however, plucked out of a military environment, her comrades were suddenly highly conscious of her female presence.

It was more than seven years since Flora Sandes had first haphazardly enlisted with the second regiment during the Serbian Army's retreat into Albania. According to her friend Dr. Katherine MacPhail, after the war Flora became a familiar sight in Belgrade, 'marching with her soldiers through the streets in the early morning and drilling them at the barracks in the fortress.'[58] Despite her reputation — her Belgrade home was full of visitors paying homage — her colleagues were disconcerted by Flora in women's clothes and could no longer treat her as an equal. When she visited her former commanding officer in Southern Serbia, he threw up his hands in horror when Flora appeared on his doorstep in a newly-purchased hat and dress. He ordered his wife to run upstairs to find an old uniform for Flora to wear; he insisted she be properly attired before they could talk. 'He didn't know where he was with me,' wrote Sandes, 'nor how to talk to me.'[59]

Once deprived of her masculine identity, the return to femininity launched some women on a relentless pursuit for an intangible replacement. Some found comfort in their roles as wife and mother, forgetting the horrors of war in the peace of domestic life. But for others the brief foray into the male world created an unquenchable thirst for an active life imbued with more meaning than the responsibilities of home, children and marriage. Flora Sandes wrote that the legacy of her life in the Serbian army was 'a permanent incapacity to settle down to anything.'[60] In 1927 she married a fellow officer, Yurie Yudenitch, a Russian and former White Army General, but her restlessness continued unabated. Although she remained a regular member of the Reserve Officers and Soldiers, her retirement from active service spurred her to take up new challenges. In 1924 she was granted a speed boat licence; she wrote a second autobiography and moved temporarily to Paris where she and Yurie purchased Belgrade's first taxi. Flora worked as a matron to a dancing troupe, the John Tiller girls, before her return to Yugoslavia where she supplemented her military pension by teaching English lessons.[61]

There was no role for her within the post-war government equivalent to the years she spent fundraising for the Serbian cause and working as an unofficial ambassador. Even before her retirement from active service, however, Flora had to fight attempts to overlook her military record. In April 1919 when the army's list of promotions was issued, raising all sergeant-majors to second lieutenants, Flora's name was not among them. There had never been a woman or a foreigner made an officer in the Serbian army so after protests to her commanding officer, her rank had to be commissioned by a special Act of Parliament and passed by the Skupshtina.[62] On her first public appearance, she marched with her company through Belgrade's streets lined with residents shouting, 'Bravo Sandes' while a windowful of girls sarcastically sprinkled the Lieutenant with rose petals.[63] On 11 September 1926 she was promoted to Captain.

Flora found 'becoming a woman' again extremely difficult. As she walked through Belgrade after demobilization in 1922, she kept her hand clenched to prevent the embarrassment of automatically saluting or removing her hat when entering a restaurant or a house. The passivity that automatically accompanied her resumption of 'femininity' made her grit her teeth with frustration. She had grown comfortable with giving orders to men and having her authority respected. Now she was expected to wait for male companions to make decisions for her. 'It was impossible at first,' she wrote, '. . . to wait till I was asked instead of saying, "Come along, where shall we go to-night?"'[64] Flora had experienced equality in the Serbian army even within the military's social and sexual hierarchy that she respected. She was accepted as an individual who posed no fundamental ideological challenge because she signalled no continuing challenge to the military's structure. Upon her retirement Flora Sandes relinquished her claims to the male world without protest but she mourned her loss for the rest of her life.

Cut off from her companions, deprived of an identity that had shaped her life for seven years and raised her to the level of an international heroine, Flora Sandes grew nostalgic about the war. She inadvertently romanticized the horror that was the context for the warmth and friendship she so vividly experienced. Intimately tied to these memories was a sense that Flora Sandes was literally another person, a man, during those years in the army. As she wrote in 1927:

> Sometimes now, when playing family bridge for threepence a hundred in an English drawing-room, the memory of those wild, jolly nights comes over me and I am lost in another world. So far away it all seems now that I wonder whether it was really myself, or only something I dreamed. Instead of the powdered nose of my partner I seem to be looking at the grizzled head and unshaven chin of the Commandant, and the scented drawing-room suddenly fades away into the stone walls of a tiny hut lighted by a couple of candles stuck into bottles and thick with tobacco smoke, where five or six officers and I sit crowded on bunks or camp stools. . . . I return to the prosaic drawing-room with a start, and the realization that I am a "lady" now and not a "soldier and a man."[65]

Life as a 'lady' had never appealed to Flora Sandes who had so longed for the independence she found in Serbia during the war. According to her niece Betty Russell, Flora was always most comfortable adopting the pose of her army days — sitting with a cigarette in one hand, a drink in the other and her knees planted firmly apart. As she grew into old age she quietly accepted the frustration that accompanied her awkward status.

Flora Sandes was once again called up for service in the Yugoslav army before the bombing of Belgrade in April 1941, even though her previous war injuries had left her permanently disabled. She and her husband Yurie were briefly interned under the German occupation and were forced to report regularly to the Gestapo. Before her release Flora was forced to sign a paper saying, 'I would not speak to anyone but Serbs, nor receive letters (must show them to the Gestapo) nor say anything to offend Germany.'[66] Yurie returned home the same day but was extremely ill and died two months later with Flora by his side. She wrote in her diary: 'At 1:30 heard a little gasp and then a sound — the death rattle — rushed to Yurie but it was all over. Yurie had died in his sleep. Could not believe it and spoke to him frantically but no heartbeat and no pulse.'[67] Flora returned to England via Italy, Palestine and South Africa in August 1946 with the help of the British Adriatic Mission and retired to a cottage in Suffolk, a few miles from Marlsford Rectory where her father once ministered.[68] Her mobility restricted, Flora travelled round the country lanes of her childhood in an electric car and settled into a life that she described as, 'very safe but not very exciting!'[69] In a more direct moment she revealed: 'I hate old age and retirement. I'm bored to tears. I missed soldiering — I loved it.'[70]

More than other retired soldiers perhaps, Flora was still plagued by the contradictions of her situation. When the Salonika Reunion Association organized their annual parade in 1950, Flora was not sure where she should march. 'I'm wondering where I'll stand as I can't, of course, go with the men and I don't belong to the nursing sisters and I don't know anyone,' she wrote, firmly convinced that none of her former comrades would remember her since she was now, 'a very old lady not a bit like the Sergeant you knew.'[71] Flora walked with the nurses in a skirt but displayed her medals on her chest and afterwards 'had a jolly good chinwag' with her male contemporaries.

Did she miss soldiering or did she long for the social privileges of men that the military granted her? To Flora Sandes they were one and the same. Hers was never a struggle against the ideals that forced her back into a dull and uninspiring female life. Rather she continued to identify herself most strongly, although privately, as a retired soldier for whom peace lacked the passion of warfare. Among her papers in her Suffolk cottage, Flora kept a article by J. G. Lucas entitled, 'Nostalgia for War,' its most relevant passages underlined in black ink. 'You don't forget learning in war that a man could love the other more than himself,' wrote Lucas, 'I didn't know that kind of living before I went to war. I haven't known it since. I miss it. The absence of it, the brutal contradiction of it in peace makes it harder to forget.'[72] These, however, were private considerations and according to a close family friend, Flora Sandes rarely talked about her war experiences.[73]

What had proved most difficult, was an attempt to create a life devoid of the constraints she had abandoned in August 1914. Her war injuries — she received a comfortable income of 300 dinars per month as a disability pension from the Yugoslav government— severely limited her options.[74] Perhaps post-war English society could have offered her more but Flora Sandes remained committed to the country that was her escape and where she had redefined herself. Jenny Merkus, who had also fled from the restrictions that a single 'lady' faced in late nineteenth-century European society, only returned home to the Netherlands in old age. She had served in the Serbian Army in 1876 and dedicated much of her life to philanthropic work in Jerusalem. Like Flora Sandes, she brought little of her other life back home with her. A cousin's childhood memories of her were that, 'She was thin, of medium height with short grey hair, a sort of raincoat and a cigar! . . . I do not believe she ever told anything about her experiences.'[75]

When necessity no longer required the former combatant to publicize her case, many sought the troubled peace of anonymity. Russian soldier Marina Yurlova who published her memoirs of life in the Tsar's Army in 1934, carefully veiled any references to her current circumstances. She ended her story looking out from the deck of a ship leaving Vladivostock in 1919 bound for Japan. Only in a follow-up to the success of *Cossack Girl*, her original autobiography, did Marina Yurlova disclose that she left Japan for the United States with a one-year residents' permit in hand.[76] Red Cross nurse Florence Farmborough met Maria Bochkareva, leader of the Russian Women's Battalion, aboard an American ship destined for San Francisco in 1918. 'She has eluded the spy-net of the Red Guards and is making good her escape to the US,' wrote Farmborough.[77] According to the journalist, Rheta Childe Dorr, Bochkareva published her memoirs in 1919, 'dazzled by the lure of money she was to receive from her story dictated to a well-known magazine writer,' and then faded into obscurity.[78] Dorothy Lawrence's short-lived career with a British Expeditionary Force tunnelling company had an equally strange epilogue. On the ship going home after her two week stint at the

Western Front in 1915, Lawrence claimed to have met Emmeline Pankhurst and another prominent suffragette who invited her to speak at a forthcoming meeting. Lawrence was, however, forced to decline since the Defence of the Realm Act prevented her from speaking or writing about her experience.[79]

Lawrence eventually published an account of her enlistment and detection in 1919. But even as Lawrence and other female soldier's stories continued to intrigue audiences, the era when this heroine's sexual ambiguity could be playfully questioned was drawing to a close. During the post-war period, psychologists' new theories about sexual inversion fed into a backlash against women's newly acquired power. For the first time in the history of the literature, homosexuality became a serious concern. Women who coveted 'masculine' jobs and clothes were considered to suffer from an inappropriate attraction to behaviour that rightly belonged to the opposite sex. By the 1920s another cross-gender figure, the writer, Radclyffe Hall, had also gained a new public prominence. To Radclyffe Hall and other feminists wearing male clothing symbolized assertiveness, modernity and sexual freedom. And it was sexual freedom that was both the cutting edge of modernity and lay at the heart of post-war concerns about women's real emancipation.[80]

The feminists wanted not simply entry into male professions but access to the broader world of male opportunity. The war proved that women could undertake 'male' jobs and so the potential for challenging perceived understandings of sexual difference existed. Greater numbers of women enjoyed opportunities to function autonomously, outside their family or husbands' control and many experienced their first financial independence. This was, however, unlike the experiences of Flora Sandes, Maria Bochkareva or other female soldiers, seen as a threat. Attempts to cope with the consequences of the war reinforced the way in which sexuality became an issue of social control for women. The female soldiers, the only women aside from nurses, who had direct battle experience, were recast as deviants in post-war psychological analysis. Desire for a male lifestyle became conflated with homosexual impulses as psychologists actively participated in the reconstruction of sexual concepts. During the war the combatants represented a strikingly different female image even if their perceived lack of sexuality denied their absolute adoption of masculinity.

Although earlier psychologists noted in case studies of female transvestites from 1910 a particular desire to emulate the masculine occupation par excellence, the analysis of gender confusion began to take on new meaning. In 1934, the German psychologist, Magnus Hirschfeld, President of the World League for Sexual Reform, and others identified a woman's desire to enter the military as a sign of transvestism, homosexuality or even sadism. Moreover, they contended that women whose 'psychic attitude' was masculine often had a yearning for the soldier's life. The sexologist, Richard Von Krafft-Ebing, defined women's aspirations to 'male' occupations and gender-crossing as signs of lesbianism. The most masculine were the most deviant although he acknowledged, 'the consciousness of being a woman and deprived of the gay college life, or to be barred from a military career produces painful reflections.'[81] Yet to pursue masculine inclinations, he added, could reflect a congenital form of psychic disorder.

But how could distinctions be drawn between women who had longed to escape from the restrictions of their sex and those who coveted a 'masculine' identity? Particularly for those who experienced a new-found autonomy during the war, the lack of any alternative to domesticity after 1918 reinforced a belief that only by imitating male behaviour could a woman break free. The psychologists believed the answer to understanding this female frustration lay in her sexual identity and so turned their attention to the female combatants.

Krafft-Ebing's path-breaking book, *Psychopathia Sexualis*, first published in 1886, cited several cases of women suffering from 'congenital antipathic sexual instinct.' They preferred playing soldiers to playing with dolls, neglected their toilet and substituted their love for art in the pursuit of science. Krafft-Ebing described his patients as women 'with the masculine soul heaving in the female bosom.'[82] He noted in his study of Miss N. that even in earliest childhood she preferred playing games with other boys. Provoked by a desire to roam the world, Miss O., aged 23, ran away from home dressed in male disguise. C.R., a maid servant, had an inclination for boys' games and loved to hear shooting and would gladly have gone as a soldier. 'She knew,' wrote Krafft-Ebing, 'very well that all of this inclination was unwomanly but she could not help it.'[83] W., a char-woman, 'bewailed the fact that she was not born a man, as she hated feminine things and dress and would much rather have been a soldier.' Krafft-Ebing added that W. preferred cigars to sweetmeats. All of his patients were conscious of their sexual desires for other women which, he believed, were manifested in their masculine pursuits and male clothes. He labelled all the women's conflicts about their identity as examples of sexual inversion.

But it was Magnus Hirschfeld, whose work influenced Britain's sex reform movement, who was credited with the first in-depth study of female cross-dressing. Although Hirschfeld did not contradict the assumption in Krafft-Ebing's analysis that transvestites suffered from confusion about their identity, he believed the war had sexually freed both heterosexual and lesbian women. As part of the erotic enlightenment movement and as the World League's President, he argued against forces that perpetuated sexual repression. Women's economic independence and assumption of masculine roles during the war, he said, led to their social and political equality and sexual emancipation.

Despite his acknowledgement of the restrictions women faced, the desire to wear masculine clothes and to enter a male occupation were still equated with sexual confusion. Those who suffered most from this confusion were the female combatants. He wrote in 1934:

> Women who feel an uncontrollable urge and compulsion to put on masculine clothes and to practice a masculine calling and all other members of the weaker sex whose whole psychic attitude is masculine obviously will have a particular predilection for the soldier's life which has always been regarded as the masculine occupation par excellence. It is understandable then that such women, when the opportunity is offered will seize it gladly and largely devote themselves to active warfare. We must not . . . overlook the suspicion that in certain cases, the predominant motive was a sadistic one.[84]

Thus Hirschfeld introduced his work on female soldiers adding that, 'we shall certainly not be wrong in assuming that in a great number of these cases we are dealing with transvestical and homosexual impulses.' The examples quoted included Zoya Smirnova, Maria Bochkareva and Flora Sandes, among others. He even noted the story of Clara B. of Insterburg who joined the army because she was unable to find work owing to the military campaign in East Prussia. Hirschfeld speculated that this was not the first time that erroneous sex determination, 'a concept unknown before our generation,' lead women into battle. But the use of earlier case studies confirmed Hischfeld's view that all women who longed for 'the glorious independence of masculinity' were female transvestites.

The symbolic importance of wearing male clothes in defining a lesbian identity in the 1920s lent credence to Hirschfeld's argument. The adoption of a male guise had operated as an alternative to marriage and spinsterhood until this period. The psychologists, however, found it impossible to separate the quest for sexual identity from other motives women might have for assuming a man's name and clothes. That some of the female soldiers were lesbian is certain. But the powerful and enduring fantasy of 'going for a soldier' suggested that only by rejecting their femininity completely could many women imagine their independence. In many historical periods the warrior heroine presented women with a rare, even if imaginary, alternative to a circumscribed life.

The psychologists' redefinition of cross-dressing irrevocably changed the popular understanding of the female heroine who changed her identity for pragmatic or patriotic reasons. Rather than finding these women amusing, shocking or politically threatening, contemporary audiences increasingly regarded them with clinical suspicion and confusion. Newspapers still reported cases of adventurous women escaping from home in men's trousers and former combatants continued to write and publish memoirs that were eagerly snapped up. But while the female warrior heroine still drew crowds to music halls and carnival shows in the post-war period, a change was in the air.

Just at the close of the Great War, a Liverpool newspaper warned of the perils that 'romantic maidens' could fall into by pursuing adventures in male clothes. Potential 'jolly Jack Tars' and their mothers were reminded of the horrors that awaited those foolhardy females who stowed away aboard ships. The modern female tar was seen as vulnerable to sexual molestation and in need of protection rather than sexually assertive. The threat of attack was used to dissuade her from such adventures, a warning that echoed the wartime concerns about the hazards of women working with men in 'masculine' occupations. The Liverpool special investigator wrote of four recent cases of female stowaways:

> The war has bred a new spirit amongst the rising generation. It is full of glorious adventure. . . . Women were imitators ever and the history of all nations knows how women have emulated men not alone in deeds of valour but in personal habits and ideals. . . . But there is one direction in which woman's desire has been checkmated. She would have fought on the battlefield and

was not allowed to, although she managed to get to the fringe. . . . She has
imbibed the spirit of our own gallant masculine youth and she is clamouring
for an outlet for the newly-inherited spirit of adventure.[85]

Aside from the real hazard that sexual molestation posed to women every-
where, this concern was a warning to stay away from the male territory of
the battlefield or ship. The war, according to this report, had awakened in
women a dangerous desire for 'masculine' occupations and behaviour.

One of the arrests in Liverpool of female stowaways was that of a young
war widow who had served four years as a transport driver. Once demobilized she echoed Flora Sandes' frustration with the mundane alternatives
offered her. The former driver, 'could not settle again to domesticity, she
pined for adventure [and] she too rigged herself in trousers' and boarded an
American ship. When she was arrested she pleaded, 'I did not mean any
harm. It was just bravado and a bit of fun.'[86] But it was clearly more than a
'bit of fun' that provoked her to escape from what she saw as an enforced
return to femininity and to try a short-cut back to the rewards she had experienced in a 'masculine' job.

A sympathetic magistrate interviewed about this phenomenon acknowledged the constraints against which the female stowaways were obviously
fighting. 'The trouble is, these girls want an outlet for their enthusiasm,' he
was quoted as saying. 'They want freedom from restraint, the opportunity to
enjoy life and not to be compelled to spend their days in a band-box tied up
with pink ribbons. They want to come out and be in touch with realities.'[87]
Since alternatives to 'pink-ribbons' were still in short supply, women continued to register their individual protest by claiming male privileges for themselves. In 1931, Percival Christopher Wren, author of several novels about
the French Foreign Legion, published the edited diary of an English woman
he named Mary Ambree who served as a legionnaire for five years. To substantiate his claim, he cited the recent example of the Legion's reintroduction
of a bathing parade to determine whether a woman was serving in the
ranks.[88] Although reviewers proclaimed Wren's book a novel, it was considered of outstanding merit because its author, 'while always making Mary
play the man, [Wren] never forgets she is a woman.'[89] Princess
Dadeshkeliani's memoirs, *Princess in Uniform*, received equal attention and was
praised because the writer was considered 'neither . . . a virago, an amazon,

a "male impersonator", a feminist or a player of any part for which the label suggests itself.'[90] By 1937, Valerie Arkell-Smith, released after a nine-month sentence for fraud in connection with her marriage to another woman after disguising herself as a British army officer for six years, attracted spectacular crowds to her show as 'Colonel Barker' on the Blackpool marquee. Female sailor stowaways, women in the French Foreign Legion and masquerading British officers were still the stuff of popular fantasy. But as they had in every previous age, the meaning of their exploits had undergone a significant shift.

On an autumn night, fine and cold after a sudden rain, a couple of middle-aged women stand, teasing each other outside a garish seaside marquee that reads, 'On a Strange Honeymoon? Love calling, Colonel Barker, admission two pence.' A large woman giggles behind her hand and chides her friend standing next to her, 'Ere's Colonel Barker, your old friend. You'd better go and see how she's getting along.' Her friend laughs uproariously. A group of young girls stand in a defiant gang, and looking up at the sign one of them comments, 'Ay, I'm not going in there — make me blush it would.' An older woman, in her sixties, says to herself, 'Ee, isn't it a sensation!'[91] During that season, thousands of people paid to walk around a pit and glimpse down at a couple — Colonel Barker in red pyjamas and her 'bride' in a nightgown — lying in single beds. A Belisha beacon and a taped on cross-walk divided the floor between them and, according to the marquee, the couple promised not to touch each other or leave their cage until the Blackpool season ended.

Billed as 'the most famous intersexual character of our time,' the popularity of 'Colonel Barker's' seaside show drew a complex web of reactions from her mainly working-class patrons in 1937. The admission of her lesbian relationship with Elfrida Haward at her highly-publicized 1929 trial, lent the Colonel an aura of illicit eroticism. It was rumoured that her bride, Eva, was 'one of those women who like women,' and the couple were treated as curiosities. The landlady of the doss house where they had lived together said of 'Colonel Barker': 'He can be a man one minute and then be a woman. Christ knows how he does it. They should lock up that sort of person, they're no use to anybody.'[92] Claims that the Colonel was actually a transvestite and 'the first person in the world to have the now famous operation changing her sex from that of a man to a woman,' further complicated matters.[93]

Ultimately 'Colonel Barker's' appearance at Blackpool signified a renewed sexual repression rather than Hirschfeld's optimistic view of post-war liberation. It was little more than a freak show, devoid even of the praise that earlier women with legitimate military records were afforded. Since 'Colonel Barker' had never actually served in the ranks, her adoption of the female warrior heroine's mantle rang hollow to her audience. Her stark admittance of the sexual and economic advantages her uniform afforded her, lacked the comforting illusion used by her real-life counterparts. She also lacked the innocence that music hall singers like Vesta Tilley brought to their mocking portraits of men in uniform.[94] In Blackpool the enduring fantasy was perpetuated at its most naked and exploitative level.

Elsewhere during the 1930s, the conflation between women taking up arms and breaking down the barriers of sexual repression continued to dominate the popular imagination. Travel writer Rosita Forbes who, 'became a torch of inspiration for the women of those post-war years, now emancipated in large measure, were still but gingerly feeling their way along the paths trodden heretofore only by men,' took up the female sol-dier's cause.[95] To assume the quintessential masculine profession, seemed the most vivid realization of equality to Forbes who followed the burgeon-ing of women's military involvement in her weekly magazine. An article on Chinese women entitled, 'From Lily Foot to Army Boot,' identified the army as a great liberating force. 'Typical of China before her reawakening in the twentieth century were the bound feet of womenfolk,' she wrote. 'Contrast with this the feet of members of a Red Cross Detachment in boots of military pattern.'[96] Young women and girls, happily displayed their ranks in Spain's Republican militia. The female members of the Japanese Patriotic Association were shown practicing firing guns at aeroplanes, a Somaliland woman shouldered a gun across her naked chest and modern Turkish women at the University of Ankara were reported to 'have taken quickly and with eagerness to the modern idea of uniforms.'[97]

Revolutionaries and fascists were thrown together under Forbes' catego-ry of those who trod new paths to freedom even though she realized the fragile promise of equality that women's military involvement held out. Underlying the image of the woman with a gun was the illusion that her ser-vice would entitle her to power and a political voice. Forbes became trans-fixed by the story of Halide Edib, a heroine of Kemal Ataturk's revolution told to her by a group of women at a raki party in Turkey. Once someone mentioned Halide's name, 'it seemed to me a match was put to straw,' wrote Forbes. 'I saw the sparks reflected in eyes accustomed to patience and in others, younger, where resentment struggled with frustration. Hard and purposeful they told me the story of the woman who played Joan of Arc to Kemal's version of the Dauphin.'[98]

Halide had ventured from the harem to work in secret for the Committee of Union and Progress designed to overthrow the last Ottoman Sultan. She spoke out in public about freedom of speech and movement to enormous crowds in Istanbul, addressed revolutionary meetings in attics and alleys but was soon arrested. To escape she threw herself into the Bosphorous, the waterway that divides the continents of Europe and Asia, was picked up by a fishing boat and found her way to Ataturk's headquarters. She fought at the head of a Turkish battalion and as a reward for her service she extracted a promise from Ataturk that the women of Turkey should be free. '"The equal of men," she said having done a man's job.'[99] But when Halide became her country's first minister of education and attempted to liberate women from the veil, she met with violent opposition to Turkey's president. Her political opposition forced her to flee to America.

Halide's commitment to liberating women from the bonds against which she fought so vigorously made her a heroine to Forbes and her Turkish companions. Her story vividly captures some of the disparate elements in an issue, teeming with contradictions. When Halide was rewarded for her military service with a position in Ataturk's government her power to affect a real sexual revolution was quickly curtailed. Most female combatants never reached Halide's level of awareness but rather embraced their position as exceptions who posed no threat to the military structures in which they lived and worked. For centuries the female warrior heroine lived as a popular figure of emancipation, without any ability to transform the lives of other women. It was a momentary, deeply-felt rebellion that could reach out to other women only through their imaginations, compelling them to rethink their own lives.

The female warrior of heroic stories, who managed to act out her long, secret desire, remains a powerful symbol of unconventional womanhood. Although we too readily divorce her from the real horrors of war, it is her ability to transform her circumstances that holds our fascination. In 1941,

Mrs. Carrie Glover, a housewife in Virginia, sang a version of a nineteenth-century English ballad about a young woman named Flora, who follows her lover James to sea, works for five years aboard ship, and wins the respect of all the crew. The ballad has all the elements that so boldly challenged conventional assumptions of femininity; Flora is granted equality, admiration and freedom from the anxiety and drudgery of staying at home. She matches the men in her physical strength and befriends those who would, in another context, have acted as her superior. In an interview Mrs. Grover reflected on whether she ever fantasized about emulating this heroine's example. Did she ever daydream about being this kind of woman sailor, running off, carefree and in love with a lover-companion? 'I sure did,' she replied. 'I had daydreams about a good many of those songs. . . . I imagine things like this happened in days gone by . . . but now they've got laws so they couldn't get away with it.'[100] Even now, compassionate, vividly individual women are rare and we still dream of breaking laws and disrupting the oppressive order of our lives. Even now women dream of gaining equality and of sailing away into a new land of liberty and peace.

*Jenny Merkus, soldier in the Bosnian uprising against Turkish rule, and soldier in the Serbian army, 1876. (*Collection Koopstra, Algemeen Ryksarchief, The Hague*.)

Below left Sarah Emma Edmonds as a field nurse during the Civil War. (*Clarke Historical Library*.)

Below right During her public-speaking tours Flora Sandes handed out and signed postcards for the soldiers, and civilian crowds who came to hear her lectures. (*Flora Sandes Collection, Sudbourne, Suffolk*.)

Above left The Invincible Brigade or the Female Cavalry, a popular performance at Astley's theatre that used the image of the female warrior heroine, in 1802. (*Trustees of the Victoria and Albert Museum.*)

Above right Mary Anne Talbot, unhappily back in women's clothing after her discovery but still sporting a man's top hat and depicted with bulging forearms, 1804. (*The British Library.*)

Left Jane Horton, aged 19, Kirkless Hall Pits, Middle Patiscroft, Wigan, formerly a factory girl. This female miner in trousers photographed by writer A.J. Murphy typifies the yawning gap between upper and working-class images of Victorian women. As Munby's comment indicates, Jane Horton felt she had more freedom working in what was deemed a 'masculine' occupation, wearing trousers, than in the feminine confines of skirts. During the same period Munby spoke with another pit woman, a former kitchen maid at the Victoria Hotel, Southport who left service to become a collier in September 1865. She told him of another maid who had taken to mining for the same reasons. (*From the Munby Papers, reproduced by kind permission of The Masters and Fellows of Trinity College, Cambridge.*)

*One of the 'Albanian virgins' English traveller Edith Durham met on her journey through Rapsha in 1908. (*The Royal Anthropological Institute Photographic Collection.*)

Below left A songsheet of Vesta Tilley's mocking music hall portrait of 'The Bold Militiaman'. (*Raymond Mander and Joe Mitchenson Theatre Collection.*)

Below right One of the female Russian soldiers from the Women's Battalion of Death, who, according to an American journalist, 'caught the public fancy like no other feature of the great war,' in Petrograd, 1917. (*Trustees of the Imperial War Museum.*)

*Flora Sandes riding into a liberated Serbian village, 1918. (*Flora Sandes Collection, Sudbourne, Suffolk.*)

*Former Russian soldier and writer Marina Yurlova in more feminine attire, 1934.

* This illustration of Sarah Emma Edmonds, 'a comrade in war and a sister in peace' was drawn to accompany a new edition of her autobiography, *Nurse and Spy*, but she died in 1898 before completing the manuscript. (*Clarke Historical Library.*)

AN

ADDRSS,

DELIVERED WITH APPLAUSE,

AT THE *FEDERAL-STREET THEATRE*, BOSTON,

FOUR SUCCESSIVE NIGHTS OF THE DIFFERENT
PLAYS, BEGINNING *March* 22, 1802 ;

AND AFTER, AT OTHER PRINCIPAL TOWNS, A
NUMBER OF NIGHTS SUCCESSIVELY
AT EACH PLACE ;

BY MRS. DEBORAH GANNET,

THE AMERICAN HEROINE,

*Who served three years with reputation (undiscovered as a
Female) in the late* AMERICAN ARMY.

PUBLISHED AT THE REQUEST OF THE AUDIENCES.

Copy Right secured.

Dedham :

PRINTED *and* SOLD *by* H. MANN, *for Mrs* GANNET,
at the MINERVA OFFICE.—1802.

Above left Loreta Janeta Velasquez who disguised herself as Harry T. Buford, first lieutenant independent scouts CSA. The illustration from her contentious 1876 autobiography. (*The British Library*.)

Above right Phoebe Hessel, a former soldier who became a well-known character in Brighton, shown in an etching at the age of 108. (*The British Museum*.)

Left Deborah Sampson, as a married woman, returned to public life in 1802 on a public speaking tour through New England. (*The British Library*.)

*After demobilization Flora Sandes remained friends with and eventually married fellow officer Yurie Yudenitch, a former Russian White General, in May 1927. (*Flora Sandes Collection, Sudbourne, Suffolk.*)

**Below* While living in Paris with her new husband, Flora Sandes became matron to 'The Eight Extraordinarys', one of John Tiller's dancing troupes. This shot was taken at their hostel in 1927. (*Flora Sandes Collection, Sudbourne, Suffolk.*)

*After Yurie's death in September 1941 Flora Sandes returned to England and her family where she lived until her death in 1956. (*Flora Sandes Collection, Sudbourne, Suffolk.*)

Below left Serbian Captain Flora Sandes at an armistice day parade in London, circa 1954. (*Flora Sandes Collection, Sudbourne, Suffolk.*)

Below right Art imitates life in US Naval recruitment poster, First World War, by Howard Chandler Christy. (*Trustees of the Imperial War Museum.*)

*Valerie Arkell-Smith alias Colonel Barker in a side-show with her 'bride' exploiting the publicity that surrounded her 1929 perjury trial on the Blackpool marquee, 1937.

*Another angle of the Colonel Barker side-show at the Blackpool marquee, 1937.
(*Photos by Humphrey Spender, Tom Harrison Mass-Observation Archive, University of Sussex.*)

Selected Biographies

Notes

Selected Bibliography

Index

Selected biographies

Valerie Arkell-Smith 'Colonel Barker:' Born in St Clements, Jersey in 1895 to a gentleman farmer and his wife of independent means. The family moved to England in 1897 where Valerie spent much of her childhood when not attending a convent school in Brussels. After her 'coming-out' party in 1914 Valerie took up war work as a nurse, an ambulance driver and as a member of the Women's Auxiliary Air Force. By 1918 she was engaged to an Australian officer, Lieutenant Harold Arkell-Smith of the 20th Battalion, and they married on April 27. The marriage lasted only six weeks and Valerie soon became involved with another Australian, Earnest Pearce-Crouch with whom she lived until 1923. She bore him two children and then, tired of his drinking binges and violent behaviour, left him to assume her new identity as Victor Barker. As the Colonel she married Elfrida Haward at a Brighton parish church in 1923 and was charged on two counts of perjury in 1929. After the disclosure of her identity at Brixton prison her trial became a cause célèbre and she was sentenced to nine months in Holloway Prison for Women. She continued to live as a man until her death in Kessingland, East Anglia, in 1960.

Arnold, Mary Anne: Born in Sheerness, England in 1825, Mary Anne Arnold took to sea in 1836 when she realized that boys her age were 'in every way in a superior condition to her.' Borrowing a friend's trousers she signed aboard a Sutherland collier and worked on various merchant ships until her detection in December 1839.

Barry, Dr. James Miranda: Soon after the death of well-known colonial doctor Dr. James Miranda Barry in London in 1865, an article appeared in

Saunders News Letter stating that Barry was really a woman. Born in 1795, she graduated from Edinburgh medical school in 1812 and a year later was commissioned as a British Army Hospital Assistant. After working briefly in England, Barry was transferred to South Africa where she rose to become Colonial Medical Inspector. She left Cape Town in 1829 but worked as a medical officer in Jamaica, St. Helena, Barbados, Antigua, Malta, Corfu, Crimea and Montreal, Canada before returning to England where she retired in 1859.

Bochkareva, Maria: Born in Tomsk, Siberia in 1889, the third daughter in a peasant family, Maria was surrounded by violence even in childhood. At the age of 15 she married soldier Afansi Bochkarev, in part, to escape from her brutal, alcoholic father. She worked throughout Siberia as a construction labourer with her husband and quickly rose to foreman. She twice ran away from her husband who became as violent as her father. She met and married a second husband, Yakov Buk, and followed him into political exile. But after Yakov also became overbearing and abusive Maria dressed in male clothes and returned to her family in Tomsk. There she appealed to the Tsar and was granted permission to join the 25th Reserve Battalion. She fought for two years, was twice wounded and, under the provisional government, formed the Petrograd Women's Battalion of Death in the summer of 1917. They saw action on Russia's Western front but suffered devastating losses and their final act came on October 25, 1917 when they helped to defend the Winter Palace against the Bolsheviks. Bochkareva left Russia through Vladivostock and emigrated to the US where she dictated her life-story to a well-known magazine writer, Isaac Don Levine.

Dadeshkeliani, Princess Kati: Born in an eighth-century, feudal castle in the Russian state of Georgia in 1891, Kati Dadeshkeliani was the eldest child of Prince Alexander and Princess Eristavi. Her father, the inspector of State Forests, was assassinated in 1909. To secure the future of her widowed mother and her younger brother and sister Kati gave up her ambitions for medical school to marry a wealthy Baron. During the war, Kati's husband was called up and she moved to Petrograd where she became Prince Djamal. She served in an ambulance corps at the Austrian front, attached to the 4th squadron of a Tartar regiment under the Grand Duke Michael. She was wounded in 1916 on the Austrian front and hospitalized in Kiev. She returned to Georgia in 1917, which was declared an independent state in 1918, but left after the Russians took control three years later. With her family, Kati left Russia for Paris in October 1922.

Davies, Christian: Also known as Mother Ross and Kit Welsh, she was born in Dublin in 1667 to a brewing family. At the age of 17 Christian went to live with an aunt who died four years later, leaving her the owner of an inn. There she met and married her employee Richard Welsh with whom she had three sons. Four years later Richard disappeared and Christian, on a mission to find him, disguised herself as Christopher Welsh and enlisted in Captain Tichbourne's company of foot. She re-enlisted in 1701 and eventually found her husband after a separation of thirteen years. Her true identity was finally discovered by army surgeons while they dressed a skull fracture she suffered during the battle of Ramilles. She continued to work as a sutler — selling meats and wines to the troops — until 1712. She applied for and was eventually granted a military pension and died on July 7, 1739. She was buried at the Pensioners' College in Chelsea and three grand volleys were fired over her grave.

Edmonds, Sarah Emma: One of the most famous female soldiers of the American Civil War, Sarah Emma Evelyn Edmonds was born in December 1842 in New Brunswick. As a teenager she was inspired to leave a cruel and dictatorial father by emulating the heroine of Murray's novel, *Fanny Campbell or the Female Pirate Captain*. While still an adolescent Emma cut off her hair, dressed as a man and became Franklin Thompson — a bible seller for a firm in Hartford, Connecticut. She enlisted in a Michigan regiment in June 1861 and served two years with the Army of the Potomac. She deserted in April 1863 with James Reid of the 79th New York Volunteers but soon resumed her female role and dress. She eventually worked for the United States Christian Commission as a nurse, wrote a best-selling autobiography, married her childhood sweetheart Linus Seelye in 1867, had three children and spent several years petitioning the American government for a full-pension. She died at La Porte, Texas in 1898 but as part of the Memorial Day services in 1901 her body was moved to the Grand Army of the Republic portion of the Washington Cemetery in Houston.

Gunn, Isabelle: In 1781 Isabelle Fubister was born to a crofting family in Tankerness, St. Andrew's parish, in the Orkney islands. In 1806 she signed on with the Hudson's Bay Company fur trading company as John Fubister and set sail aboard the *Prince of Wales* , bound for the Nor'West on June 29. She was part of a crew in 1807 that sailed 1,800 miles along the Albany river to Pembina Post on the Red River. At the company post Isabelle gave birth to a son, her disguise dramatically revealed, and her life as John Fubister abruptly ended. That spring she and her son, the first white child born in the West of what became Canada, were sent back to Fort Albany where she worked for another year. In 1809 she and her infant returned to Orkney. Isabelle, now calling herself Gunn, died on November 11, 1861.

Guerin, Elsa Jane, 'Mountain Charley': The illegitimate daughter of Anna Baldwin and plantation owner Henry Vereau, Elsa was born near Baton Rouge, about 1837. She was raised by her step-father but educated at boarding school in New Orleans before she married a river pilot at the age of 12. Three years later her husband was killed in a fight with a ship's mate and to support her children, Elsa Jane Guerin became sailor. She worked steam ships travelling between St Louis and New Orleans, engaged as a brakeman on the Illinois Central Railroad and later became a gold prospector. According to a man who claimed to have known her, 'Mountain Charley' also served in the Iowa Cavalry during the Civil War under the name Charles Hatfield, worked as a spy and was promoted to Lieutenant. Her story was first published in Iowa in 1861.

Hessel, Phoebe: Reputed to have been born in Stepney, London in 1713, Phoebe Hessel served in many parts of Europe as a private soldier in the 5th regiment of foot. In 1745 she fought under the Duke of Cumberland at the battle of Fontenoy and received a bayonet wound in her arm. She retired to Brighton where, in her old age, she supported herself selling fruit and gingerbread. According to local legend Phoebe Hessel attracted the attention of the Prince Regent, George IV who granted her a pension in 1817. She died on 12 December 1821, allegedly 108 years old.

Lawrence, Dorothy: An ambitious young writer, Dorothy Lawrence decided the best way to further a career in journalism was to disguise herself as an enlisted soldier and write about her experiences on the Western front. In 1915 she became Sapper Denis Smith with the help of a few British Tommies and served for 10 days in a British Expeditionary Force Tunnelling Company before she divulged her real identity to her commanding officer. She was immediately taken to BEF headquarters and interrogated. Before she was shipped back to England, Dorothy was temporarily housed in a French convent and made to swear an affidavit promising not to make her experiences public. She waited until 1919 to publish her memoirs.

Merkus, Jenny: The youngest daughter of Pieter Merkus, Governor-General of the Netherlands Indies, Jenny was born in Djakarta on 11 October 1839. Her father died in 1844 and the family returned to Holland where, four years later, Jenny's mother also passed away. She then lived with her uncle, a prominent figure in the Netherlands Reformed Church, and became devoutly religious. At the age of 21 she inherited a considerable family fortune and travelled throughout France, Italy and Sicily. In 1873 she moved to Jerusalem to 'erect a building to the glory of God' and became involved with philanthropic work. Three years later she helped fund a revolt against Turkish rule in Bosnia and supplied the rebels with arms and enlisted in the Serbian army. After her experiences in the Balkans she returned to her charitable works and eventually retired to the Netherlands where she died on 11 February 1897 in Utrecht at the age of 57.

Sampson, Deborah: Born near Plymouth, Mass., on 17 December 1760. Her father died soon after her birth, and she was sent to live with a family friend in Middleborough as an infant. Between the ages of 10 and 18 she lived with Deacon Jeremiah Thomas and 'became acquainted with almost all kinds of manual labour'. In 1779 she began teaching school and three years later, after several social forays in male clothing, left Middleborough to enlist as a volunteer soldier in the American Army. Disguised as Robert Shurtleff she fought as a member of the Continental Forces in several battles, was wounded and hospitalized before she was given an honorary discharge. In 1785 she married farmer Benjamin Gannett with whom she had three children. She published her memoirs, *The Female Review*, anonymously in 1797 and toured through New England in her old uniform in 1802 lecturing about her military experiences. For her service she received a pension from both state and federal governments. After her death in 1827 the American congress passed an act for the relief of her heirs.

Sandes, Flora: The youngest child of a large rector's family, Flora was born in Poppleton, Yorkshire on 22 January 1876. At the age of nine her family moved to Marlsford, Suffolk where Flora spent the remainder of her childhood. Her father, Samuel Dickson Sandes, retired in 1894 and moved to Thornton Heath. Flora left a secretarial job at the outbreak of war to work for the Serbian Red Cross and was stationed at a large military hospital in Kragujevatz with seven other nurses in 1914. Her next post came in February 1915 where she and an American friend, Emily Simmonds, were put in charge of an operating room in Valjevo, known as 'the death trap of Serbia'. Both caught typhus but recovered and in November, Sandes became attached to the ambulance of the Second Infantry Regiment of the Serbian Army as a dresser. Twenty days later she became a private, and then rapidly rose to the rank of sergeant. In September 1916 she published her first autobiography of her experiences before returning to active service. On 15 November 1916 she was wounded and a month later received the Kara George Star for non-commissioned officers and was promoted to Sergeant-Major. Throughout her years in the Serbian army she regularly conducted speaking-tours to raise funds for the Serbian cause. In 1920 she toured Australia and met with several government ministers in a bid to improve trade-ties. By this time she had been made a Lieutenant and she was later promoted to Captain. She was demobilized in 1922 but remained in Belgrade and married fellow officer, former White Army general, Yurie Yudenich in 1927. That year she published a second autobiography before settling in Belgrade. Flora and Yurie were briefly interned under the German occupation of Yugoslavia. After her husband's death in September 1941, Flora returned to England and she died at her Suffolk home in 1956.

Snell, Hannah: Born in Worcester in 1723, Hannah Snell grew up in a working-class family of nine children. Her three brothers were all sailors or soldiers and her five sisters all married into military families. Hannah moved to London in 1740 after her parents' death and lived with her sister in Wapping. There she met and married a Dutch sailor, James Summs on January 6, 1744 who left her six months later. Hannah was then several months pregnant but gave birth to a daughter who lived only a few days. She then decided to find her husband so borrowed a suit from her brother-in-law, took his name, James Gray, and enlisted in Coventry in November 1745. She was ordered aboard the sloop of war, *Swallow* and was wounded in the British siege of Pondicherry. After her recovery she spent another few years working as a sailor, discovered that James Summs had died and retired from sea in 1750. After resuming her female identity and clothes, she became a publican, performed on stage and sold her memoirs. She remarried twice, was widowed once and gave birth to one son. In 1789 she was declared insane and admitted to Bethlehem Hospital. She died there on 8 February 1792.

Talbot, Mary Anne: An illegitimate daughter of the Lord William Talbot, Mary Anne was born at Lincoln's Inn Fields in London on February 2, 1778. Her mother died in childbirth and Mary Anne was sent to school in Chester and then to a guardian in Shropshire. The aptly-named Mr. Sucker handed over his charge to Captain Bowen who enlisted Mary Anne as John Taylor, a footboy, aboard a ship bound for Santa Domingo. Accompanied by Bowen she was enrolled as drummer-boy and taken to Flanders in 1792 and participated in the capture of Valenciennes on 28 July 1793. She deserted the regiment, made her way to France, boarded a lugger and was eventually assigned to a British ship, the *Brunswick*. Serving under Captain John Harvey she was wounded in June 1794, recovered but was captured by the French aboard the *Vesuvius* bomb and imprisoned until 1796. Her true identity was eventually disclosed to prevent her being taken by a press-gang and she went on to various careers as a theatrical performer, a jeweller, and a domestic servant. She died on 4 February 1808 at the age of 30.

Thornton, Anne Jane: At the tender age of 13, Anne fell in love with a ship's captain, Alexander Burke, in her native Donegal, Ireland. When Burke sailed back to his home in America, Anne resolved to find him. She left the home of her father, a wealthy shopkeeper, with a maid servant and a boy who helped her to find a sailor's costume and to engage as a cabin-boy aboard a ship bound for America. Anne turned up at her lover's home only to discover that he was already married, and decided to continue her life as a boy. She sailed for 31 months with various crews in the Mediterranean before a ship mate discovered her identity while she was bathing. She sailed to London in 1835 where she was reunited with her father.

Velasquez, Loreta Janeta: Born in Havana, Cuba in 1842, Loreta Janeta Velasquez secretly married a young American officer in 1856 and eloped to the US. When her husband enlisted in the Confederate Southern Army at the outbreak of Civil War, Loreta disguised herself as Harry T. Buford, a member of the Independent Scouts, CSA. She raised her own regiment and met her 'amazed' husband at his camp in Pensacola. Loreta claimed to have fought in the Battle of Bull Run and to have served under several Confederate generals including Jackson and Bragg. She was wounded in the foot during a skirmish at Fort Donelson under the command of General Pillow but fearing detection she left for Jackson, Mississippi and then worked as an independent officer. While in the army of East Tennesse she was wounded again, retired from active service and instead became a military spy. Her other adventures included working as a bounty and substitute broker in New York; a prospector in California; living among the Mormons and travelling in Europe and South America. She was thrice married and published a widely-read autobiography in 1876.

Yurlova, Marina: Born in a small village in 1914 in the Southern Caucasus mountains of Russia, Marina Yurlova was accidentally pulled into the First World War as a combatant. While standing amidst a crowd of women and children accompanying the soldiers to war, Marina was pushed onto a railway car. At the front she changed her name to Marina Kolesnikova and was befriended by a Cossack officer who found her a uniform, a job grooming horses and a regiment. Without disguising her identity she became an unofficial soldier and was twice wounded. After her second wound, she suffered severe battle fatigue and was placed in a mental asylum in Omsk. Eventually Marina was released and left Russia for the U.S.A. from Vladivostock in 1919. She published two autobiographies.

Notes

CHAPTER ONE: The Persistence of a Phenomenon

1. Quoted in O. P. Gilbert, *Women in Men's Guise*, John Lane, London, 1932, p. xvii.
2. Ibid, p. xii.
3. 'Colonel Barker Prosecuted', *The Times*, March 28, 1929.
4. 'Colonel Barker in the Dock at the Old Bailey', *Daily Herald*, 25 April 1929.
5. 'Old Bailey Acquittals', *The Times*, July 15, 1927.
6. 'Woman's Strange Life as a Man', *Daily Express*, March 6, 1929.
7. 'Colonel Barker Prosecuted', *The Times*, March 28, 1929.
8. 'How the Colonel's Secret was Revealed', *Daily Sketch*, March 6, 1929.
9. Radclyffe Hall to Audrey Heath, March 19, 1929 quoted in Michael Baker, *Our Three Selves: The Life of Radclyffe Hall*, Hamish Hamilton, London, 1985, p. 254.
10. Ibid, p. 254.
11. 'Colonel Barker in the Dock at the Old Bailey', *Daily Herald*, April 25, 1929.
12. Ibid.
13. 'Perjury Charge', *The Times*, April 26, 1929.
14. 'My Amazing Masquerade', *Empire News and Chronicle*, Februrary 19, 1956.
15. 'Colonel Barker Sent for Trial', *Daily Sketch*, March 28, 1929.
16. 'Old Bailey Trial for Colonel Barker', *Daily Express*, March 28, 1929.
17. 'Colonel Barker Sentenced', *The Times*, April 26, 1929.
18. 'Pop' cartoon strip, *Daily Sketch*, May 16, 1929.
19. Valerie Arkell-Smith, 'I posed as a man for 30 years!', *Empire News and Chronicle*, Februrary 19, 1956.
20. Trinity College Library, Cambridge, A. J. Munby, diary, vol. 34, February

18, 1866 and March 24 , 1866.

21. For more on the Amazons, see Mandy Merck, 'The City's Achieve-
ments: The patriotic Amazonomachy and Ancient Athens', in Susan
Lipshitz, ed., *Tearing the Veil: Essays on Femininity*, Routledge & Kegan
Paul, London, 1978.

22. Natalie Zeamon Davis, *Society and Culture in Early Modern France*,
Stanford University Press, Stanford, 1975, p. 130.

23. J. H. Wilson quoted in Pat Rogers, 'The Breeches Part', in Paul-Gabriel
Boucé ed., *Sexuality in Eighteenth-Century Britain*, Manchester
University Press, Manchester, 1982, pp. 244–257, p. 249.

24. Simon Shepherd, *Amazons and Warrior Women: Varieties of Feminism in
Seventeenth Century Drama*, Harvester, Brighton, 1981, p. 69 and Lisa
Jardine, *Still Harping on Daughters: Drama in the Age of Shakespeare*,
Harvester, Brighton, 1983.

25. Lynne Friedl, 'Women Who Dressed as Men', *Trouble and Strife*, No. 6,
Summer 1985; Anna Clark, 'Popular Morality and the Construction of
Gender in London 1780–1845', Ph.D. thesis, Rutgers University,
Rutgers, New Jersey; Louise Anne May, 'Worthy Warriors and Unruly
Amazons: Sino-Western Historical Accounts and Imaginative Images of
Women in Battle', Ph.D. thesis, University of British Columbia, 1985.

26. Dianne Dugaw, *Warrior Women and Popular Balladry, 1650–1850*,
Cambride University Press, Cambridge, 1989.

27. Nadezhda Durova translated by Mary Fleming Zirin, *The Cavalry
Maiden: Journals of a Russian Officer in the Napoleonic Wars*, Indiana
University Press, Bloomington, 1988.

28. Charlotte Bremer, *Life, Letters and Posthumous Works of Fredrika Bremer*,
Hurd and Houghton, New York, 1868, p. 31 and O. P. Gilbert, op. cit.

29. Rudolf Dekker and Lotte van de Pol, *The Tradition of Female Cross-
Dressing in Early Modern Europe*, Macmillan, London, 1989.

30. Philip Ziegler, *Addington: A Life of Henry Addington, First Viscount
Sidmouth*, Collins, London, 1965, p. 114.

31. 'Women in Red Cloaks as Soldiers', *Notes and Queries*, 7th series III, 4
June 1887, p. 452 and *Notes and Queries*, 7th series IV, July 9, 1887, p. 37.

32. 'Women's Fitness for Soldiering', *The Times*, October 9, 1917.

33. Sara Maitland, *Vesta Tilley*, Virago Press, London, 1986, p. 101.

34. 'Woman's Strange Life as a Man', *Daily Express*, March 6, 1929.

35. 'How the Colonel's Secret was Revealed', *The Daily Sketch*, March 6,
1929.

36. Robert Benewick, *The Fascist Movement in Britain*, Penguin,
Harmondsworth, 1972, p. 37.

37. 'Another Female Sailor', *Weekly Dispatch*, December 17, 1843 and
'Another Female Sailor', *Weekly Dispatch*, July 25, 1841.

38. Jonathan Katz, *Gay American History: Lesbians and Gay Men in the USA*, Crowell, New York, 1977, p. 318
39. Marina Warner, *Joan of Arc: The Image of Female Heroism*, Pan Books, London, 1981, p. 153.
40. Rita Mae Brown, *High Hearts*, Bantam Books, London, 1987.
41. Joan Bethke Elshtain, *Women and War*, Harvester Press, Brighton, 1987, p.17.
42. Anonymous, *The Female Soldier or the Surprising Life and Adventures of Hannah Snell*, Richard Walker, London, 1750, p. 31.
43. Colonel Frederick Schneider, 'Sarah Emma Edmonds-Seeley: The Female Soldier', Lansing, *State Republican*, 19 June 1900.
44. Anonymous, *The Life and Adventures of Mrs. Christian Davies, the British Amazon, Commonly Call'd Mother Ross*, Richard Montagu, 1741, part II, p. 16.
45. 'Female Pugilism', *Weekly Dispatch*, October 6, 1813.
46. Flora Sandes Private Collection, Sudbourne, Suffolk (hereafter called FS Coll.).
47. George MacAdam, 'When Women Fight', *New York Times Magazine*, September 2, 1917, p. 3.
48. Chief Commander S.M. Crawley, 'The Use of Woman-Power in the Army', *The Army Quarterly*, Vol. LVI, No. 2, pp. 217–225, p. 217.
49. Magnus Hirschfeld, *The Sexual History of the World War*, The Panurge Press, New York, 1934, pp. 114–118.
50. Wendy Chapkis, ed., *Loaded Questions: Women in the Military*, Transnational Institute, Amsterdam, 1981, pp. 4–5.
51. Lynne Segal, *Is the Future Female? Troubled Thoughts on Contemporary Feminism*, Virago Press, London, 1987, p. 162.
52. Cynthia Enloe, *Does Khaki Become You? The Militarisation of Women's Lives*, Pandora Press, London, 1989.
53. Barton Hacker, 'Women and Military Institutions in Early Modern Europe: A Reconnaissance', *Signs*, Summer 1981, Vol. 6, No. 4, pp. 643–671.
54. Sergeant-Major Edward Cotton, *A Voice from Waterloo*, B.L. Green, London, 1849, p. 55, footnote.
55. Myna Trustram, *Women of the Regiment: Marriage and the Victorian Army*, Cambridge University Press, Cambridge, 1984, p. 14–22.
56. See for example, *The Soldier's Companion or Martial Recorder, consisting of biography, anecdotes, poetry and other miscellaneous information peculiarly interesting to those connected with the military profession*, Edward Cock, London, 1824, pp. 73, 349.
57. Trustram, op. cit., p. 28.
58. Menié Muriel Dowie, ed., *Women Adventurers: The Adventure Series*, Vol. 15, Unwin Brothers, London, 1893, p. xvii.

59. H. Havelock Ellis, *Studies in the Psychology of Sex*, Vol. 1, 'Sexual Inversion', The University Press, London, 1897, pp. 9–10.
60. Quoted in John Laffin, *Women in Battle*, Abelard-Schuman, London, 1967, p. 12.

CHAPTER TWO: And Then Annie Got Her Gun

1. Frank Schneider, *Post and Tribune*, Detroit, October 1883, in Clarke Historical Library, Central Michigan University.
2. Ibid.
3. Ibid.
4. Ibid.
5. Schneider, op. cit.
6. Ibid.
7. Ibid.
8. Betty Fladeland, 'Alias Frank Thompson', in *Michigan History*, Vol. 42, No. 3, September 1958, pp. 435–462, p. 439.
9. Ibid.
10. Sylvia G. L. Dannett, *Noble Women of the North*, Thomas Yoseloff, New York, 1959.
11. Dianne Dugaw, 'Balladry's Female Warriors: Women, Warfare and Diguise in the Eighteenth Century', *Eighteenth Century Life*, January 1985, No. 9, pp. 1–20.
12. Dianne Dugaw, *Warrior Women in Popular Balladry, 1600–1850*, Cambridge University Press, Cambridge, (forthcoming 1989).
13. Anonymous, *The Life and Adventures of Mrs. Christian Davies, the British Amazon, Commonly Call'd Mother Ross*, Richard Montagu, London, 1740, p. 20, part 1.
14. Anonymous, *The Life and Adventures of Mrs. Christian Davies, the British Amazon, Commonly call'd Mother Ross*, Richard Montagu, London, 1741, pp. 1–2.
15. 'Gleanings from Dark Annals', *Chambers's Journal*, May 30, 1863, No. 491, p. 350.
16. Madeline Moore, *The Lady Lieutenant, or the Strange and Thrilling Adventures of Miss Madeline Moore*, Barclay and Co., Philadelphia, 1862, p. 17.
17. Loreta Janeta Velasquez, C. J. Worthington, ed., *The Woman in Battle*, T. Belknap, Hartford, Conn., 1876, p. 6.
18. For further information about women soldiers during the American

Civil War, see Jane Shultz, 'Woman at the Front: Gender and Genre in the Literature of the American Civil War', Ph.D. thesis, University of Michigan, Ann Arbor, MI.

19. Philip P. Sheridan, *Personal Memoirs of P.H. Sheridan, United States Army*, C.L. Webster, New York, 1888, Vol. 1, p. 254.

20. A. Jackson Crossley to Samuel Bradbury, Headquarters, Army of the Potomac, May 29, 1864, Manuscript department, William R. Perkins Library, Duke University, North Carolina.

21. Mary Livermore, *My Story of the War*, Hartford, Conn., 1888, p. 120.

22. Schneider, op. cit.

23. Delia T. Davis, 'Saw Active Service: Woman Disguised as a Man', 1917, in Clarke Historical Library, Central Michigan University.

24. 'Interesting Scrapbook is Discovered', *Concord News*, 1937 and 'Pvt. Frank Thompson', *Citizen Patriot*, May 28, 1960, in Clarke Historical Library, Central Michigan University.

25. Dianne Dugaw, *Warrior Women*.

26. Maria Bochkareva, as told to Isaac Don Levine, *Yashka: My Life As Peasant Officer and Exile*, Frederick A. Stokes, New York, pp. 18, 27.

27. Ibid, p. 28.

28. Ibid, p. 28.

29. Ibid, p. 33. Maria and Yakov Buk, a 'handsome young man aged 24', were married by civil agreement without the sanction of the church which was a very common practice in Russia before the revolution since divorce was so difficult to obtain.

30. Ibid, p. 66.

31. Quoted in Bochkareva, op. cit., p. ix.

32. Ibid, p. viii.

33. Lt-Col. R. F. Fitzgerald, 'Women's Work in the Great War', Unidentified Sydney newspaper, March 13, 1920, FS Coll.

34. Bessie Beatty, *The Red Heart of Russia*, The Century Co., New York, 1918, p. 92.

35. Bochkareva, op. cit., p. 76.

36. Ibid, pp. 76, 80.

37. Beatty, op. cit., p. 100.

38. Ibid, p. 102.

39. Louise Bryant, *Six Red Months in Russia: An Observer's Account of Russia Before and During the Proletarian Dictatorship*, Heinemann, London, 1918, p. 212 and Richard Stites, *The Women's Liberation Movement in Russia: Feminism, Nihilism and Bolshevism, 1860–1930*, Princeton University Press, Princeton, N.J., 1978, p. 280.

40. Marina Yurlova, *Cossack Girl*, Cassell and Co., London, 1934, pp. 18–19.

41. Ibid, pp. 32–33.

42. Ibid, p. 36.

43. Ibid, p. 36.

44. Anne Eliot Griesse and Richard Stites, 'Russia: Revolution and War', in Nancy Loring Goldman, ed., *Female Soldiers — Combatants or Non-Combatants: Historical Perspectives*, Greenwood Press, London, 1982, p. 65.

45. 'Warrior Women', *Literary Digest*, June 19, 1915, p. 1460.

46. Rosita Forbes, *Women Called Wild*, Grayson and Grayson, London, 1935, p. 65.

47. Flora Sandes, *The Autobiography of a Woman Soldier: A Brief Record of Adventure with the Serbian Army, 1916–1919*, Witherby, London, 1927, p. 9.

48. Velasquez, op. cit., p. 16.

49. FS Coll.

50. Dora Sigerson Shorter, *The Vagrant's Heart*, first published in *The Troubadour and Other Poems*, Hodder and Stoughton, London, 1907.

51. Flora Sandes notes for her 1920 Australian tour, FS Coll.

52. Flora Sandes diary, August 17 and August 24, 1914, FS Coll.

53. Flora Sandes notes for her 1920 Australian tour, FS Coll.

54. Ibid.

55. Ibid.

56. Ibid.

57. Monica Krippner, *The Quality of Mercy: Women at War, Serbia 1915–1918*, David and Charles, London, 1980, p. 110.

58. Flora Sandes diary, February 18, 1915, FS Coll.

59. Flora Sandes' lecture notes and diary, February 22, 1915, FS Coll.

60. Flora Sandes lecture notes, FS Coll.

61. Isabel Emslie Hutton, *With a Woman's Unit in Serbia, Salonika and Sebastopol*, Williams and Norgate, London, 1928, p. 37/38.

62. Flora Sandes diary, November 3, 1915, FS Coll.

63. Hutton, op. cit., pp. 67–68.

64. Sandes, *Autobiography*, p. 12.

65. Flora Sandes diary, November 20, 1915, FS Coll.

66. Sandes, *Autobiography*, p. 12.

67. Flora Sandes diary, November 28, 1915, FS Coll.

68. Sandes, *Autobiography*, p. 13.

69. Ibid, p. 13.

70. Flora Sandes, *An English Woman-Sergeant in the Serbian Army*, Hodder and Stoughton, London, 1916, p. 47.

71. Sandes, *Autobiography*, p. 77.

72. Edith Durham, *High Albania*, Virago, London, 1985, p. xii–xv.

73. 'The Autobiography of a Woman Soldier', *Times Literary Supplement*, May 20, 1927, p. 378.

74 'Jeanne Merkus', Algemeen Ryksarchief, the Hague, Collection

Koopstra, 1030/63, p. 5.

75. Public Record Office, Admiralty Minute Book, Adm. 2, vol. 79, 1772.

76. 'Female Sailors', *Notes and Queries*, VII series, IV, December 17, 1887, p. 486.

77. 'A female sailor' *The Times*, December 28, 1839, p. 7.

78. 'Tale of 1807: Orkney Woman's Trials', *The Orcadian*, December 28, 1922, p. 3.

79. Rudolf Dekker and Lotte van de Pol, *The Tradition of Cross-Dressing in Early Modern Europe*, Macmillan, London, 1989.

80. 'Phoebe Hessel', *The Circulator of Useful Knowledge, Literature, Amusement and General Information*, London, March 5, 1825, No. X, p. 147.

81. Velasquez, op. cit., p. 27.

82. Anonymous, *The Surprising Adventures of Almira Paul*, C.E. Daniels, NewYork, 1840, pp. 13–14.

83. Elsa Jane Guerin, introduction by F. W. Mazzulla and William Kostka, *Mountain Charley or the Adventures of Mrs E. J. Guerin, Who Was Thirteen Years in Male Attire*, University of Oklahoma Press, Norman, 1968, p.18.

84. Dorothy Lawrence, *Sapper Dorothy Lawrence: The Only English Woman Soldier, Late Royal Engineers, 51st Division, 179th Tunnelling Company, BEF*, John Lance, London, 1919, pp. 41–42.

85. Ibid, p. 40.

86. Ibid, p. 48.

87. Ibid, p. 58.

88. 'Woman's Attempt to Join the Army', *Hornsey Journal*, August 18, 1917.

89. Ibid.

90. Berta Ruck, 'Why Women Masquerade as Men: the craving they endure in this day of big things', *Illustrated Sunday Herald*, August 27, 1916.

91. Howard Chandler Christy, First World War American recruiting poster, Imperial War Museum, Cat. No. 0246.

92. *Hornsey Journal*, op. cit.

93. For further information about women aboard navy and commercial ships, see Gordon Grant, *The Life and Adventures of John Nicol, Mariner*, Cassell and Co., London, 1937 and Michael Lewis, *A Social History of the Navy 1793–1815*, Allen and Unwin, London, 1960, p. 282.

94. Mary Anne Talbot, 'The Intrepid Female: Or Surprising Life and Adventures of Mary Anne Talbot, otherwise John Taylor', in *Kirby's Wonderful and Scientific Museum*, Vol. II, London, 1804, pp. 160–225.

96. 'Female Sailor', *The Times*, November 12, 1807.

97. Anne Chambers, *Granuaile*, Wolfhound Press, Dublin, 1986.

98. Daniel Defoe, *A General History of the Pyrates*, Dent, London, 1972, pp. 153–165.

CHAPTER THREE: Becoming One of the Boys

1. Jackie Bratton, 'King of the Boys', *Women's Review*, Number 20, 1987, p. 12.
2. Martha Vicinus, *Independent Women: Work and Community for Single Women: 1850–1920*, Virago, London, 1985, p. 261.
3. On the image of the military nurse in Britain, pre-1914 see Anne Summers, *Angels and Citizens: British Women as Military Nurses, 1854–1914*, Routledge and Kegan Paul, London, 1988.
4. Marina Yurlova, *Cossack Girl*, Cassell, London, 1934, p. 45.
5. Ibid, p. 53.
6. Flora Sandes, *An Englishwoman in the Serbian Army*, Hodder and Stoughton, London, 1916, p. 18.
7. Flora Sandes, *The Autobiography of a Woman Soldier: A Brief Record of Adventure with the Serbian Army, 1916–1919*, Witherby, London, 1927, p. 149.
8. Ibid, p. 138.
9. John Adams Vinton, 'The Female Review: Life of Deborah Sampson, the Female Soldier in the War of the Revolution, with an introduction and Notes', *The Magazine of History with Notes and Queries*, Extra No. 47, Boston, 1916, p. 131.
10. Maria Bochkareva as told to Isaac Don Levine, *Yashka: My Life as Peasant Officer and Exile*, Fredrick A. Stokes, New York, 1919, p. 76.
11. Ibid, p. 78.
12. Ibid, p. 82.
13. Ibid, p. 102.
14. Ibid, p. 88.
15. Ibid, p. 88.
16. Princess Kati Dadeshkeliani, *Princess in Uniform*, translated by Arthur J. Ashton, G. Bell, London, 1934, p. 111.
17. Lul Gardo, *Cossack Fury: The Experiences of a Woman Soldier with the White Russians*, Hutchinson and Co., London, 1938, p. 103.
18. Sandes, *Autobiography*, pp. 85–86.
19. Anonymous, *The Life and Adventures of Mrs. Christian Davies, the British Amazon, Commonly Call'd Mother Ross etc.*, Richard Montagu, London, 1741, part 1, p. 20.
20. Ibid, part 1, p. 27.
21. Ibid, part 1, p. 77.
22. Anonymous, *The Life and Extraordinary Adventures of Susanna Cope: The British Female Soldier*, Cheney, Banbury, 1810? n. p.
23. Anonymous, *Hannah Snell, the Female Soldier etc*, Richard Walker, London, 1750, p. 87.
24. Mary Anne Talbot, 'The Intrepid Female or Surprising Life and Advent-

ures of Mary Anne Talbot, otherwise John Taylor', in *Kirby's Wonderful and Scientific Museum*, Vol. II, London, 1804, pp. 160–225, 182.

25. Ibid, p. 217.
26. Vinton, op. cit., p. 150, footnotes.
27. Ibid, p. 153, footnotes.
28. Dadeshkeliani, op. cit., pp. 118–119.
29. Ibid, pp. 119–120.
30. Madeline Moore, *The Lady Lieutenant or the Strange and Thrilling Adventures of Miss Madeline Moore*, Barclay and Company, Philadelphia, 1862, p. 33.
31. See for example Henry Fielding, *The Female Husband*, Liverpool University Press, 1960 and for contemporary work on the subject, Anna Clark, 'Dandy Men and Manly Women: Gender Trangression in Late Eighteenth and Early Nineteenth Century England,' Chapter VI in *Popular Morality and the Construction of Gender in London 1780–1845*, Rutgers University, Ph.D. thesis.
32. Sandes, *Autobiography*, 1927, p. 84.
33. Ibid, p. 82.
34. Ibid, p. 212.
35. Ibid, p.85.
36. Jerome Robbins diary, November 1, 11, 1861, Michigan Historical Collection, Bently Historical Library, University of Michigan, Ann Arbor, MI, (hereafter MHC).
37. Ibid, November 11, 1861.
38. Ibid, November 16, 1861.
39. Ibid, November 17, 1861.
40. Ibid, November 19, 1861.
41. Ibid, December 22, 23, 1861.
42. Ibid, November 11, 1861.
43. Ibid, December 23, 1861.
44. Ibid, December 20, 1862.
45. Ibid, March 3, 1863.
46. Ibid, April 20, 1863.
47. Ibid, April 20, 1863.
48. Ibid, April 4, 1863.
49. Emma Edmonds to Jerome Robbins, Washington, D.C., May 10, 1863, MHC.
50. Emma Edmonds to Jerome Robbins, Falmouth, Virginia, January 16, 1865, MHC.
51. Emma Edmonds to Jerome Robbins, Washington, D.C., May 10, 1863, MHC.
52. Jerome Robbins diary, April 20, 1863, MHC.

53. Colonel Frederick Schneider, 'The Female Soldier' *The State Republican*, June 21, 1900.

54. Vinton, op. cit., p. 123.

55. Loreta Janeta Velasquez, C.J. Worthington, ed., *The Woman in Battle*, T. Belknap, Hartford, Conn., 1876, p. 35.

56. Ibid, p. 17.

57. Dadeshkeliani, op. cit., p. 74.

58. 'Young Girls Fighting on the Russian Front', *Current History*, May 1916, Vol. 4, No. 2, pp. 365–367, p. 366.

59. Dorothy Lawrence, *Sapper Dorothy Lawrence: The Only English Woman Soldier Late Royal Engineers, 51st Division, 179th Tunnelling Company*, BEF, John Lance, 1919, p. 93.

60. Ibid, p. 110.

61. Louise Mack, *A Woman's Experience in the Great War*, Mills and Boon, London, 1915; Lady Isabella St. John, *A Journey in Wartime*, Lane, London, 1915; and Dr. Katherine MacPhail to her mother, from Bellevue Samoensa, October 9, 1916, Women's Work Collection, Imperial War Museum, October 9, 1916.

62. Quoted in Susanne J. Kessler and Wendy McKenna, *Gender: An Ethnomethodological Approach*, John Wiley, New York, 1978, p. 127.

63. W. H. Davies, *The Autobiography of a Super-Tramp*, Oxford University Press, Oxford, 1986, p. 84.

64. Ibid, pp. 86, 84.

65. Elsa Jane Guerin, *Mountain Charley, or the Adventures of Mrs. E. J. Guerin, Who Was Thirteen Years in Male Attire*, University of Oklahoma Press, Norma, 1968, p.29.

66. Ibid, p. 22.

67. Charles Dickens, 'British Amazons', *All the Year Round*, April 6, 1872, Vol. 7, No. 175, pp. 448–452.

68. Anonymous, *Hannah Snell*, op. cit., p. 36.

69. Ibid, p. 72.

70. Isobèl Rae, *The Strange Story of Dr. James Barry*, Longman, London, 1958, p. 22.

71. Velasquez, op. cit., p. 6.

72. Valerie Arkell-Smith, 'My Amazing Masquerade', *Empire News and Sunday Chronicle*, February 19, 1956.

73. 'At the Mansion House', *Weekly Dispatch*, London, July 5, 1840.

74. Sandes, *Autobiography*, 1927, pp. 125–126, emphasis in original.

75. Ibid, pp. 27, 86.

76. Ibid, p. 68.

77. Ibid, p. 69.

78. Yurlova, op. cit., p. 66.

79. Ibid, pp. 126–132.
80. Ibid p. 120 and see references in Kathy Bond-Stewart, ed., *Young Women in the Liberation Struggle*, Zimbabwe Publishing House, Harare, Zimbabwe, p. 8 for contemporary accounts of female combatants in all-male regiments whose male identification manifests itself physiologically as well. Gladys Moyo who fought with Zimbabwe's liberation army ZANLA in the struggle for independence in the 1970s, wrote of her experiences: 'In Zambia I was trained with men and I ended up feeling like a man. . . . I went on guard and didn't even attend to my monthly periods. I lived like a man.'
81. Velasquez, op. cit., p. 8.
82. *Current History*, op. cit.
83. Rosemary McKechnie, 'Living with Images of a fighting elite: Women and the French Foreign Legion', in Sharon MacDonald, et. al., eds., *Images of Women in Peace and War*, MacMillan Education, Oxford, 1987, pp. 122–147. 'In the past joining the Legion was a renunciation in the grand style: of the past, of one's name and nationality, of a normal role in society — and possibly, of life itself.' (p. 127.)
84. Gardo, op. cit., p. 96.
85. Ibid, p. 125.
86. Ibid, p. 163.
87. Bessie Beatty, *The Red Heart of Russia*, The Century Co., New York, 1918, p. 93.
88. Richard Stites, *The Women's Liberation Movement in Russia: Feminism, Nihilism and Bolshevisim 1860–1930*, Princeton University Press, Princeton, New Jersey, 1975, p. 322.
89. Bochkareva, op. cit., p. 163.
90. Ibid, p. 209.
91. Flora Sandes to ----, 'at the very front of the front', October 14, 1916, FS Coll.
92. Sandes, *Autobiography*, 1927, p. 75.
93. Yurlova, op. cit., p. 79.
94. Ibid, p. 94.
95. Magnus Hirschfeld, *The Sexual History of the World War*, Panurge Press, New York, 1934, p. 66.
96. Bochkareva, op. cit., p. 174.
97. Dadeshkeliani, op. cit., p. 111.
98. Lawrence, op. cit., p. 93.
99. Anonymous, *Hannah Snell*, p. vi.
100. Vinton, op. cit., p.132.
101. 'Mansion House', *The Times*, October 10, 1803.
102. 'Another Female Sailor', *Weekly Dispatch*, December 17, 1843.

103. Emma Cole, *The Life and Sufferings of Miss Emma Cole, Being a Faithful Narrative of Her Life*, M. Aurelius, Boston, 1844, p. 15.

104. Quoted in Linda Grant De Pauw, *Seafaring Women*, Houghton, Mifflin and Co., Boston, 1982, pp. 97–98, originally appeared as *The Adventures of Louisa Baker, whose life and character are particularly distinguished*, Luther Wales, New York, 1815.

105. Bochkareva, op. cit., p. ix.

106. Frank Mundell, *Heroines of History*, the Sunday School Union, London, 1898 p. 40.

107. Sandes, *Autobiography*, 1927, p. 141.

CHAPTER FOUR: The Denouement

1. 'Modern Amazons', *Chambers's Journal*, May 30, 1863, p. 348.

2. Dorothy Lawrence, *Sapper Dorothy Lawrence: The Only English Woman Soldier, Late Royal Engineers, 51st Division, 179th Tunnelling Co., BEF*, John Lance, London, 1919, p. 128.

3. Ibid, p. 131.

4. Ibid, p. 133.

5. Ibid, p. 136.

6. Ibid, p. 160.

7. Ibid, p. 151.

8. Ibid, p. 149.

9. Ibid, p. 152.

10. Ibid, p.175.

11. 'Soldier Hides Wife on Army Transport', *New York Times*, July 16, 1917 and 'Mrs. Hazel Carter of Douglas, Arizona was determined to go to France', *New York Times*, July 17, 1917.

12. Ibid, July 17, 1917.

13. Elsa Jane Guerin, *Mountain Charley or the Adventures of Mrs. E. J. Guerin, Who was Thirteen Years in Male Attire*, University of Oklahoma Press, Norman, Oklahoma, 1968, p. 29.

14. 'Another Female Sailor', *Weekly Dispatch*, Dec. 17, 1843.

15. *Morning Star*, March 31, 1868.

16. 'At Mansion House', *Weekly Dispatch*, July 5, 1840.

17. 'A Female Sailor; Extract of a letter from an officer of the "Robert Small" off the Cape of Good Hope, Oct. 20, 1839', *The Times*, Dec. 28, 1839, p. 7

18. Ibid, Dec. 28, 1839, p. 7.

19. 'At Mansion House', *Weekly Dispatch*, July 5, 1840.

20. Ibid.
21. Ibid.
22. 'Another female sailor', *Weekly Dispatch*, July 25, 1841.
23. 'Flogging Female Prisoners', *Weekly Dispatch*, June 10, 1838.
24. Elliot Coues, ed. *New Light on the Early History of the Greater Northwest: The Manuscript Journals of Alexander Henry and of David Thompson, 1799–1814*, Minneapolis, 1965 p. 426.
25. Peter Fidler, *Journal of a Journey from Swan to the Red River* , ref: 3/3 fo. 58, Provincial Archives of Manitoba, Hudson's Bay Company Archives, Winnipeg, Manitoba.
26. Letter from William Harper to William Watt, Albany Fort, Sept. 5, 1808 in the Earnest Marwick collection, Orkney Parish Archives, Kirkwall, Orkney.
27. 'Young girls fighting on the Russian Front', *Current History*, May 1916, Vol. IV, No. 2, pp. 365–367, p. 367.
28. 'A female sailor — a romantic adventure', *Weekly Dispatch*, Feb. 8, 1835.
29. Robert S. Kirby, *Wonderful Museum*, London, 1804, Vol. ii, p. 160.
30. Hannah Snell, *The Female Soldier; or the Surprising Life and Adventures of Hannah Snell*, Richard Walker, London, 1750.
31. Anonymous, *The Life and Adventures of Mrs. Christian Davies, the British Amazon*, R. Montagu, London, 1741, part I, p. 53.
32. Ibid, part I, p. 77.
33. Anonymous, *Christian Davies*, 1740, part 1, p. 45.
34. Ibid, part 2, p. 15.
35. Ibid, part 1, p. 31.
36. O. P. Gilbert, *Women in Men's Guise*, John Lane, London, 1932, p. 88.
37. Lady Charlotte Guest's Manuscript Journal, April 1851, Paris. I am indebted to Angela John for this reference.
38. Gilbert, op. cit., p. 80, account by the French poet M. de Fernig.
39. Ibid, pp. 80 and 81.
40. Ibid, p. 87.
41. John Adams Vinton, 'The Female Review: Life of Deborah Sampson, the Female Soldier in the War of the Revolution', in *The Magazine of History with Notes and Queries*, Extra No. 47, Boston, 1916, p. 155.
42. Ibid, p. 23.
43. *The Annual Register*, 1807, W. Otridge, et al., London, 1809, p. 496.
44. Mary A. Livermore, *My Story of the War*, Hartford, Conn., 1888, p. 119.
45. Harry Besancon Papers, diary May 26, 1864, Manuscript Department, William R. Perkins Library, Duke University.
46. A. Jackson Crossly to Samuel Bradbury, Headquarters, Army of the Potomac, May 29, 1864, Manuscript Department, William R. Perkins Library, Duke University.

47. J. W. Staats Evers, *Criminal Justice in Gelderland or Important Criminal Cases which have occured there from 1811 to 1859*, D.A. Thieme, Arnhem, 1859, translated by Hendrick van Kerkwijk.

48. Rudolf M. Dekker and Lotte C. van de Pol, *The Tradition of Female Cross-dressing in Early Modern Europe*, MacMillan, London, 1988.

49. Princess Kati Dadeshkeliani, *Princess in Uniform*, G.Bell and Sons, London, 1934, p. 161.

50. Velasquez, op, cit., p. 36.

51. Ibid, pp. 39–40.

52. Isaac Don Levine, *Yashka: My Life as Peasant Officer and Exile*, New York, 1919, p. 116.

53. Flora Sandes, *The Autobiography of a Woman Soldier: A Brief Record of Adventure with the Serbian Army 1916–1919*, Witherby, London, 1927, p. 31.

54. Flora Sandes to Sophie Sandes, November 21, 1915, FS Coll.

55. Ibid, p. 176.

56. Flora Sandes to Sophie Sandes, Oct. 14, 1916, FS Coll.

57. 'Jeanne Merkus', Algemeen Ryksarchief, The Hague, Collection Koopstra, F. 1030/63, p. 3.

58. Anonymous, *The Life and Adventures of Mrs. Christian Davies, the British Amazon*, R. Montagu, London, 1741, part II, p. 45.

59. Menié Muriel Dowie, (ed.), *Women Adventurers: The Adventure Series*, Vol. 15, The Gresham Press, London, 1893, p. 173.

60. Ibid, p.115.

61. Ibid, p. 116.

62. Sandes, op cit., p. 161.

63. Yurlova, op. cit., p. 80.

64. Emma Edmonds to Jerome Robbins, Washington D.C., May 10, 1863, Michigan Historical Collections, Bentley Historical Library, University of Michigan, Ann Arbor, MI.

65. Sarah Emma E. Edmonds, *Nurse and Spy in the Union Army: Comprising the Adventures and Experiences of a Woman in Hospitals, Camps and Battle-Fields*, 29, W. S. Williams and Co., Hartford, Conn., 1865, p. 271.

66. Guerin, op. cit., p. 51.

67. Ibid, p. 32.

68. Sandes, op. cit., p. 16.

69. Flora Sandes to Sophie Sandes, Oct. 14, 1916, Salonika, FS Coll.

70. Flora Sandes to -- , Oct. 14, 1916, FS Coll.

71. Yurlova, op cit., p. 156.

72. Ibid, p. 21.

CHAPTER FIVE: When the World Looked On

1. 'Serbia's Heroine', *Morning Herald*, Sydney, June 9, 1920.
2. 'Flora Sandes's arrival', *Sun*, Sydney, June 9, 1920.
3. Ibid.
4. 'Flora Sandes' programme, King's Hall, Hunter St., Sydney, June 8, 1920.
5. 'For Serbia's Sake', *Herald*, Evening, June 7, 1920.
6. 'Sydney Day by Day', unidentified Melbourne newspaper, June 1920, FS Coll.
7. 'Like a Joan of Arc', unidentified English newspaper, 1920, FS Coll.
8. 'Serbia's Heroine', unidentified Sydney newspaper, June 9, 1920, FS Coll.
9. 'For Serbia's Sake', *Herald*, Evening, June 7, 1920, 'A Woman's Letter', *The Bulletin*, July 8, 1920, and 'Flora Sandes of Serbia', *PFA Magazine*, June, 1920.
10. 'Serbia's Heroine, *Herald*, June 9, 1920.
11. Brisbane newspaper, n. d., July, 1920, FS Coll.
12. *The Australian Bystander*, July 8, 1920.
13. Flora Sandes, *An English Woman-Sergeant in the Serbian Army*, Hodder and Stoughton, London, 1916, p. 210.
14. FS lecture notes, FS Coll.
15. Brisbane, unidentified newspaper, nd., FS Coll.
16. 'Flora Sandes of Serbia', *PFA Magazine*, June, 1920.
17. Sandes, op. cit., p. 124.
18. Flora Sandes, *The Autobiography of a Woman Soldier: A Brief Record of Adventure with the Serbian Army, 1916–1919*, Witherby, London, 1927, p. 128.
19. 'Jeanne Merkus', Algemeen Ryksarchief, the Hague, Collection Koopstra, 1030/63, p. 5.
20. 'At the Mansion House', *Weekly Dispatch*, July 5, 1840.
21. 'A female sailor — romantic adventure', *Weekly Dispatch*, Feb. 8, 1835.
22. *The Interesting Life and Wonderful Adventures of that Extraordinary Woman Anne Jane Thornton, the Female Sailor; Disclosing Important Secrets, Unknown to the Public*, written by herself, n. p., London, 1835.
23. 'The Female Sailor', American Broadside, 1830s, Brown University, quoted in Dianne Dugaw, *Warrior Women*, Cambridge University Press, Cambridge, 1989.
24. Mrs. Ellen Stephens, *The Cabin Boy Wife*, C.E. Daniels, New York, 1840.
25. Quoted in Dianne Dugaw, *The Female Warrior Heroine in Anglo-American Popular Balladry*, University of California, Los Angeles, 1982,

unpublished Ph.D. thesis, appendix II.

26. 1861 Census, entry: Stromness, Main Street, in Old Parish Register, Kirkwall, Orkney and Register of Births, Deaths and Marriages (Scotland), Stromness, Orkney, 1861.

27. C. N. Bell, *Transcripts of the Historical and Scientific Society of Manitoba*, No. 37, 1889, p. 18.

28. Charles Napier Bell, 'First White Woman in Western Canada', *Winnipeg Free Press*, June 23, 1934, p. 8.

29. 'What Can Women Do?' *Chamber's Journal*, Oct. 5, 1872, no. 458, p. 636.

30. Warwick Wroth and Arthur Edgar Wroth, *The London Pleasure Gardens of the Eighteenth Century*, MacMillan, London, 1896, pp. 35–36.

31. Deborah Gannett, 'An Address Delivered at the Federal Street Theatre, Boston', n.p. Dedham, 1802.

32. Robert S. Kirby, *Wonderful Museum*, London, 1804, Vol. ii, p. 160.

33. Dennis Arundell, *The Story of Sadler's Wells, 1683–1977*, London, 1965, p. 71.

34. Playbill, Royal Ampitheatre, Astleys, Gabrielle Enthoven Collection, Victoria and Albert Theatre Museum.

35. Derek Hudson, *Munby: Man of Two Worlds: The Life and Diaries of Arthur J. Munby 1828–1910*, Abacus, London, 1974, p. 188.

36. Trinity College Library, Cambridge, A.J. Munby diaries, vol. 12, January 27, 1862, p. 54.

37. A.J. Munby diaries, vol. 13, June 4, 1862, p. 209.

38. A.J. Munby diaries, vol. 11, November 30, 1861, p. 217.

39. Hudson, op. cit., July 23, 1862, p. 131.

40. 'The Belle of Cairo', *Edinburgh Evening Despatch*, May 16, 1903.

41. Dianne Dugaw, *The Female Warrior Heroine in Anglo-American Popular Balladry*, University of California, Los Angeles, 1982, unpublished Ph.D. thesis, p. 92.

42. Charles Hindley, *Curiosities of Street Literature*, Vol. 2, Broadsheet King, London, 1966, p. 141.

43. Hudson, op. cit., February 20, 1867, p. 237.

44. 'Gleanings from dark annals; Modern Amazons', *Chambers's Journal*, May 30, 1863.

45. *The Adventures of Louisa Baker, whose life and character are particularly distinguished*, Luther Wales, New York, 1815, and Ellen Stephens, *The Cabin-boy Wife* C.E. Daniels, New York, 1840, p. 12.

46. Pat Rogers, 'The Breeches Part', in Paul-Gabriel Boucé, ed., *Sexuality in Eighteenth Century Britain*, Manchester University Press, Manchester, 1982, pp. 244–257, p. 249.

47. Dr. Kirko Barjaktarevic, *The Problem of Tobleije*, in *Glasnik Ethnografskog Museja*, Belgrade, Krjiga, 1965–66, pp. 273–286. Translated by Mira

Harding.

48. Rose Wilder Lane, *The Peaks of Shala: Being a Record of Certain Wanderings Among the Hill-Tribes of Albania*, Chapman and Dodd, Ltd., London, 1922, p. 172.

49. Edith Durham, *High Albania*, Virago Press Ltd., London, 1985, p. 80.

50. Anne Kindersley, *The Mountains of Serbia: Travels through Inland Yugoslavia*, John Murray, London, 1976, p. 81.

51. Menié Muriel Dowie, (ed.) *Women Adventurers: The Adventure Series*, (Vol. 15), Unwin Brothers, London, 1893, p. x.

52. Ethel F. Heddle, 'Celebrated Lady Travellers', I, Menié Muriel Dowie, (Mrs. Henry Norman), *Good Words*, Vol. 42, (1901), p. 18.

53. James Caulfield, *Portraits, Memoirs and Characters of Remarkable Persons*, Vol. II, London, 1819, p. 112.

54. Ibid, p. 111.

55. Myna Trustram, *Women of the Regiment, Marriage and the Victorian Army*, Cambridge University Press, Cambridge, 1984, p.28.

56. James Parton, *Eminent Women of the Age*, Hartford, Connecticut, 1869, pp. 206–207.

57. Barton Hacker, 'Women and Military Institutions in Early Modern Europe: A Reconnaissance', *Signs*, 6(4), pp. 634–671.

58. *The Soldier's Companion or Martial Recorder*, London, 1824, Vol. I, p. 349.

59. Thomas Carter, *Curiosities of War and Military Studies: Anecdotal, Descriptive and Statistical*, London, 1860, p. 90.

60. For further information about the role of nurses, see Anne Summers, *Angels and Citizens: British Women as Military Nurses 1854–1914*, Routledge and Kegan Paul, London, 1988.

61. Ibid, p. 98.

62. *The London Gazette*, June 1, 1847.

63. Commander W. B. Rowbotham, R.N., 'The Naval Service Medal, 1793–1840', *The Mariner's Mirror: The Journal of the Society for Nautical Research*, Vol. 23, July 1937, pp. 366.

64. Ellen C. Clayton, *Female Warriors: Memorials of Female Valour and Heroism, from the Mythological Ages to the Present Era*, (Vols. I and II), Tinsley Brothers, London, 1879, Vol. I, p. 3.

65. Ibid, Vol. I, p. 2, emphasis in original.

66. Sir John Carr, *Descriptive Travels in the Southern and Eastern Parts of Spain and the Balearic Isles*, Sherwood, London, 1809, p. 32.

67. Ibid, p. 33.

68. Ibid, p. 37.

69. Dowie, op. cit., p. x.

70. 'Female Soldiers and Sailors', *Notes and Queries*, Feb. 19, 1881, 6th series, Vol. III, p. 228.

71. Michael Hiley, *Victorian Working Women*, Gordon Fraser, London, 1979, p. 176.
72. Dowie, op cit., p. xxii.
73. 'What Can Women Do?' *Chambers's Journal*, Oct. 5, 1872, no. 458, p. 635.
74. Anna Harriette Leonowens, *The English Governess at the Siamese Court: Being Recollections of Six Years in the Royal Palace at Bangkok*, Truber, London, 1870, p. 94.
75. A. J. Munby, diary, vol. 65, June 22, 1893, p. 174.
76. Richard F. Burton, *A Mission to Gelele, King of Dahome*, Tinsley Brothers, London, 1864, and John Duncan, *Travels in Western Africa in 1845 and 1846; comprising a journey through the Kingdom of Dahomey, etc.*, London, 1847. *Times* correspondent Jules Gerard, Commodore Wilmot, Commander Forbes, Mr. Beecroft, M. Wallon and Mr. Enschott are all cited by Burton as fellow writers on the King of Dahomey and his Amazonian guards in this period.
77. Leslie Stephen, ed., *Dictionary of National Biography*, Vol. 14, London, 1888, p. 133.
78. These notes appear on the British Library's edition of J. Wilson, *The British Heroine: Or An Abridgement of the Life and Adventures of Christian Davies, Commonly Call'd Mother Ross*, J. Newberry and C. Micklewright, Reading, 1742.
79. 'Ultra-Centenarisanism', *Notes and Queries*, September 20, 1873, 4th series, XII, pp. 221–222 and 'Ultra-Centenarianism, *Notes and Queries*, 5th series, SL, March 21, 1874, pp. 221–223.
80. Hannah Snell, *Notes and Queries*, December 3, 1892, 8th series, II, p. 171.
81. 'Female Soldiers and Sailors', *Notes and Queries*, Feb. 19, 1881, 6th series, III, p. 283.
82. Dispatch Printing Co., Houston, Texas in Clarke Historical Library, Central Michigan University, Mount Pleasant, MI.
83. Sarah Emma Edmonds, *Nurse and Spy in the Union Army: The Adventures and Experiences of a Woman in Hospitals, Camps and Battlefield*, W.S. Williams and Co., Hartford, Conn., 1865, p. 6.
84. Sarah Emma Edmonds, 'The Female Soldier', *The State Republican*, June 19, 1900, p. 7.
85. Edmonds, *Nurse and Spy*, p. 333.
86. *The London Graphic*, Oct. 21, 1916 and *Liverpool Weekly Post*, Oct. 7, 1916.
87. 'Russian Girl Troops Mob Commander', *New York Times*, Sept. 22, 1917.
88. Isaac Don Levine, *Yashka: My Life as Peasant Officer and Exile*, New York: 1919, p. 162.
89. Richard Stites, *The Women's Liberation Movement in Russia: Feminism, Nihilism and Bolshevism*, Princeton University Press, Princeton, 1978, pp. 297–298.

90. Ibid, p. 168.
91. 'Russian Women Warriors Denounce Men', *New York Times*, June 25, 1917, p. 7.
92. 'Warrior Women', *Literary Digest*, June 19, 1915, p. 1460.
93. Louise Bryant, *Six Red Months in Russia: An Observer's Account of Russia Before and During the Proleterian Dictatorship*, Heinemann, London, 1918.
94. George MacAdam, 'When Women Fight', *The New York Times Magazine*, September 2, 1917, p. 3.
95. Ibid, p. 3.
96. Bessie Beatty, *The Red Heart of Russia*, The Century Co., New York, 1918, p. 114.
97. 'Root lauds Russian women', *New York Times*, Aug. 8, 1917.
98. Rheta Childe Dorr, *A Woman of Fifty*, Funk and Wagnalls, New York, 1924, pp. 367–368.
99. Florence Farmborough, *Nurse at the Russian Front: A Diary 1914–1918*, Constable, London, 1974, pp. 299–300, 304–305.
100. 'Letter from an American girl in France', Miscellaneous 4, item 60, Women's Work Collection, Imperial War Museum.
101. Farmborough, op. cit., pp. 306–307.
102. Flora Sandes to Fanny Sandes, July 24, 1917, 'in the trench', FS Coll.
103. Bryant, op. cit., p. 212.
104. Stites, op. cit. p. 298.
105. Bryant, op cit., p. 216.
106. Ibid, p. 218.
107. Jess Dixon, *'The Little Grey Partridge': The Diary of Isobel Ross, Serbia 1916–1917*, unpublished diary, Imperial War Museum, pp. 25, 18.
108. *Nursing Times*, Sept. 19, 1915.
109. Elsie Corbett, *Red Cross in Serbia 1915–1919: A Personal Diary of Experiences*, Banbury, Cheney, 1964, p. 163.
110. *The Coffs Harbour and Dorrigo Advocate*, Aug. 21, 1920.
111. *The Sydney Sun*, June 18, 1920.

CHAPTER SIX: Wounds That Would Not Heal

1. 'Deborah Gannett', *Sharon Historical Society of Sharon, Massachusetts*, No. 2, April , C.H. hight, Boston, 1905, p.192.
2. Deborah Gannett, *An Address Delivered with Applause, At the Federal-Street Theatre, Boston, 4 Successive Nights of the Different Plays, beginning March 22, 1802*, published at the request of the audience, Dedham, 1802, p. 6.
3. Ibid, p. 9.

4. John Adams Vinton, 'The Female Review: Life of Deborah Sampson, the Female Soldier in the War of the Revolution, with an Introduction and Notes', in *The Magazine of History with Notes and Queries*, Extra No. 47, Boston, 1916, p. 24.

5. Ibid, p. 90.

6. Ibid, p. 90.

7. Ibid, p. 21.

8. Gannett, *Address*, p. 12.

9. Ibid, p. 14.

10. Providence, Rhode Island, May 5, 1802, cited in *Sharon Historical Society*, p.192.

11. *Address*, op. cit., p. 4.

12. *Sharon Historical Society*, p. 193.

13. Vinton, op. cit., p.18.

14. Ibid, p. 18.

15. *Sharon Historical Society*, p.17.

16. Linda Grant De Pauw, 'Women in Combat: The Revolutionary War Experience', in *Armed Forces and Society*, Vol. 7, No. 2, Winter 1981, pp. 209–226, p. 218–219.

17. E. E. Seeley to Albert E. Cowles, Fort Scott, Kansas, Aug. 15, 1883, emphasis in original.

18. Colonel Frederick Schneider, 'Sarah Emma Edmonds-Seeley; The Female Soldier', Lansing, *State Republican*, June 21, 1900.

19. 'Franklin Thompson alias Sarah E.E. Seeley' in *House Reports*, No. 820.

20. *State Republican*, June 26, 1900, see also, Betty Fladeland, 'Alias Franklin Thompson', *Michigan History*, Vol. 42, No. 3, Sept. 1958, pp. 435–462.

21. E. E. Seeley letter to R.H. Halstead, La Porte, Texas, Sept. 21, 1897, emphasis in original, MHC.

22. Schneider, op. cit., June 21, 1900.

23. E.E. Seeley, letter to R.H. Halstead, Fort Scott, Kansas, Jan. 27, 1885.

24. Emma Edmonds to Jerome Robbins, Washington, D.C. May 10, 1863, MHC.

25. Schneider, op. cit., June 26, 1900.

26. Loreta Janeta Velasquez to General Jubal Early, Rio de Janiero , Brazil, May 18, 1878, in Tucker Family Papers, Southern Historical Collection, University of North Carolina Library, Chapel Hill, NC, (hereafter SHC).

27. General Jubal Early to W. F. Slemons, Lynchburg, Virginia, May 22, 1878, in Tucker Family Papers, SHC.

28. Early to Slemons, SHC.

29. Early to Slemons, SHC.

30. Loreta Janeta Velasquez to General Jubal Early, op. cit. SHC.

31. Early to Slemons, SHC.

32. James Longstreet to E.W. Park, Gainsville, Georgia, June 18, 1888, William R. Perkins Library, Duke University.

33. Menié Muriel Dowie, ed., *Women Adventurers: The Adventure Series*, Vol. 15, Unwin Brothers, London, 1893, p. 51.

34. Gerard P. Clausius, 'The Little Soldier of the 95th: Albert D.J. Cashier', *Journal of Illinois State Historical Society*, Vol. 51, No. 4, Winter 1958, pp. 380–387.

35. Mary Anne Talbot, 'The Intrepid Female or Surprising Life and Adventures of Mary Anne Talbot, otherwise John Taylor', in *Kirby's Wonderful and Scientific Museum*, Vol. II, London, 1804, pp. 160–225, p. 193.

36. Ibid, p. 162.

37. Ibid, p. 187.

38. Ibid, p. 188.

39. Ibid, p. 216.

40. A guinea was a gold coin worth £1.05.

41. *Morning Herald*, November 1, 1799.

42. Kirby, op. cit., p. 224.

43. Dowie, op. cit., from a reprint of R.S. Kirby's *Life and Surprising Adventures of Mary Ann Talbot*, London, 1809.

44. Anonymous, *The Life and Adventures of Mrs. Christian Davies, the British Amazon*, Richard Montagu, London, 1741, part II, p. 79.

45. Ibid, p. 82.

46. Ibid, p. 91.

47. Ibid, p. 101.

48. A. J. Boyer, *The Political State of Great Britain for the Month of July 1739*, T. Cooper, London, 1739, p. 90.

49. 'Phoebe Hessel', *The Gentleman's Magazine*, Dec. 1817, p. 550.

50. Alderman Martin, *History of Brighton*, Brighton, 1871, p. 83 and *Gentleman's Magazine*, op. cit., p. 550.

51. William Andrews, *Curious Epitaphs*, London, 1899, p. 63.

52. Anonymous, *The Female Soldier; or the Surpring Adventures of Hannah Snell*, Richard Walker, London: 1750; Hannah Snell, *De vrouwelyke soldaat of de verbazende levensgevallen van Anna Snell*, Gerrit de Groot, Amsterdam, 1750 and for information concerning Snell's pension see, 'The Female Marine', *The Scots Magazine*, Vol. XII, W. Sands et al., Edinburgh, 1750.

53. Anonymous, *The Female Soldier.*, p. 128.

54. Rev. Daniel Lysons, *The Environs of London; Being an Historical Account of the Towns, Villages and Hamlets within 12 miles of that capital*, Vol. II, T. Cadell, London, 1795, p. 164.

55. *Universal Chronicle*, Nov. 3–10, 1759, p. 359 and Sidney Lee, ed. *Dictionary of National Biography*, Vol. XVIII, Smith and Elder, London,

1909, p. 613–614.

56. Clausius, op. cit., pp. 380–387.

57. Flora Sandes, *The Autobiography of a Woman Soldier: A Brief Record of Adventure with the Serbian Army, 1916–1919*, Witherby, London, 1927, p. 221.

58. Jean Bray, *Biography of Dr. Katherine Stuart MacPhail*, unpublished Imperial War Museum manuscript, p. 48.

59. Sandes, op. cit., p. 221.

60. Ibid, p. 221.

61. Various documents from FS Coll, translated by Eva and Zika Antonijevic´.

62. 'The Autobiography of a Woman Soldier', *Times Literary Supplement*, May 20, 1927, p. 378.

63. Sandes, op. cit., p. 200.

64. Ibid, p. 220.

65. Ibid, p. 38.

66. FS diary, July 5, 1941, FS Coll.

67. FS diary, September 11, 1941, FS Coll.

68. Flora Sandes Yudenitch to Colonel L. R. Smellie, Wickham Market, Suffolk, Jan. 4, 1950, Imperial War Museum, Women's Work Collection.

69. Sandes to Smellie, Jan. 4, 1950, IWM.

70. *Woman's Sunday Mirror*, 1956.

71. Sandes to Smellie, Sept. 10, 1950, IWM.

72. J.G. Lucas, 'Nostalgia for War', *Readers Digest*, 1946.

73. In conversation with Mira Harding, Dittisham, Devon, April, 1987, who knew Flora Sandes in Belgrade, she said she remembered her visits as a child: 'She was wearing a skirt and she was Mrs. Yudenitch but I knew that she was a soldier.'

74. Serbian National Invalid Fund to Flora Sandes Yudenitch, Dec. 28, 1939 and Invalid's Certificate, Feb. 20, 1930, I am grateful to Eva and Zika Antonijevic´ for this translation.

75. 'Jeanne Merkus', Algemeen Ryksarchief, The Hague, Collection koopstra 1030/63, p.6.

76. Marina Yurlova, *Russia Farewell*, Michael Joseph, London, 1936, p. 287.

77. Florence Farmborough, *Nurse at the Russian Front: A Diary 1914–1918*, Constable, London, 1974, p. 368. Maria Bochkareva's departure from Russia is further complicated by claims that she made a bold appeal to Lenin and Trotsky who gave her permission to travel home to Siberia and then by various means to the U.S.; see, for example, 'The Battalion of Death', *Times Literary Supplement*, July 31, 1919, p. 407.

78. Rheta Childe Dorr, *A Woman of Fifty*, Funk and Wagnalls, New York, 1924, p. 367.

79. Dorothy Lawrence, *Sapper Dorothy Lawrence: The Only English Woman Soldier, Late Royal Engineers, 51st Division, 179th Tunnelling Co., BEF*, John Lane, London, 1919, p. 189.

80. Esther Newton, 'The Mythic Mannish Lesbian: Radclyffe Hall and the New Woman', *Signs*, Vol. 9, No. 4, University of Chicago Press, Chicago, Summer 1984, pp. 558–575.

81. Richard Von Krafft-Ebing, *Psychopathia Sexualis: With Special Reference to the Antipathetic Sexual Instinct*, Staplis Press, London, 1965, p. 265.

82. Ibid, p. 264.

83. Ibid, p. 280.

84. Hirschfeld, op. cit., p. 111.

85. 'Girls Love of Adventure', *Liverpool Weekly Courier*, December 13, 1919, p. 3.

86. Ibid.

87. Ibid.

88. Percival Christopher Wren, ed., *Sowing Glory: The Memoirs of 'Mary Ambree' the English Woman-Legionary*, John Murray, London, 1931; 'Paris day-by-day — Woman in the Foreign Legion', *Daily Telegraph*, June 19, 1931, p. 11.

89. 'Sowing Glory', *Times Literary Supplement*, October 1, 1931, p. 750.

90. 'Princess in Uniform', *Times Literary Supplement*, December 27, 1934, p. 916.

91. Indoor Entertainment II, Freak Shows, Box 59-D, Tom Harrison Mass Observation Archive, University of Sussex.

92. Ibid, interview with Blackpool landlord Jack Gallimore about Colonel Barker's seven week stay.

93. Ibid.

94. Jackie Bratton, 'King of the Boys — Music Hall Impersonators', *Women's Review*, No. 20, 1987, pp. 12–14.

95. Introduction by E. Royston Pike, Rosita Forbes, (ed.), 'Some strange women of my travels', *Women of All Lands: Their Charm, Culture and Characteristics*, Amalgamated Press, London, 1938.

96. Ibid, p. 38.

97. Ibid, 'Rifle Practice', p. 132; 'Woman-at-Arms', p. 9, and 'Miss Turkey Steps Out', p. 189.

98. Rosita Forbes, *Women Called Wild*, Grayson and Grayson, London, 1935, p. 172.

99. Ibid, p. 174.

100. Library of Congress, Archive of Folksong, tape 4463, A2, B1, 2, quoted in Dianne Dugaw, *The Female Warrior Heroine in Anglo-American Popular Balladry*, University of California, Los Angeles, 1982, unpublished Ph.D. thesis, p. 261.

Selected Bibliography

Biographies and Autobiographies:

Anonymous, *The Female Soldier or the Suprising Life and Adventures of Hannah Snell . . . without her sex ever being discovered*, Richard Walker, London, 1750.

Anonymous, *The Life and Adventures of Mrs. Christian Davies, Commonly Call'd Mother Ross . . . Great Scenes of Action*, Richard Montagu, London, 1740.

Anonymous, *The Life and Adventures of Mrs. Christian Davies, the British Amazon, Commonly Call'd Mother Ross . . . Uncommon Martial Bravery*, Richard Montagu, 1741.

Anonymous, *The Life and Extraordinary Adventures of Susanna Cope: The British Female Soldier*, Cheney, Banbury, 1810?

Michael Baker, *Our Three Selves: The Life of Radclyffe Hall*, Hamish Hamilton, London, 1985.

Bessie Beatty, *The Red Heart of Russia*, the Century Co., New York, 1918.

Maria Bochkareva as told to Isaac Don Levine, *Yashka: My Life as Peasant Officer and Exile*, Frederick A. Stokes, New York, 1939.

Malvina Bolus, 'The Son of I. Gunn', *The Beaver*, Winter, 1971, pp. 23–26.

Charlotte Bremer, *Life, Letters and Posthumous Works of Fredrika Bremer*, Hurd and Houghton, New York, 1868.

Louise Bryant, *Six Months in Red Russia: An Observer's Account of Russia Before and During the Proletarian Revolution*, Heinemann, London, 1918.

Anne Chambers, *Granuaile*, Wolfhound Press, Dublin, 1986.

Gerard P. Clausius, 'The Little Soldier of the 95th: Albert D. J. Cashier', *Journal of the Illinois State Historical Society* Vol. 51, No. 4, Winter 1958, pp. 380–387.

Emma Cole, *The Life and Surpising Adventures of Louisa Baker whose life and character are particularly distinguished*, Luther Wales, New York, 1815.

Princess Dadeshkeliani, *Princess in Uniform*, C. Bell, London, 1934.

W. H. Davies, *The Autobiography of a Super-Tramp*, Oxford University Press, Oxford, 1986.

Rita Childe Dorr, *A Woman of Fifty*, Funk and Wagnalls, New York, 1924.

Menié Muriel Dowie, ed., *Women Adventurers: The Adventure Series*, Vol. 15, Unwin Brothers, London, 1893.

Edith Durham, *High Albania*, Virago Press, London, 1985.

Nadezhda Durova, translated by Mary Fleming Zirin, *The Cavalry Maiden: Journals of a Russian Officer in the Napoleonic Wars*, Angel Books, London, 1988.

Sarah Emma E. Edmonds, *Nurse and Spy in the Union Army: Comprising the Adventures and Experiences of a Woman in Hospitals, Camps and Battle-Fields*, W.S. Williams and Co., Hartford, Conn., 1865.

Florence Farmborough, *Nurse at the Russian Front: A Diary 1914–1918*, Constable, London, 1974.

Betty Fladeland, 'Alias Franklin Thompson', *Michigan History*, Vol. 42, No. 3, September 1958, pp. 435–462.

Betty Fladeland, 'New Light on Sarah Emma Edmonds, Alias Franklin Thompson', *Michigan History*, Vol. 49, No. 4, December 1963, pp. 357–362.

Rosita Forbes, *Women Called Wild*, Grayson and Grayson, London, 1935.

Lul Gardo, *Cossack Fury: The Experiences of a Woman Soldier with the White Russians*, Hutchinson and Co., London, 1938.

Elsa Jane Guerin, introduction by F.W. Mazzulla and William Kostka, *Mountain Charley or the Adventures of Mrs. E. J. Guerin, who was Thirteen Years in Male Attire*, University of Oklahoma Press, Norman, 1968.

Dorothy Lawrence, *Sapper Dorothy Lawrence: The Only English Woman Soldier: Late Royal Engineers, 51st Division, 179th Tunnelling Company, BEF*, John Lance, London, 1919.

Rose Wilder Lane, *The Peaks of Shala: Being a Record of Certain Wanderings Among the Hill-Tribes of Albania*, Chapman and Dodd, Ltd., 1922.

Mary Livermore, *My Story of the War*, Hartford, Conn., A. D. Worthington and Co., 1876.

Sara Maitland, *Vesta Tilley*, Virago Press, London, 1986.

Madeline Moore, *The Lady Lieutenant, or the Strange and Thrilling Adventures of Miss Madeline Moore*, Barclay and Co., Philadelphia, 1862.

Isobel Rae, *The Strange Story of Dr. James Barry*, Longman, London, 1958.

June Rose, *The Perfect Gentleman: The Remarkable Life of Dr. James Miranda Barry, the Woman Who Served as an Officer in the British Army from 1813 to 1859*, Hutchinson, London, 1977.

Deborah Sampson, *The Female Review*, Herman Mann, Dedham, 1797.

Deborah Gannett née Sampson, *An Address Delivered with Applause, at the Federal-Street Theatre, Boston*, n.p., Dedham, 1802.

Flora Sandes, *An English Woman-Sergeant in the Serbian Army*, Hodder and Stoughton, London, 1916.

Flora Sandes, *The Autobiography of a Woman Soldier: A Brief Record of Adventure with the Serbian Army 1916–1918*, Witherby, London, 1927.

Stephen Scobie, *Isabel Gunn*, Quarry Press, Kingston, Ontario, 1987.

Ellen Stephens, *The Cabin-boy Wife*, C. E. Daniels, New York, 1840.

Mary Anne Talbot, 'The Intrepid Female or Surprising Life and Adventures of Mary Anne Talbot, otherwise John Taylor', *Kirby's Wonderful and Scientific Museum*, Vol. II, London, 1804.

Anne Jane Thornton, *The Interesting Life and Wonderful Adventures of that Extraordinary Woman Anne Jane Thornton, the Female Soldier; Disclosing Important Secrets, Unknown to the Public*, np., London, 1835.

Loreta Janeta Velasquez, C. J. Worthington, ed., *The Woman in Battle*, T. Belknap, Hartford, Conn., 1876.

James Adams Vinton, 'The Female Review: Life of Deborah Sampson, the Female Soldier in the War of Revolution', *The Magazine of History, Notes and Queries*, Extra No. 47, Boston, 1916.

J. Wilson, *The Life and Adventures of Mrs. Christian Davies, Commonly Call'd Mother Ross . . . Great Scenes of Action*, T. Cooper, London, 1742.

J. Wilson, *The British Heroine: Or An Abridgement of the Life and Adventures of Christian Davies Commonly Call'd Mother Ross . . . Great Scenes of Action*, J. Newberry and C. Micklewright, Reading, 1742.

Percival Christopher Wren, *Sowing Glory: The Memoirs of 'Mary Ambree', the English Woman-Legionary*, John Murray, London, 1931.

Marina Yurlova, *Cossack Girl*, Cassell and Co., London, 1934.

Marina Yurlova, *Russia Farewell*, Michael Joseph, London, 1936.

Related Sources:

Peter Ackroyd, *Dressing Up: Transvestism and Drag: The History of an Obsession*, London, Thames and Hudson, 1979.

Martin Binkin and Shirley Bach, *Women and the Military*, Brookings Institute, Washington, D.C., 1977.

Dea Birkett, *Victorian Women Explorers*, Basil Blackwell, Oxford, 1988.

Dea Birkett, *Mary Kingsley*, MacMillan, London, 1989.

Kathy Bond-Stewart, ed., *Young Women in the Liberation Struggle*, Zimbabwe Publishing House, Harare, Zimbabwe, 1984.

Jackie Bratton, 'King of the Boys', *Women's Review*, Number 20, 1987.

Gail Braybon and Penny Summerfield, *Out of the Cage: Women's Experiences in Two World Wars*, Pandora Press, 1987.

Rita Mae Brown, *High Hearts*, Bantam Books, London, 1986.

Anne Chambers, *Granuaile*, Wolfhound Press, Dublin, 1986.

Wendy Chapkis, ed., *Loaded Questions: Women in the Military*, Transnational Institute, Amsterdam, 1981.

Anna Clark, 'Popular Morality and the Construction of Gender in London,

1780–1845', Ph.D. thesis, Rutgers University, New Jersey, 1987.

Diana Condell and Jean Liddard, *Working for Victory? Images of Women in the First World War 1914–1918*, Routledge and Kegan Paul, 1987.

Sylvia G. Dannett, *Noble Women of the North*, New York, Thomas Yoseloff, 1959.

Natalie Zemon Davis, *Society and Culture in Early Modern France*, Stanford University Press, Stanford, 1975.

Rudolf Dekker and Lotte van de Pol, *The Tradition of Female Cross-Dressing in Early Modern Europe*, MacMillan, 1988.

Dianne Dugaw, 'Balladry's Female Warriors: Women, Warfare and Disguise in the Eighteenth Century', *Eighteenth Century Life*, January 1985, No. 9, pp. 1–20.

Dianne Dugaw, *Dangerous Examples: Warrior Women and Popular Balladry, 1600–1850*, Cambridge University Press, Cambridge, 1989.

H. Havelock Ellis, *Studies in the Psychology of Sex*, Vol. 1, the University Press, London, 1897.

Jean Bethke Elshtain, *Women and War*, Harvester Press, Brighton, 1987.

Cynthia Enloe, *Does Khaki Become You? The Militarization of Women's Lives*, Pandora Press, 1988.

Jeannette H. Foster, *Sex Variant Women in Literature*, The Naiad Press, 1985.

Lynne Friedli, 'Women Who Dressed as Men', *Trouble and Strife*, No. 6, Summer 1985.

O. P. Gilbert, *Women in Men's Guise*, John Lane, London, 1932.

Anne Eliot Griesse and Richard Stites, 'Russia: Revolution and War', in Nancy Loring Goldman, ed., *Female Soldiers —Combatants or Non-Combatants: Historical Perspectives*, Greenwood Press, London, 1982.

Barton Hacker, 'Women and Military Institutions in Early Modern Europe: A Reconnaissance', *Signs*, Summer 1981, Vol. 6, No. 4, pp. 643–671.

Diane Hamer, 'Contemporary Lesbian Identity', M.Phil., Department of Contemporary Cultural Studies, Birmingham University, 1989.

Derek Hudson, *Munby: Man of Two Worlds: The Life and Diaries of Arthur J. Munby, 1828–1910*, Abacus, London, 1974.

Lisa Jardine, *Still Harping on Daughters: Drama in the Age of Shakespeare*, Harvester Press, Brighton, 1983.

Estelle C. Jelinek, 'Disguise Autobiographies: Women Masquerading as Men', *Women's Studies International Forum*, Vol. 10, No. 1, pp. 53–62.

Jonathan Katz, *Gay American History: Lesbians and Gay Men in the USA: A Documentary*, Crowell, New York, 1977.

Susan J. Kessler and Wendy McKenna, *Gender: An Ethnomethodological Approach*, John Wiley, New York, 1978.

Anne Kindersley, *The Mountains of Serbia: Travels through Inland Yugoslavia*, John Murray, London, 1976.

Monica Krippner, *The Quality of Mercy: Women at War, Serbia 1915–1918*,

David and Charles, London, 1981.

Michael Lewis, *A Social History of the Navy, 1793–1815*, Allen and Unwin, London, 1960.

Sharon Macdonald, Pat Holden and Shirley Ardener, *Images of Women in Peace and War: Cross-Cultural and Historical Perspectives*, MacMillan Education, Oxford, 1987.

Mandy Merck, 'The City's Achievements: The patriotic Amazonmachy and Ancient Athens,' in Sue Lipshitz, ed., *Tearing the Veil: Essays on Femininity*, Routledge and Kegan Paul, London, 1978.

Esther Newton, 'The Mythic Mannish Lesbian: Radclyffe Hall and the New Woman', *Signs*, Vol. 9, No. 4, University of Chicago Press, Summer 1984, pp. 558–575.

Linda Grant de Pauw, 'Women in Combat: The Revolutionary War Experience', in *Armed Forces and Society*, Vol. 7, No. 2, Winter 1981, pp. 209–226.

Linda Grant de Pauw, *Seafaring Women*, Houghton, Mifflin and Company, Boston, 1982.

Julian Putkowski and Julian Sykes, *Shot at Dawn*, Wharncliff, 1989.

Pat Rogers, 'The Breeches Part', in Paul-Gabriel Boucé, ed., *Sexuality in Eighteenth-Century Britain*, Manchester University Press, Manchester, 1982.

Commander W. B. Rowbotham, 'The Royal Navy Service Medal, 1793–1840', *The Mariner's Mirror: The Journal of the Society for Nautical Research*, Vol. 23, July 1937, pp. 366.

Jane Schultz, 'Woman at the Front: Gender and Genre in the Literature of the American Civil War', Ph.D. thesis, University of Michigan, Ann Arbor, MI, 1988.

Lynne Segal, *Is the Future Female? Troubled Thoughts on Contemporary Feminism*, Virago Press, London, 1987.

Simon Shepherd, *Amazons and Warrior Women: Varieties of Feminism in Seventeenth Century Drama*, Harvester, Brighton, 1981.

Dora Sigerson Shorter, *The Troubador and Other Poems*, Hodder and Stoughton, London, 1907.

Barbara Sichtermann, *Femininity: The Politics of the Personal*, Basil Blackwell, 1983.

Richard Stites, *The Women's Liberation Movement in Russia: Feminism, Nihilism and Bolshevism, 1860–1930*, Princeton University Press, Princeton, New Jersey, 1975.

Anne Summers, *Angels and Citizens: British Women as Military Nurses, 1854–1914*, Routledge and Kegan Paul, London, 1988.

Myna Trustram, *Women of the Regiment: Marriage and the Victorian Army*, Cambridge University Press, Cambridge, 1984.

Sylvia Van Kirk, *'Many Tender Ties': Women in Fur-Trade Society in Western Canada, 1670–1870*, Watson and Dwyer Publishing Ltd., Winnipeg, Manitoba, 1980.

Martha Vicinus, *Independent Women: Work and Community for Single Women, 1850-1920*, Virago Press, London, 1985.

Marina Warner, *Joan of Arc: The Image of Female Heroism*, Pan Books, London, 1981.

Jeffrey Weeks, *Sex, Politics and Society: The Regulation of Sexuality Since 1800*, Longman, London, 1981.

Julie Wheelwright, 'Amazons and Military Maids: An examination of female military heroines in British literature and the changing construction of gender', *Women's Studies International Forum*, Vol. 10, No. 5, pp. 489-502, 1987.

Julie Wheelwright, 'British Medical Women in Serbia, 1914-1918: The Case of Lt. Flora Sandes', in John Allcock and Antonia Young, *Black Lambs and Grey Falcons: Women Travellers in the Balkans*, forthcoming, 1990.

Anne Wiltshire, *Most Dangerous Women: Feminist Peace Campaigners of the Great War*, Pandora Press, 1985.

Index

Also available from Pandora Press:

BACK TO HOME AND DUTY
Women Between the Wars, 1918–1939

Deirdre Beddoe

Deirdre Beddoe makes an explorative journey through the two decades which spanned the end of the First World War and the outbreak of the Second in order to discover what happened to those 'gallant girls' of wartime when they were told to go *Back to Home and Duty*.

She explores the lives of women of all classes, from debutantes to domestic servants. She looks at the many images held up to women by the media, the education of all classes, employment, home life and leisure time, health and politics, and highlights the impact of the 'back to the home' movement upon women's lives and aspirations. Those gallant girls were transformed into dole scroungers, pin money girls and became women who 'stole men's jobs' unless, that is, they were to enter domestic service.

Whilst there are many parallels between the 1920s and 1930s and today, that world is deceptively familiar. Many of the women whose stories are told here, for example, would not receive secondary education, worked alongside men for a fraction of the male wage, would not, for much of this period have the vote and would face increasingly high risks of dying in childbirth.

Vividly realised, with evidence from many and varied sources, and illustrated with photographs, *Back to Home and Duty* comprehensively fills a gap in our knowledge of women's past.

0-04-440515-4
£9.99 pbk.

BANANAS, BEACHES AND BASES

Making Feminist Sense of International Politics

Cynthia Enloe

This radical new analysis of international politics reveals the crucial role of women in implementing governments' foreign policies – be it Soviet *Glasnost*, Britain's dealings in the EEC or the NATO alliance.

Cynthia Enloe pulls back the curtain on the familiar scenes – governments restricting imported goods, bankers negotiating foreign loans, soldiers serving overseas – and shows that the *real* landscape is less exclusively male.

She shows how thousands of women tailor their marriages to fit the demands of state secrecy; how foreign policy would grind to a halt without secretaries to handle money transfers or arms shipments; and how women are working in hotels and factories around the world in order to service their governments' debts.

Cynthia Enloe also challenges common assumptions about what constitutes 'international politics'. She explains, for example, how turning tacos and sushi into bland fast foods affects relations between affluent and development countries, and why a multinational banana company needs the brothel outside its gates. And she argues that shopping at Benetton, wearing Levis, working as a nanny (or employing one) or booking a holiday are all examples of foreign policy in action.

Bananas, Beaches and Bases does not ignore our curiosity about arms dealers, the President's men or official secrets. But it shows why these conventional clues are not sufficient for understanding how the international political system works. In exposing policy makers' reliance on false notions of 'femininity' and 'masculinity', Cynthia Enloe dismantles a seemingly overwhelming world system, exposing it to be much more fragile and open to change than we are usually led to believe.

0–04–440368–2
£8.99 pbk

BLOOD AT THE ROOT

Motherhood, Sexuality and Male Dominance

Ann Ferguson

Blood at the Root presents a new feminist theory of the connections between motherhood, sexuality, male dominance and economic systems.

The 1980s was a watershed period for feminists in western societies. Women have gained significant rights and freedoms and our sexual options are widening. These positive gains are being threatened by a fierce backlash against feminism as we experience the growth of the New Right. A starting point for Ann Ferguson's important book is that no existing feminist theory can provide an adequate explanation for this paradoxical position of feminism today. She sets out to develop the concept of 'modes of sex/affective production': historical ways of organising sexuality and parenting on which systems of social dominance like patriarchy, racism and class-divided economies are importantly based.

In Part One of *Blood at the Rood*, Ann Ferguson borrows from marxism, radical feminism, freudianism and classical theories of sexuality to develop an original theory of the self and sexuality. Part Two develops this theory of sex/affective production in order to defend the hypothesis that women are a new radical sex class. Part Three deals with some political questions concerning motherhood, the feminist sex debate on such issues as pornography, S/M sexuality and lesbian separatism and offers us a model for socialist-feminist transformation of society.

0-04-440445-X
£8.95 pbk

Also available from Pandora Press